Explo

Language

& Literature

A Practical Guide to AS and A-Level English Language and Literature

Steven Croft
Robert Myers

OXFORD
UNIVERSITY PRESS

OXFORD
UNIVERSITY PRESS

Great Clarendon Street, Oxford OX2 6DP

Oxford University Press is a department of the University of Oxford.
It furthers the University's objective of excellence in research, scholarship,
and education by publishing worldwide in

Oxford New York

Athens Auckland Bangkok Bogotá Buenos Aires Calcutta Cape Town
Chennai Dar es Salaam Delhi Florence Hong Kong Istanbul Karachi
Kuala Lumpur Madrid Melbourne Mexico City Mumbai Nairobi
Paris São Paulo Singapore Taipei Tokyo Toronto Warsaw

with associated companies in
Berlin Ibadan

Oxford is a registered trade mark of Oxford University Press
in the UK and in certain other countries

A CIP catalogue record for this book is available from the British Library

ISBN 0 19 831457 4

Designed by Mike Brain Graphic Design Limited, Oxford

Typeset by AFS Image Setters Ltd, Glasgow

Printed in Great Britain by Cambridge University Press

Orders and enquiries to Customer Services:
Tel. 01536 741068   Fax 01536 454519

Contents

Acknowledgements

Rob Myers would like to personally thank the following for their part in helping him with this book:

My good friend and mentor Shaun O'Toole who provided the stimulus for many of the ideas in the sections on language production and textual recasting in this book; all of the students who were guinea-pigs for many of the activities which are used in the book; my colleagues in the English Department at Whitby Community College; the staff at the Associated Examining Board, especially Caroline Wilkins; and finally, and by no means least, Ruth and Tom Myers for their endless patience whilst writing this book during holiday times and weekends!

The authors and publisher are grateful for permission to re-print the following copyright material:

Simon Armitage: 'I Say, I Say, I Say', 'On an Owd Piktcha', 'White Christmas' and 'The Anaesthetist' from *The Dead Sea Poems*, reprinted by permission of the publisher, Faber & Faber Ltd.
BBC Radio: transcripts from BBC Radio Cleveland live football commentaries by Ray Simpson and Kevin Smith of Darlington v Wolverhampton Wanderers FA Cup Third Round match and Fourth Round replay, reprinted by permission of BBC Radio Cleveland.
BBC Television: transcript of interview between Michael Parkinson and Billy Connolly from *Parkinson* (December 1999); and transcript of an interview with two elderly ladies from *Century Road* (BBC2, 1999)
Pat Barker: extract from *The Ghost Road* (Viking, 1995), copyright © Pat Barker 1995, reprinted by permission of Penguin Books Ltd.
Alan Bennett: extract from 'Bed Among the Lentils' from *Talking Heads* (BBC, 1988), copyright © Alan Bennett 1988, reprinted by permission of BBC Worldwide Ltd and PFD on behalf of the author.
Louis de Bernieres: extract from *Captain Corelli's Mandolin* (Secker & Warburg, 1994), reprinted by permission of the Random House Group Ltd.
Joanna Briscoe: extract from *Skin* (Phoenix, 1997), reprinted by permission of the Orion Publishing Group Ltd.
Christopher Brookmyre: extract from *Quite Ugly One Morning* (Abacus, 1996), reprinted by permission of Little, Brown and Company (UK).
Bill Bryson: extract from *Notes from a Small Island* (Black Swan, a division of Transworld Publishing, 1998), copyright © Bill Bryson 1998, reprinted by permission of the publishers. All rights reserved.
Sir Winston Churchill: extract from 'Their Finest Hour' speech, copyright © Winston S. Churchill, reprinted by permission of Curtis Brown Ltd, London on behalf of the Estate of Sir Winston S. Churchill.
Wendy Cope: 'Strugnell in Liverpool' from *Making Cocoa for Kingsley Amis*, reprinted by permission of the publisher, Faber & Faber Ltd.
E. E. Cummings: 'Anyone Lived in a Pretty How Town' from *Complete Poems 1904–1962* edited by George J. Firmage, copyright © 1991 by the Trustees for the E. E. Cummings Trust and George J. Firmage, by permission of the publishers, W. W. Norton & Company.
Kinky Friedman: extract from *Roadkill* (1997) reprinted by permission of the publisher, Faber & Faber Ltd.
Jane Gardam: extract from 'Stone Trees' in *Pangs of Love* by Jane Gardam (Hamish Hamilton), reprinted by permission of David Higham Associates.
David Guterson: extract from *Snow Falling on Cedars* (Bloomsbury, 1995).
Susan Hill: extracts from 'Mr Proudham and Mr Sleight', 'In the Conservatory' and 'The Custodian' all in *A Bit of Singing and Dancing* by Susan Hill, (Hamish Hamilton), copyright © Susan Hill, 1971, 1972, 1973, reprinted by permission of Sheil Land Associates Ltd.
Michael Hodges: Report of Middlesbrough v Leicester City football match in *Sunday Times* Sports Section.
Alistair Horne: extract from *Death of a Generation – From Neuve Chappelle to Verdun and the Somme* (Macdonald 1972), reprinted by permission of Little, Brown and Company (UK).
Rebecca Hughes: lexical example from *English in Speech and Writing* (Routledge, 1996).

Ted Hughes: 'Football at Slack', reprinted by permission of the publisher, Faber & Faber Ltd.
Rory Johnson: extract from 'Storylines' article first published in *The Guardian*, 9.9.91, copyright © Rory Johnson 1991, reprinted by permission of Guardian Newspapers Ltd.
Marcel Junod: 'Visiting Hiroshima, 9 September 1945', extract from *Warrior Without Weapons* translated by Edward Fitzgerald (Jonathan Cape, 1951), reprinted by permission of the Random House Group Ltd.
Martin Luther King: extract from 'I have a dream' speech, reprinted by permission of the Joan Daves Literary Agency.
D. H. Lawrence: 'To Women, As Far As I'm Concerned' and 'Discord in Childhood' from *The Complete Poems of D. H. Lawrence*, reprinted by permission of Laurence Pollinger Limited and the Estate of Frieda Lawrence Ravagli.
Eric Lomax: extracts from *The Railway Man* (Jonathan Cape, 1995), reprinted by permission of the Random House Group Ltd.
Toni Morrison: extract from *Beloved* (Chatto & Windus, 1987), copyright © Toni Morrison 1987, reprinted by permission of International Creative Management, Inc.
Grace Nichols: 'Hey There Now!' and 'Iguana Memory' from *The Fat Black Woman's Poems* (Virago Press, 1984), copyright © Grace Nichols 1984, reprinted by permission of Curtis Brown Ltd, London on behalf of Grace Nichols.
The Onion Bag article 'The Lowdown . . . Paul 'Ga-Ga' Gascoigne' from *The Onion Bag* (Issue 12).
Dorothy Parker: 'Resume' from *The Portable Dorothy Parker*, reprinted by permission of the publisher, Gerald Duckworth and Company Ltd.
Harry Pearson: extract from *Racing Pigs and Giant Marrows* (Abacus, 1997), reprinted by permission of Little, Brown and Company (UK).
PGL holiday advertisement leaflet extract reprinted by permission of PGL Travel Ltd.
Philip Pullman: extract from *Clockwork* (Corgi Yearling, a division of Transworld Publishing, 1997), copyright © Philip Pullman 1997, reprinted by permission of the publishers. All rights reserved.
E. Annie Proulx: extracts from *The Shipping News* (Fourth Estate Ltd, 1993), copyright © E. Annie Proulx 1993, reprinted by permission of the publishers.
Anthony Quinn: 'Oh What a Lonely War!', review of William Boyd's *The Trench* from *The Independent*, 17.9.99, copyright © The Independent, reprinted by permission of Independent Newspapers (UK) Ltd.
Jean Rhys: extract from *Wide Sargasso Sea* (Penguin), reprinted by permission of Sheil Land Associates Ltd.
The Sun editorial 'Sick making' from *The Sun*, 23.10.99, copyright © News International Newspapers Ltd 1999, reprinted by permission of News International Syndication.
John Updike: 'Winter Ocean' from *Telephone Poles and Other Poems* (Viking/Deutsch), copyright © John Updike, reprinted by permission of Penguin Books Ltd.
Alice Walker: extract from *The Color Purple* (The Women's Press Ltd, 1983), reprinted by permission of David Higham Associates.

The publisher would like to thank the following for permission to reproduce photographs: Hulton Getty (pages 36 and 145); Roger Ressmeyer/Corbis UK Ltd (page 97); Moviestore (page 160); John Tramper/Globe Theatre (page 195); Imperial War Museum (page 237); Sporting Pictures (page 257).

We are also grateful to the following students for allowing us to use their responses as examples: Neil Armitage, Eleanor Chalkley, Victoria Grice, Sandra Haigh, Rebecca Harbin, Michael Lomas, Helen Mitchell, Joanne Rudsdale, Amrit Saroya, Ben Thorp, Becci Thorpe, Eoin Walker; and to the following for permission to reproduce material from examination papers and specimen papers: The Associated Examining Board (AEB), Assessment & Qualifications Alliance (AQA), Northern Examinations and Assessment Board (NEAB). Any example answers to examination questions or hints on answers used in this book are the sole responsibility of the authors and have not been provided or approved by the examining boards.

We have tried to trace and contact all copyright holders before publication. If notified the publishers will be pleased to rectify any errors or omissions at the earliest opportunity.

SECTION I: AS-LEVEL

Laying the Foundations of Literary and Linguistic Study

This particular course is exactly what its name implies: it is the study of both English Language and Literature and the specification has been designed with the total integration of these two aspects of the subject in mind. Consequently, you will be asked to study a range of writing representing a variety of genres, including the main literary types of prose, poetry and drama, from both literary and linguistic viewpoints. You will be expected to study a selection of non-literary texts, especially those that could feature as stimulus materials for your own language production (Unit 1) and your adaptation of language (Unit 5) as well as those that might be used to test synopticity (Unit 6). You will also study the features of speech and be expected to analyse a range of speech situations, including transcripts of spontaneous speech.

This course aims to foster a deeper understanding of both English Language and English Literature than that gained at GCSE level, by examining **texts** from both literary and linguistic viewpoints.

Text	A text is simply a piece of writing or a piece of speech. Michael Halliday famously outlined the possible range of texts as being 'prose or verse, dialogue or monologue, it may be anything from a single proverb to a whole play, from a momentary cry for help to an all-day discussion on a committee.'

By examining a variety of texts in this way, you should be able to see whether a literary, linguistic or integrated analytical approach helps you to understand a text more fully. You will be encouraged to do this by applying differing analytical **frameworks**.

Framework	A framework is a critical skeleton around which you can build the body of your analysis. Different frameworks may be more suited to different texts and it will be up to you to learn which one best serves your analysis.

Frameworks can be made up of a variety of critical 'bones', and this book will help you learn the most effective ways of constructing your own frameworks for analysis, when to apply them and how to review their effectiveness.

However, it is also necessary for you to be able to apply the detail of the frameworks to different texts; for you to do this it is necessary for you to know about the different 'bones' that join together to make different frameworks. You will have learned some of these 'bones' at GCSE level (alliteration, imagery and metaphor for instance), but there will be many more that you need to become familiar with so as to increase the breadth and effectiveness of your analytical interpretations and responses.

The advantage of engaging in combined literary and linguistic study is that you will have the best of both worlds: you can use terms from both disciplines seamlessly to inform your analyses, and you will learn which terms and which frameworks help you to deconstruct texts most effectively. It is essential that you do this, as the final synoptic unit of the specification will test your ability to use, and then reflect on your use of, different critical approaches to textual analysis.

There are other points that must be taken into account before we engage in the study of the content relevant to each part of the course. There are certain underlying principles that you need to be aware of when you are engaged in either AS or A2 study. You will need to study a minimum of four set texts (for any specification). At AS level for AQA Specification A, you will need to study a prose work and a volume of poetry, one of which must have been written before 1900. You will also need to work on unseen texts, particularly examples of non-literary writing, as well as undertaking detailed study of speech acts of various kinds. At A2 level of this specification, your studies will become more penetrating and include comparative work. You will need to study a piece of dramatic writing written before the Romantic period (that is, pre-1770), study one other text, and engage in comparative study in two Units of the course. We will guide you through these sections which will require you, at all times, to consider the purpose, audience and context of each piece of writing you study, as well taking other points into consideration, such as comparison, textual adaptation and authorial attitudes. These principles will be pointed up at each opportunity in this book and we will show you how they fit into the study and assessment of the course.

Because textual analysis is a skill that you need to learn from the outset, we will spend a little time straight away building a framework for analysis which you can then apply throughout this book, adapting it and refining it as you see fit. Textual analysis lies at the heart of this subject, and the application of it (through whichever framework or method you choose) will enable you to become a more confident, informed and skilful critic of English Language and Literature.

As you will see in the following section, all texts whether written or spoken have a purpose, audience and context; these terms are all dealt with in much greater detail in the following section. Essentially, the terms refer to what a text does, who it is written for and where it appears. When you are engaging in textual analysis, it is always a good idea to start with these three areas as they help you to find a route into the text. When you have identified these, you can continue by examining the text at a variety of levels, moving from individual words through phrases, sentence structures and other grammatical and syntactical issues, to how the text is put together, and finally on to what it looks like as a whole.

Use the flow chart below to help you use one method of deconstructing any text you are studying; once you have become accustomed to the methodology, you can adapt it for your purposes.

One method of textual analysis

What? Who? Where?

1 What is the text trying to do? → Purpose

2 Who is it trying to communicate these ideas to? → Audience

3 Where will the text appear? → Context

4 What does it look like? → Form

⬇

How?

5 Use of specific words or terms from a certain area → Semantic field

6 Use of certain types of words and word classes → Grammar

7 Use of other constructions in phrases and sentences → Syntax

8 Use of sound features and other rhetorical devices → Phonology

9 How the text fits together → Cohesion

10 What the text looks like and how it is laid out → Graphology

⬇

Effect?   Evaluation of . . .

11 Does the text do what it sets out to? → Purpose

12 Does it hit its target readership? → Audience

13 Does the place where it appears help the text? → Context

14 Does its layout help? → Form

Of course, analysing a text in such a way does not construct an argument for you. A simple and effective way to do this is simply to chain your points together by using a three-point critical sentence. In this you would:

1 identify the point you want to discuss

2 give an example from the text

3 comment on how it works within the text in terms of purpose and audience.

This is a tried and tested method that helps you to focus on each example that you choose to discuss. You will be able to practise textual analysis at many points in this book, which will help you to engage with the textual analysis required in the synoptic paper.

ACTIVITY

Read the text *Racing Pigs and Giant Marrows*, below.

1 Identify the range of examples and ideas that you could use in a textual analysis.

2 Tabulate your findings: this will give you a series of points that you can use as the basis for your response.

3 Using the flow chart above, organize your findings into relevant sections.

4 Write out your textual analysis of the piece.

Text *Racing Pigs and Giant Marrows* by Harry Pearson

We drove up over the big emptiness of Stanhope Moor. It was another boiling hot day. The cloudless sky was the colour of a blackbird's egg and even here, at a thousand feet above sea level, the tarmac of the road hissed and shimmered. Groups of red grouse were bobbing busily about among the shooting butts like veterans revisiting a battle site. As we passed they glanced up briefly then went back to their business. A cursory inspection of our car was enough to satisfy them we weren't wealthy enough pose a threat. Game birds are an arrogant lot. Sometimes assistants in expensive shops develop, through association with the rich and powerful, the misguided impression that they too are socially superior. Should anyone in anything so common as training shoes attempt to cross the threshold of their emporia they will freeze them out with a frosty glare. Game birds suffer from similar delusions. Every once in a while a cock pheasant would turn up in our garden and begin gobbling up the peas. I'd rush out and clap my hands to shoo him off and he'd just turn and appraise me slowly down the length of his beak, as if to say, 'And just who do you think you are, you tedious little man?' I used to suffer severe crop damage from hoity-toity pheasants. Then I got my dog. The pheasants don't act so haughty with him. This is partly because he has a long and impressively aristocratic pedigree. Mainly, though, it is because he is prepared to bite the bum off anything that gets within range.

➡

In one of the tiny ex-lead-mining villages of Weardale a terrier show was in progress. Dog shows are normally rather precious events. I once entered my own dog in one of the larger ones – in the face of considerable protest from him, I might add. He felt a dog show was little more than a cattle market. My abiding memory of it is going into a tent in which row after row of busy owners were lacquering the bouffants of their standard poodles. It was like a backstage scene at a convention of Little Richard impersonators. The build-up of hairspray fumes was such that one match would have seen half the pedigree poodle population of Britain go up in a puff of smoke. I can't say I wasn't tempted.

There was nothing twee about this terrier show, however. It was strictly for working dogs: a gang of bustling roughnecks any one of which wouldn't have looked ill at ease with a Woodbine in the corner of his mouth and a copy of the *Racing Post* tucked under a foreleg. Like hot-water bottles, zip-up cardigans with suede elbow patches and the serving of tomato juice as a starter, terriers are a peculiarly British phenomenon – and one of which, if anything, we can be even prouder. When the Romans arrived here our plucky little pets were about the only thing that impressed them about our native isle. They wrote letters home gushing with praise for the amazing little dogs that never ducked a fight. In so doing the Romans helped forge one of the most fundamental of all human beliefs: that someone who is small and belligerent is a doughty and admirable character, while someone who is large and belligerent is a moronic psychopath.

The Romans would be delighted to see that, though nearly 2,000 years have passed since they first came across them, terriers remain a pugnacious lot. On the edge of a football field overhung by gaunt fell, you could see the owners struggling to keep their charges apart. They were Jack Russells and Borders mainly. Most terriers are up for a scrap, but Borders take the biscuit. Brindle-haired, bristly and pug-nosed, they walk with a stiff-legged, minatory strut.

In the far corner of the field, steering clear of any conflict, a group of men were walking their Bedlingtons. A cross between a whippet and Dandie Dinmont (a grey-and-white terrier that looks like an ageing dachshund in an ill-fitting toupee), the Bedlington steps along on tippy-toes, its greyish, curly coat giving it the appearance of an effete and anorexic lamb. The look is deceptive. The Bedlington is a true pit man's dog, quick and sharp-toothed, nippy in every sense of the word and a remorseless and successful hunter. There are people who lived through the Depression in the Northumberland and Durham coalfields who will tell you at times it was hard to tell whether it was the family that kept the Bedlington, or the Bedlington who kept the family.

1 Language Production and Practical Writing

One aspect of GCSE English that many students enjoy is writing creatively, whether it is under examination conditions and with a particular purpose in mind, or whether it is writing at length as part of a coursework folder. This A-level Language and Literature specification starts with a Unit asking students to undertake a particular type of writing, that is writing for a specific task where audience, purpose, context and style are each of paramount importance.

As with any language production task, a knowledge of different types of writing and familiarity with differing textual examples is very important. We suggest that you use this section of the book as a useful route into the course. First, read carefully the different kinds of text that are given here, and then analyse them by using a framework to find out what gives each text its particular qualities. Secondly, look at the tasks linked to each piece and practise writing in response to the kinds of questions that might be set for Unit 1 of this specification. Finally, familiarize yourself with the methods you should use to make comments about your own writing and learn how you can reflect effectively on the choices you have made in producing your own new text.

The basics: purpose and audience

It is vital for you to recognize that any text that is produced always has a **purpose** and a particular **audience** in mind. These are two key terms, and they form the backbone of any framework for language production. To help you see at first hand the differences between these two, try your first piece of textual analysis by looking closely at the two texts printed below.

Extract 1 *Clockwork:* Philip Pullman

Once upon a time (when time ran by clockwork), a strange event took place in a little German town. Actually, it was a series of events, all fitting together like the parts of a clock, and although each person saw a different part, no-one saw the whole of it; but here it is as well as I can tell it.

It began on a winter's evening, when the townsfolk were gathering in the White Horse Tavern. The snow was blowing down from the mountains, and the wind was making the bells shift restlessly in the church tower. The windows were steamed up, the stove was blazing brightly, Putzi the old black ➡

cat was snoozing on the hearth; and the air was full of the rich smell of sausage and sauerkraut, of tobacco and beer.

Extract 2 *Captain Corelli's Mandolin*: Louis de Bernières

Dr Iannis had enjoyed a satisfactory day in which none of his patients had died or got any worse. He had attended a surprisingly easy calving, lanced one abscess, extracted a molar, dosed one lady of easy virtue with Salvarsan, performed an unpleasant but spectacularly fruitful enema, and had produced a miracle by a feat of medical prestidigitation.

He chuckled to himself, for no doubt this miracle was already being touted as worthy of St Gerasimos himself. He had gone to old man Stamatis' house, having been summoned to deal with an earache, and had found himself gazing down an aural orifice more dank, be-lichened, and stalagmatic even than the Drogarati cave.

ACTIVITY

These are the beginnings of two novels with distinct purposes and audiences in mind.

❏ What does each writer concentrate on or aim to do (**purpose**) in the opening of each novel? You might like to focus on such matters as character, setting and plot when you look at each writer's purpose in this way.
❏ What clues are there that help you to see who the readership (**audience**) is intended to be for each of these extracts? You should concentrate on lexis (the words used), grammar (the way the words are strung together) and phonological features (the sounds or representation of sounds).

In the activity above, you will no doubt come up with a variety of answers to each of the questions. You will have seen that the first extract is essentially a simple piece of writing that aims to set the scene, whereas the second piece is more complex and concentrates on establishing one of the central characters. You should have ascertained that *Clockwork* is aimed at a young audience and that *Captain Corelli's Mandolin* is much more adult in its appeal.

For the purposes of this book, we will use the following definitions of purpose and audience. As you work through this textbook, you may find it helpful to build up a critical vocabulary in an exercise book or note-book of your own, to use in your specific analytical frameworks.

Purpose	What the text is trying to communicate to its target audience and the responses it seeks from the reader(s) or listener(s)
Audience	Who the text is written for or aimed at; the audience can vary from the very general (such as adults) to the very specific (female twenty-somethings who work in the city)

Context and topic

Any text must have a purpose, and the purpose may be a combination of a number of ideas. But many students make the mistake, when analysing texts, of thinking that the purpose stands alone and there are no other elements to be considered. For instance, when students analyse texts, they commonly write that a text's purpose is 'to persuade' or 'to entertain'. However, they are missing a crucial point here – the text must have been written 'to persuade *someone to do something*' or 'to *entertain a particular audience in some way*'. In other words, it is a pointless exercise to look at the different purposes a text might have without considering the audience the text is aimed at, and the **context** within which it is produced. Any text will also have a certain amount of content or a central **topic**, which can also be linked to the context. Look closely at the two texts printed below and answer the questions in the activity, and you will see how these two features play a vital part in any text.

Text PGL Adventure Holiday advert

NEVER A DULL MOMENT

Abseiling, pony trekking, windsurfing, motorsports, canoeing, learning to drive, training to be a lifeguard – PGL offer over 60 different activities at 23 centres across the UK and France for 6–18 year olds.

Whether you have a young child or a teenager, they won't experience a single dull moment on a PGL holiday!

Text Football commentary from BBC local radio

An' the ball goes out of play for another throw-in to Darlo (1.0) just over twenty minutes remainin' (1.0) Darlington nil (1.0) Wolverhampton Wanderers two (1.5) an' it looks as if Wolves (.) are headin' to south London (0.5) to play Charlton (.) in the fourth round (.) in ten days' time (2.0) unless we see a mighty comeback (1.0) from Darlington (1.0) in these remainin' minutes.

Key:
(1.5) indicates a pause in seconds
(.) indicates a micropause

ACTIVITY Examine the two texts closely.

❑ What evidence is there that these two texts are dependent upon their context?

❑ What pointers are given as to the subject matter of each text?

❏ Having answered the previous two questions, can you say what purpose each text has? Remember to make your estimation of the purpose transitive, and give sufficient evidence to account for each of your answers.

As you will no doubt have noticed, the place of production of each of the above texts is all-important. If the first text were found in the middle of a recipe for lasagne, it would be totally inappropriate; but it is part of a leaflet advertising a holiday company, so it is contextualized and we accept its appropriateness, even if we do not want to patronize the company. If we heard the second text in the middle of a dinner party, we would again find that the piece is out of context; but if we switched on the car radio and heard it, we would readily accept it.

The subject matter of these two texts is also obvious. In the advert, we see a number of nouns that are all part of the **semantic field** of sporting activities: *abseiling, canoeing, windsurfing*. In the second text, there are a number of terms that belong to the semantic field of soccer: *throw-in, ball, fourth round, Wolverhampton Wanderers*. It is easy, therefore, to recognize what the texts are about and that in turn helps us to put them into context.

There is one other crucial difference that you will have noted about these two texts: one is written and the other is spoken (it is represented here in the form of a transcript). These differences of **mode** will be discussed at length in Chapter 4. To add to our framework of the terminology used in analysing language production, we can define context and topic in the following way.

Context	The situation in which the text takes place, is used or is intended to happen
Topic	What the text is about, its subject matter or 'topicality', which can be recognized by words used in a particular semantic field

Form and style

As we have already noted, a number of other factors can affect textual production but do not always come into play. One of these matters is the **form** that the text takes, or the representation of the text. If we look at the following text, we can see simply by its appearance that it is an advertisement, despite the fact that there are no images. The layout, the use of words, the inclusion of a location, telephone number and website address all help to convey this.

Text Advert for Shyness Clinic

> *OVERCOME SHYNESS*
> **BUILD SELF-ESTEEM**
> Combat fear, conversation blocks and
> physical symptoms in a new group,
> led by skilled psychotherapist.
> Achieve success and build
> self-confidence. Proven results.
> **CALL FOR FREE CONSULTATION**
> **The Shyness Clinic**
> Devonshire Place, W1
> *Tel: 0797 000 0000*
> www.bashful.com

So we can define form in the following way:

Form	The way that the text is represented, seen or heard, the recognized format of textual representation that is applied by the writer to the whole of the text

One vital area we must also consider is the **style** in which a text is written (or spoken). This will be linked very closely to the purpose, and consequently to the audience, with any stylistic issues having been decided beforehand. Style is a term you will also come across when you study literary texts; indeed, you should already have a good grasp of what constitutes a writer's literary style from your study of literature at GCSE. We can define it for textual production purposes by breaking it down into five major areas.

Style	The way that the text is written. It includes such matters as **lexis** (the words used), **grammar** (the ways in which single words are organized into meaningful chunks of text), **phonology** (the way sounds are used and combined to help convey textual meaning), **cohesion** (the way the text is ordered and hangs together) and **graphology** (what the text looks like).

Language production

It is essential that you take all of the above areas into consideration when you plan and produce texts (as well as when you analyse texts), and you must always ensure that you are able to justify your choice of any of them in your commentary.

The chart below is a diagrammatic representation of the issues that we have discussed so far.

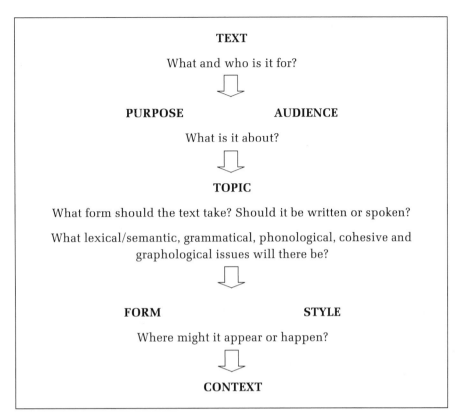

You can see that with this flow-chart model each stage of production is dependent on the choices made in the preceding ones and has implications for the next stage also. But, as the model below shows, the decisions do not necessarily have to be made in a linear fashion. We can also consider the text as being at the centre of a production 'circle', where each stage of production is linked to the other stages and the text needs all of them in order to work.

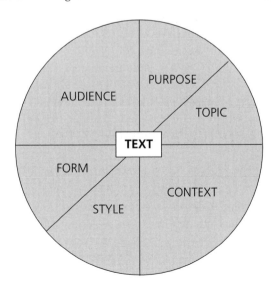

In this diagram we see that each segment must be satisfactory and all must be working together before the 'whole' can operate as a text.

Whichever of these models you feel is most appropriate and works for you is the 'framework' you should use when you come to write texts of your own. The framework will also help you to reflect upon which areas have been given most prominence in your production, when you come to write your commentary. We will deal with this aspect of the course later in the chapter.

In conclusion, you should be aware that no texts are produced in a vacuum; you should therefore always assume that any writing you do on this course has a **practical** angle to it and a particular purpose and audience at its heart. Once these two areas have been identified, considerations can be given to topic, form, style and context. If texts are produced without these considerations, it is likely that they will not be effective.

What purposes might I be given for language production?

It is impossible to give an exhaustive list of the types of purposes for writing that you might be given in an examination task. However, the specification says that you may be asked to do any of the following:

> *information-based writing, argument-based writing, discursively-based writing, persuasive writing, writing to entertain, expositional work,* or any reasonable *combination* of these.

As you can see, this constitutes a vast range of purposes, and when you take all other considerations into account, such as audience and context, then it seems that an almost infinite combination of tasks could be given to you. This is why there is so much written material in our world; and when you add in spoken texts, the weight of material becomes enormous! Bearing this in mind, we will look at some of the more common types of task you might be asked to do. We will do this firstly by examining a variety of textual springboards, to familiarize you with the idea of textual analysis, and then give you some tasks to tackle that are linked to the original texts.

Writing to entertain (and divert) us

If you have to write in an entertaining fashion, you will be given a specific brief from which to write. You will still need to provide some ideas and 'plot', but you will be given a specific starting point. Use the framework cited earlier in this chapter as a planning tool. Once you have done your planning you can start your piece of writing.

Possible story lines

Many writers have claimed that there are only a certain number of story lines and that any narrative is a variation on a theme. In an article in *The Guardian*, Rory Johnson outlines what he believes are the eight basic plot lines available to any writer. These are useful in that they can provide you with a structure, should you struggle to come up with one in the examination room. Don't forget, however, that your narrative does not need to be complete. There is a limit to what you can produce in 45 minutes!

Johnson's eight basic plots are:

1 The **Cinderella** story, where an unrecognized virtue is finally given due credit. Cinderella is not always female and a love interest does not have to be the basis for the plot. (Example: *Jane Eyre* by Charlotte Brontë)

2 The **Achilles** story, which highlights the fatal flaw that leads to inevitably tragic consequences. (Example: *King Lear* by William Shakespeare)

3 The **Orpheus** story, which shows what happens when apparent good fortune is taken away for a particular reason. (Example: *Vile Bodies* by Evelyn Waugh)

4 The **Romeo and Juliet** story, which shows what happens when strangers meet and fall in love. It does not have to be a tragic ending. (Example: *Pride and Prejudice* by Jane Austen)

5 The **Irrepressible Hero** story, where a series of hurdles are placed in front of the protagonist and he or she always succeeds. A variant of this is the David and Goliath story. (Example: Widmerpool in Anthony Powell's *A Dance to the Music of Time*)

6 The **Circe** story, where an unsuspecting character is drawn into a devious plot by a villain. (Example: Boxer in *Animal Farm* by George Orwell)

7 The **Tristan** story, which sets out the workings of the eternal triangle; this can be two men and one woman, or vice versa. (Example: *Far From the Madding Crowd* by Thomas Hardy)

8 The **Faust** story, where a pact is made with the devil, and the debt must finally be paid. (Example: *Macbeth* by Shakespeare)

Each of these plots can be styled in various fashions, such as given a comic or melodramatic treatment, or can shift the basic plot details around. They can also have various issues or themes superimposed upon them, to add interest to the narrative. If you feel you need to make overt use of any of the above ideas, try to be original in the way in which you deal with the story line.

Practising language production

Below are a series of activities for you to work on, each drawing from a slightly different source, thus requiring different treatment (and evaluation in your commentary).

Text 1 The start of a novel

(Adapted from) *Roadkill* by Kinky Friedman

You could say the whole adventure began the day I looked in the bathroom mirror and saw the gypsy. That explanation might not hold up in a court of law, but as far as I'm concerned it's close enough. I'd come in rather late the night before and as I slept I was visited by a strange and singularly vivid dream. Without going into graphic details, let me just say that I finally came across the girl in the peach-coloured dress who was being held captive . . .

ACTIVITY 1

Using the start of the novel given above, write the continuation of it, paying special attention to the following:

❑ Continue in the same narrative style, using the first-person viewpoint, moving the narrative on in a logical fashion.
❑ Do not fall into the trap of making this a stereotypical dream story; any reference to the dream should be carefully contextualized.
❑ Finish your section by returning as naturally as you can to the references of the first sentence.

Text 2 Adaptation of speech into a narrative

(from Talking Heads) *Bed Among the Lentils* by Alan Bennett

I stand up and say, 'My name is Susan. I am a vicar's wife and I am an alcoholic.' Then I tell my story. Or some of it anyway. 'Don't pull any punches,' says Clem, my counsellor. 'Nobody's going to be shocked, believe me love, we've all been there.' But I don't tell them about Mr Ramesh because they've not been there. 'Listen, people. I was so drunk I used to go and sleep with an Asian grocer. Yes, and you won't believe this. I loved it. Loved every minute.' Dear oh dear. This was a real drunken lady.

'So how did you come to AA?' they ask. 'My husband,' I say. 'The vicar. He persuaded me.' But I lie. It was not my husband, it was Mr Ramesh.

ACTIVITY 2

This is an extract from a monologue spoken from Susan's point of view. A certain amount of information is given here which you should work into your narrative. Imagine you are a member of the Alcoholics Anonymous group that Susan attends.

- ❏ Relate her story from your point of view, adapting Susan's speech and her reported speech as naturally as you can.
- ❏ Work in as much detail of her story as you can, being as realistic as possible.
- ❏ Reflect the atmosphere of the group in your piece of writing.

Text 3 Argumentative and persuasive writing

(from *The Sun* Editorial, October 23, 1999)

Sick Making

The double-dealing of the French is exposed for all to see

They defy European law and ban British beef because they claim it still has BSE – which the experts say it doesn't.

But all the time they have been feeding their own animals with human sewage and illegal animal waste.

It is enough to make your stomach churn – at the blatant abuse of hygiene standards and at their flagrant hypocrisy.

Britain has slaughtered five million cattle at a cost of **£4.2 BILLION** to make its beef safe from BSE.

Farmers have been driven to bankruptcy as meat prices have gone through the floor.

None of that has been good enough for the French farmers, who have a shocking record of using every trick in the book to protect their own inefficiency at the expense of others.

The French claim they don't have BSE. That's because every time a cow catches it, the animal is killed and buried without any official record being made.

France must be made to stick to the rules and clean up its act.

If it refuses, its products should be banned from other EU countries.

ACTIVITY 3 This editorial appeared in the tabloid newspaper *The Sun* after the French government had refused to lift its ban on British beef. In the same week, it was revealed that French farmers had fed their cattle with human and animal waste.

- ❏ Write a letter to the broadsheet newspaper *The Independent*, outlining how limited you feel these views are.
- ❏ Refer to the detail of this editorial in your letter.
- ❏ Use appropriate lexis and grammatical structure.

(You may want to read the detail in Chapter 4 on rhetorical and persuasive techniques before you tackle this particular activity.)

Once you have completed these activities you need to look at the next section of this chapter; in your examination, you will be asked to reflect on parts of your writing in a brief commentary. However, it is important to practise your production skills first, since you cannot reflect on anything you have written until it is completed!

Writing a commentary

It is perhaps a little inaccurate to call this second part of the question a 'commentary', since you are required to comment on only *some* aspects of your writing. The more detailed commentary appears in the A2 section of the course, specifically in Unit 5 Section B. However, it is always good practice to articulate your own choices. You can note these choices as you are writing your text, since this will help you focus on why you are making particular decisions while you are engaged in the act of production. Once you have written your text, you will then be able to comment on the overall impact and effect you wanted to create, since you will have a more objective view of your work. Finally, if at this early point in the course you familiarize yourself with the types of issues that are related to commentaries, you will be much more effective in dealing with the more detailed commentary necessary for Unit 5 in the A2 part of the specification.

Possible frameworks for commentaries

When you are given a specific task, the second part of the question will require you to write a commentary. You will be asked to examine specific parts of your production work; this will give you the broad structure for your answer. It is, in effect, a mini textual analysis. Whatever the detail of the question, you should always concentrate on your text by:

❏ showing what you have done through carefully chosen examples
❏ showing how it adds to the effect of the text, by commenting on audience and/or purpose
❏ contrasting the example with the original if required.

You should remind yourself of the section in the previous chapter on how to adopt an analytical framework, and what constitutes the analytical sentence. This will help you focus on the analytical aspects needed to answer this part of the question; you can identify what you want to say in your commentary, pick out some examples to illustrate the points you want to make, quote them and then show how they work. By stringing together your analytical sentences, you will construct a mini commentary which should address the issues you have identified.

One possible way of focusing on the way you have written your text is to use the following framework as a structure around which you can build your analysis and systematically construct your commentary. Use the following questions to help you:

1 Issues of audience
   ❏ What have you done to make your material suitable for the intended audience?
   ❏ Why have you made these choices? How will they help you target the right audience?

2 Issues of purpose
   ❏ What types of stylistic choices have you made to help the overall purpose of the piece?
   ❏ Why have you chosen these particular ideas? How do you think they help the purpose? What do they do that other choices would not do?

3 Issues of form
   ❏ Are there any particular points of form you have taken into account in your written production, which underpin the audience and purpose?
   ❏ Why have you chosen to focus on these? How do they mesh with the other issues you have highlighted?

4 Issues of subject matter and topic
   ❏ How have you adapted any subject content you were given?
   ❏ Why have you done so?
   ❏ What is the effect of these adaptations?

5 Any other issues
   ❏ What other points have you taken into consideration in your piece?
   ❏ What effect do you intend by including this?
   ❏ How does it contribute to the overall effect of your piece of writing?

By using this framework you will be able to cover most of the eventualities that you will be faced with in this particular unit.

We will return to the activities that you tackled at the end of the last section, now that you are in a position to be able to answer the commentary questions that follow each of the production questions. Remember that the more you know about the way language works, the more accurate your commentaries and analysis will be.

Here are the commentary questions for each of those production questions. Allow yourself about half an hour to complete each one of these. Ideally, they should be done immediately after you have completed your production work. You will need to refer only to certain parts of the framework above, as not all aspects will apply to each question.

Activity 1

Key words for consideration in your commentary, taken from the production task:

❏ the start of the novel
❏ continuation

❏ the same narrative style
❏ first-person viewpoint
❏ moving the narrative on in a logical fashion
❏ *not* a stereotypical dream story
❏ the references of the first sentence.

COMMENTARY ON ACTIVITY 1

Focusing on some of the particular stylistic choices you have made in your continuation, show how and why you have made certain narrative decisions in your production work.

Activity 2

Key words for consideration in your commentary, taken from the production task:

❏ monologue from Susan's point of view
❏ information . . . work into . . . narrative
❏ imagine you are a member
❏ her story from your point of view
❏ realistic adaptation of Susan's speech
❏ reflect the atmosphere of the group.

COMMENTARY ON ACTIVITY 2

Write a brief commentary on your piece of work.

1 Show how you have shifted the viewpoint of the story and the effect this has on the narrative and the atmosphere.

2 Comment on how you have adapted some of Susan's speech for your production purposes.

Activity 3

Key words for consideration in your commentary, taken from the production task:

❏ (original) editorial appeared in the tabloid newspaper
❏ French farmers had fed their cattle with human and animal waste
❏ write a letter . . . broadsheet newspaper . . . *The Independent* . . . limited you feel these views are
❏ refer to the detail of this editorial
❏ use appropriate lexis and grammatical structure.

COMMENTARY ON ACTIVITY 3

Reflect on the letter you have written by examining the following:

1 the methods you use to counter/refute the limited views outlined in *The Sun*

2 how you have used specific words and grammatical constructions to underpin your argument.

Obviously, the type of commentary question you are asked in Unit 1 will be directly linked to the type of production task you have to do, and will test your knowledge of the techniques you have used and your ability to reflect upon those techniques, by commenting on *how* you have used them.

APPROACHES TO EXAMINATION QUESTIONS

Look at the following question, which has already been set on an examination paper, and then read the answer and commentary given by the student.

Question 1: Production Task

Read the piece of spontaneous speech printed below. It is taken from a conversation between three people. It includes pauses, overlaps, elongation of sounds and non-fluency features.

A: I (.) I thought er we was (.) were never going to find it (2.0)

C: You went right ro::und the (0.5) city

A: Yeah

B: God it was frustratin' (1.0) I

                 [

C: so what er (.) what did you (1.0)

A: [Well we er (0.5)

B: [Er we::ll (1.0)

A: couldn't go back cos we knew they er was behind us (2.0) somewhere an' we had a::bsolutely no:: idea where it was did we (.)

B: No::: (.) yeah thas right we er went down this re::ally dark road an (.)

A: Yeah I forgot about that (2.0) an' it was pissin' down an' all (2.0)

C: Did they not get (.) give you a (.) er map or summat (.)

A: Nah

     [

B: They should a (0.5) but we well we er never thought that it was gonna be that er we::ll (1.0) dangerous, did we eh (1.0)

A: Nah

     [

B: that street was so::: pitch ss black we hadn't a clue (0.5) where ter go (3.5)

C: How long did er (.) it..

            [

A: must a been at le::ast twenty no thir (.) half an hour wan it (.)

B: God at le:::ast

Use this spontaneous speech as the basis of an exchange between three characters towards the start of a novel or short story. You should include any relevant detail that would enhance the adaptation of this piece into a piece of narrative prose. You are free to choose your audience, setting and viewpoint, as well as the genre of your piece of fiction. You should draw closely on your study of prose and the representation of speech within prose, whilst endeavouring to make the piece as interesting as possible.

Question 2: Commentary

Write a commentary that explains the choices you have made in your piece of fiction. You should comment on the following:

- ❏ your choice of lexis and grammatical structures
- ❏ how your style is suited to your audience
- ❏ how you have adapted spontaneous speech for a particular context, explaining the adaptations you have made and why you made them

---

Student response

They ran on, genuine fear in their hearts, minds and faces, desperately searching for something. Something. But what? They stopped and looked around. The rain blurred their vision and added to their confusion.

All of a sudden, they spotted something familiar. A beacon of hope in a darkening, despairing landscape. With renewed hope and energy, they struck on towards the light, the sign, the sanctuary. Summoning reserves from within, they battled on.

Just as relief was seeping into their bodies, breathing feeling into numb limbs, a voice cried out behind them. Close. Too close to stop. All tiredness was forgotten and pure fear carried them on. Neither dared even consider their feelings of weariness, for that would condemn them to stop, and to stop would be to perish.

So they fought on. Against the rain. Against the pain. Against the rising feeling of emptiness, of despair eating away at their stomachs. They fought on. Now it was getting too much. It needed to stop.

Now!

Wait! What's that? The light appears again, flashes on and off, on and off, but this time they can reach it. This time they do reach it. They pass beneath the light, relief flooding through heavy limbs, diluting and flooding away fears of failure. They have made it. They're here.

Jim and David, two seven-year-old boys, cross the road at the flashing pelican crossing, as their monster – an overly playful, mangy, stray dog – fidgets, scratches itself, stranded on the other side of the river of traffic.

Bubbling with excitement and exhilaration, and bursting to tell Steven about their adventure, they run up to the house and go straight in without knocking. They find Steven at the kitchen table, eating his tea.

'I thought we was never going to find it,' says Jim, resting his hands on his knees.
'You went round the whole city?' asks Steven looking up from his egg and chips.
'Yeah.'
'God! It was frustrating,' exclaims David, keen to emphasize their ordeal, using a word he had heard his dad use more than once about him, although not really certain as to its meaning.
'So what happened?' asks Steven.

This is the question both boys have been waiting for. Supporting each other, filling in the parts the other misses, together they give their account of the events prior to their arrival at the house.

'Well we . . . '
'Yeah, we . . . ' They both speak together. David continues.
'. . . couldn't go back 'cause we knew they was behind us somewhere and we had absolutely no idea where it was, did we?'
'No. Yeah. That's right. We went down this really dark road . . . '
'. . . yeah! I forgot about that. It was pissing down as well.'

Steven coughs at the use of the forbidden word and tries to direct them back onto the track of the story.

'Didn't they give you a map or something?'
'Nah.'
'They should have, but we never thought it would be that dangerous, did we, eh?'
'Nah.'
'That street was so pitch black!' The last two words are given supreme emphasis. 'We didn't know where to go!'
'How long did it . . . ?' Steven begins to ask.
'Oh, it must have been twenty or thirty minutes! Wasn't it?'
'God, at least!'

And there, their story ends. Details missed, sentences sparse, explicit meaning the least of their concerns. Instead, through sheer excitement, they have produced a stream of information characteristic of boys their age.

Steven, however, knows exactly what they meant.

Commentary

When writing this beginning to a novel, using the supplied speech excerpt as a stimulus, I made a series of choices relating to plot, structure, language use and character to make my work more appealing to my chosen audience. I decided to write my piece with a mature audience in mind. I felt that because I was part of this target group, it would be easier for me to judge the progressive success of the piece because I could simply refer to what I myself found satisfying in a piece of literature. So I have tried to construct this piece with an adult audience in mind.

*I decided to base my piece on children, because I felt that the stimulus material gave clear examples of child-like use, or misuse, of language. For example, the incorrect third person plural agreement of verbs, as in 'they was behind us'. This, to me, is indicative of someone still learning the language, still making errors, and so it seemed obvious to use children as the protagonists of my piece. I also feel that the spontaneity of the narrative lends itself to use of these forms and it was something I chose to highlight by **not** changing all the non-standard forms.*

There is, however, a darker side to the supplied material. The speakers refer to something that is 'behind them' and that it was 'dangerous'. This element of mystery gives the piece a sinister, hidden side that we cannot understand through what is actually said, and could perhaps indicate that they are not children after all. However, I interpreted this as a characteristic of younger children such as the hyperbolic expressions to describe things that we would deem to be quite dull. So, the stray dog turns into a 'monster', the alleys are not dark, they are 'pitch black'. It is not just raining, it is 'pissing down'. However, I felt that I had to give a 'gloss' to this word by indicating its taboo nature to boys of this age. The risk and danger exists solely in the children's over active imagination, and was not real, or what we would consider to be frightening. An adult audience can recognize this, whereas a younger one may perceive what the boys experience as being genuinely life-threatening.

These conflicting and contrasting ideas – what is and isn't said – made it very easy for me to structure my piece. I began by attempting to portray the unsaid elements as a physical experience, with feelings and emotions. This builds character profiles and establishes a connection with the reader. I tried to make this as real as possible, because to the boys this would be a real experience. The dog would be a monster and so forth. So, to feel what the boys feel, the reader cannot know the real situation until it is over.

I also adjusted my language use for the different sections. In the first, I used varying sentence length, ranging from one-word fragments and paragraphs, to long-winded, complex sentences. I also used techniques such as metaphor and alliteration. In the second section, however, to highlight the fact that it was only boys' imagination, I used reasonably basic structure and vocabulary such as 'bubbling', representative of how young and naïve the boys are. I also tried to indicate a distinct change in the two sections, separated by the single paragraph 'Now', by shifting the tense from the past to the present. I also think this helps relate the breathlessness of the boys' experience.

Finally, I made several changes to the conventions of transcription. I adapted the speech of the boys by including narrative insertions, such as the comment on the word 'frustrating', as well as the more conventional 'Jim says'. I tried to vary the verbs of speech to reflect the way each of the boys speaks. I also cut out pauses and some of the overlaps, although I retained one of these for effect when the two boys are so keen to tell their story.

Whilst there are some flaws in the decision to choose child protagonists, I feel I have succeeded in adapting the piece for an adult audience in an entertaining fashion.

Examiner's comments

This is obviously the work of a talented student who has an overview of the production task and how to reflect in the commentary upon the choices made. The production piece highlights a number of points about the nature of these types of questions.

1 In completing the task the writer draws on his or her understanding of how a text works and the way in which narratives can be shaped using a minimum of material.

2 The material is not complex, the plot is simple and understandable and a readable, accessible style is maintained throughout.

3 The springboard text is totally assimilated into the story line: the mystery of the chase, the pace of the conversation, and the interchange between the characters are all included in a meaningful way.

4 The choices of setting and viewpoint are natural and there is a sense of the writer having total control of the material throughout.

The commentary also conveys many strengths, not least the ability to reflect in a meaningful way on the whole of the text.

1 The commentary deals with a number of issues: audience, purpose, adaptation of the springboard text, use of language, cohesion, and use of subject matter and content.

2 There is some use of quotation as evidence from the text, but there could be more reflection on the use of language, particularly in the first section.

3 There is evidence of the writer's acknowledgement of the limitations of the way the springboard material is used or adapted.

How this Unit links to other sections of the course

In the English Language and Literature course, each Unit has a direct link into other Units so that the skills learned in the AS section of the course can be built on and enhanced at A2 level. Unit 1 of this specification is designed to feed into Unit 5 Section B, but there are also other parts of the course that have overlaps with this particular Unit.

The table below shows the major links between this Unit and others on the course; there are, however, other links which do not carry the same weight.

Question	Skills learned	Links to other parts of the Specification
Language Production Question	Writing for different purposes	• Recasting question Unit 5 Section B • Synoptic question Unit 6 Question 2
	Identification of audience and writing for a specific audience	• Recasting question Unit 5 Section B • Synoptic question Unit 6 Questions 1 and 2
	Learning to use, select and adapt source material	• Recasting question Unit 5 Section B
	How to use a framework for production	• Synoptic question Unit 6 Question 2
Commentary	Reflecting on choices made in own writing	• Recasting question Unit 5 Section B
	Use of quotation to evidence stylistic points in own writing	• Recasting question Unit 5 Section B
	Assimilation of subject matter and content of texts	• Recasting question Unit 5 Section B
	Reflecting on how language is used to help target an audience; reflecting on context and form	• Language of Speech Unit 3 Section B • Recasting question Unit 5 Section B • Synoptic question Unit 6 Question 1

2 Poetic Study

In this Unit you will focus on the ways in which language is used in poetry texts. At the centre of this study will be the choices that poets make in terms of **language**, **form** and **structure** in order to achieve the **effects** that they want. In the examination that you are working towards, the study of poetry texts will involve looking at both linguistic and literary issues in the texts and understanding the ways that poets use language to achieve and enhance literary effects and issues.

In the examination, the section on Poetic Study will offer you a choice of texts (three modern poetry texts and three pre-1900 poetry texts). In order to meet the requirements of the examination you will need to answer one question on one of the set texts. We will look at the kinds of questions you might expect a little later on, but they will be of the kind that will allow you to employ the frameworks for linguistic and literary analysis that you have studied during your course.

Whichever text you study and whichever question you choose to answer, you will be assessed on your ability to:

❑ use literary and linguistic frameworks and terminology to describe key features of poetry as well as commenting on variation in meaning and form
❑ explain and interpret the language of poetry, including sound features, vocabulary and meaning, grammar and structure as appropriate, showing how it provides insights into literary interpretations.

As well as identifying these key objectives, the specification offers the following advice.

❑ Candidates will be required to comment on specific poems or sections of longer poems, in their analyses.
❑ Candidates should focus on linguistic matters as a route into explaining and discussing matters of content.
❑ Candidates may be required to comment on other literary interpretations and readings.

In this Unit we will be looking carefully at exactly how these objectives translate into aspects of the study of your chosen text, the kinds of things that you could be asked to do in the examination, and ways of approaching these tasks.

The nature of poetry

Like prose, poetry cannot be neatly categorized and the question of what exactly poetry is – what it is that marks it out as being different from prose – is a question that has tested writers, critics, philosophers and all concerned with literature for centuries. Certainly poets can choose from a whole range of different forms, structures, techniques and styles when writing their poetry. They can play with language and manipulate it, even invent a 'new' language to express their feelings, ideas and themselves. Because, generally, the ideas in poems are expressed in fewer words than are used in prose, the messages or ideas expressed in a poem are sometimes more difficult to understand than if they were expressed in prose. Also, the poet may be expressing himself or herself in a unique way – it is more acceptable for the language of poetry to deviate from generally observed rules. This 'poetic licence' allows poets to experiment with language, perhaps playing around with word order, or using dialectal forms, or using lexical or syntactical patterning to create or reinforce meaning. Of course, prose writers can use these techniques too, but they will be much more frequently found in the language of poetry.

ACTIVITY Throughout your life you will probably have encountered various kinds of poetry, at school, college, in reading for pleasure, on the radio, television, etc. Based on your experience write down all the features you can think of that makes poetry different from other kinds of writing.

Features of poetry

Poetry is an extremely varied genre in every respect – in content, structure, style, intention and every other way. Some poems present narratives that tell stories; some are written to be performed; some explore philosophical, emotional, or spiritual concepts and ideas; some are amusing, some are sad. In fact, it is probably safe to say that in one way or another poetry covers the whole range of human experience and the features that it possesses can be many and varied. Poems can rhyme or not, they can use figurative language or not, they can be organized in stanzas or not, they can be written in conventional English or they can break all the rules of grammar. In other words every poem is an individual piece of work with a range of features peculiar to itself. When you are reading a poem for the first time, therefore, it is important to establish what the poet is saying to the reader – in other words, what the **purpose** of the poem is. Having identified that, you can then go on to examine *how* the poet says whatever it is that he or she wishes to say.

The purpose of poetry

In poetry, language is used in both poetic and expressive ways to convey meaning to the reader, and the **purpose** of the poem could be to serve any one of a wide range of functions. For example, a poem could:

- ❑ entertain
- ❑ describe
- ❑ arouse emotions
- ❑ tell a story
- ❑ provoke thought
- ❑ inform
- ❑ console
- ❑ celebrate
- ❑ express grief

or any combination of these things.

Of course the lexis, style, form and other linguistic choices that a poet makes are closely linked to the purpose of the poem, and all provide useful clues as to what the poet's intentions are.

In order to comprehend fully any message that a poem might carry for us, it is important to look at the linguistic and stylistic features of the poem. Poets can draw upon many varied linguistic features and it is not possible to consider them all in detail here. However, there are certain devices and forms that are well worth examining and we will look at some of them now.

Manner

The first thing to consider when encountering a poem for the first time is to establish the **manner** in which it is written. Basically the manner can be either formal or informal, depending on the kind of relationship the poet wants to establish with the reader. Of course, there can be different levels of formality or informality. Poetry is often associated with a heightened use of language – the poet generally uses fewer words than the prose writer and therefore the language is in a more concentrated form. Not all poems work on a 'heightened' level, however. Some poets use poetry to mirror the language of everyday speech to, create a quite different tone.

Tone, mood and atmosphere

The overall effect that a poem creates in the mind of the reader is very closely linked to the mood and tone that it creates. The 'voice' of the poem can create a certain **tone** that conveys to the reader certain messages about the poem itself. Obviously there are many different kinds of tone.

ACTIVITY   Think of as many words as you can to describe tone.

Tone can be difficult to delineate exactly, but there are many words that can be used to describe it. This is not an exhaustive list – add any more you have on your own list. It may help you when you are uncertain as to how to describe a particular tone. (Make sure you know what all the words mean.)

Playful	Ironic	Assertive	Frivolous	Gloomy
Humorous	Sarcastic	Cynical	Calm	Heavy
Melancholy	Sardonic	Dogmatic	Serious	Personal
Mocking	Light-hearted	Dramatic	Impersonal	Angry
Sad	Philosophical	Flat	Intimate	Wistful
Evaluative	Clinical	Sharp	Solemn	Religious

Just as you might pick up clues as to how a friend feels through the tone of voice that he or she uses, so you can pick up clues from the 'voice' of the poem.

The **mood** of the poem, although closely linked to the tone, is a slightly different thing – it refers to the atmosphere that the poem creates. Very often tone and mood are closely linked and a certain tone produces a certain mood. For example, if a poet uses a lively, humorous tone it is far more likely to produce a light atmosphere than a melancholy one. In your Language and Literature course you will not only need to recognize the tone, mood and atmosphere of poems but you will also need to examine the ways in which poets use language to create their tones, moods and atmosphere.

ACTIVITY

Read the following poems carefully and think about the **manner** in which they are written. What kind of relationship do you think each poet wishes to establish with the reader? Comment on the tone, mood and atmosphere created in each poem and the ways in which the poets use language to create it.

Hey There Now!

(*For Lesley*)

Hey there now
my brownwater flower
    my sunchild branching
from my mountain river
        hey there now!
my young stream
    headlong
        rushing

➡

I love to watch you
when you're
sleeping
blushing

Grace Nichols

Advent

Earth grown old, yet still so green,
Deep beneath her crust of cold
Nurses fire unfelt, unseen;
Earth grown old.

We who live are quickly told;
Millions more lie hid between
Inner swathings of her fold.

When will fire break up her screen?
When will life burst through her mould?
Earth, earth, earth, thy cold is keen.
Earth grown old.

Christina Rossetti

I Say I Say I Say

Anyone here had a go at themselves
for a laugh? Anyone opened their wrists
with a blade in the bath? Those in the dark
at the back, listen hard. Those at the front
in the know, those of us who have, hands up,
let's show that inch of lacerated skin
between the forearm and the fist. Let's tell it
like it is: strong drink, a crimson tidemark
round the tub, a yard of lint, white towels
washed a dozen times, still pink. Tough luck.
A passion then for watches, bangles, cuffs.
A likely story: you were lashed by brambles
picking berries from the woods. Come clean, come good,
repeat with me the punch line 'Just like blood'
when those at the back rush forward to say
how a little love goes a long long long way.

Simon Armitage

One student had clear ideas about what the poems meant to her. Read her responses through carefully. How close are her responses to your own thoughts on these poems? Remember, responses to poetry can be very individual.

Grace Nichols appears to have written the poem 'Hey There Now!', in celebration of someone she loves very dearly. Writing in an informal manner, she appears to invite the reader into sharing in this celebration. The poem has a loving tone which Nichols has created through the sentiments she expresses and which is enhanced by her use of language. For example, Nichols repeats the personal pronoun 'my' when referring to the subject of the poem, emphasizing ownership of the subject. In addition, the subject is described in affectionate terms, 'my sunchild', 'my brownwater flower'. The vitality if her love for the subject is complimented by Nichols's use of natural imagery which also adds to the celebratory mood. 'Flower', 'stream', 'river' and 'mountain' are all natural images included in the poem and they present the idea of a 'forever' love which is natural and pure. The sense of 'forever', as in an unending love, is further enhanced by the use of present continuous verb forms: 'branching', ' rushing', 'sleeping', 'blushing'. These verb endings give the poem 'movement' and add to the lively tone. The repetition of the exclamatory phrase, 'Hey there now!' also adds to the lively tone enhancing the celebratory mood of the poem as a whole.

Although natural imagery is contained in Christina Rossetti's poem, 'Advent', the mood of the poem is somewhat sorrowful. Writing in a formal manner, the poet adopts a melancholy tone in her presentation of 'Earth grown old'. The language that Rossetti uses helps to create a mood of sadness. For instance, the earth is described as 'cold', 'earth, earth, thy cold is keen', which suggests that it is an unwelcoming, uncomfortable place to be. The formal manner in which the poem is written, further enhances the detachment from her surroundings that the poet feels. Rather than seeing Advent as a time which precedes the warmth of Spring, Rossetti presents the near-end of the year as a time of unfulfilment and decay and this is evident in the poem's vocabulary: 'unseen', 'unfelt', 'mould'. The hope of Spring, a 'better' time, is questionable and uncertain in this poem: 'when will fire break up her screen?' adding to the melancholy tone by creating a sense of despair. The unyielding nature of the earth, as seen by the poet, is expressed and enhanced by the apparent rigidity and restrictiveness of the rhyme sequence.

The disturbing content of the poem, 'I Say I Say I Say' is made more so as it is places us in a context in which we would expect to be in a 'happy' environment. As readers, we are placed in the audience of the poet as a 'stand-up' comedian. Using informal words and phrases we would expect to hear light-hearted humour from the comedian on stage: 'Anyone here had a go at themselves for a laugh?', 'Those in the back in the dark', 'Those at the front'. However, the poet shocks the audience with his subject of attempted suicide. An uncomfortable atmosphere is therefore created as a sad, solitary act, an attempted suicide, is given centre stage, the poem acting as an exposé, 'Let's tell it like it is'. However, the poet expresses the difficulty of 'telling it like it is' though various means and use of language in the poem. For instance, he describes how one would 'cover up' the marks on the wrists left after a suicide attempt by developing a 'passion then for watches, bangles, cuffs'. In addition, he includes a 'cover story', a 'likely story' in which 'you were lashed by brambles picking berries from the woods'. Indeed, the whole poem avoids 'telling it like it is' as it fronts the disturbing act of attempted suicide with a light-hearted, comical approach: 'I Say I Say I Say'. Individual phrases in the poem are also seen to avoid directness. For instance, by writing, 'between the forearm and the fist', which almost sounds like a comical attempt at Cockney rhyming slang, the poet avoids using the word 'wrist'. When people are faced with uncomfortable situations, it is often difficult to know what to say and they often resort to using clichés. Consequently, Armitage concludes the poem with a clichéd response from 'those at the back', those who are not 'in the know'. This clichéd response confirms and enhances the uncomfortable, disturbing mood of the poem, 'A little loving goes a long long long way'. The unsuitability of this expected response is further stressed as an extra 'long' has been inserted into this well-known cliché.

Examiner's comments

This is a mature and perceptive response to these poems, in which the student shows a close focus on the poets' use of language and the effects created through tone, mood and atmosphere. The student is greatly advantaged in expressing her ideas on these poems by her knowledge of both literary and linguisitic terminology, which makes the expression of ideas much more straightforward than it would be if basic vocabulary were missing. For example, being able to identify 'my' as a personal pronoun and see its repetition as emphasizing a kind of 'ownership' is a point well made. So is the point about verb endings giving a sense of 'movement', thereby adding '. . . to the lively tone' and 'enhancing the celebratory mood of the poem as a whole'.

Her appreciation of the effects of imagery is also a great merit here, and once again the close focus on language and the use of specific examples from the texts is extremely helpful. With the Armitage poem the student also shows an awareness of the effects of juxtaposing the stand-up comedian's 'I say I say I say' with the disturbing theme of attempted suicide. Overall, a sophisticated response.

Form and structure

Form and **structure** can also tell the reader something about the poet's intentions. The way that the language of the poem is laid out will have been carefully chosen by the poet to enhance or reflect the meaning of the poem. There are many different ways in which poems can be structured, and in looking at the structure of a particular poem we must ask ourselves why the poet has chosen to use a particular form.

Form can refer to the way that the poem is actually written on the page, or the way that the lines are organized or grouped. Basically, poetry can be divided into general categories. First there is the kind where the lines follow on from each other continuously without breaks. Long narrative poems often take this form, and poems such as Wordsworth's *The Prelude* or Keats's *Lamia*. The technical term for this kind of poetic form is **stichic** poetry.

The other kind of poetry is that where the lines are arranged in groups, which are sometimes incorrectly called 'verses'. The correct term for these groups of lines is **stanzas**. This kind of poetic form is called **strophic** poetry and examples of its use are in poems such as Keats's *Eve of St. Agnes*, Christina Rossetti's *An Apple Gathering* or Simon Armitage's *C.V.*

Stanzas can be organized in many different ways. Here are some examples.

The sonnet

The sonnet is a very popular form in English poetry, and one that poets have used for centuries. Basically a sonnet consists of fourteen lines with a structured rhyme scheme and a definite rhythm pattern (usually iambic pentameter). There are two main kinds of sonnet, the petrarchan or Italian sonnet (so called because it is named after the medieval Italian writer, Petrarch). The Petrarchan sonnet divides the fourteen lines into an octave (eight lines) and a sestet (six lines). The rhyme scheme (see page 54) can vary but generally the pattern is *abbaabba cdecde* or *abbaabba cdcdcd*. The octave sets out the theme or key idea of the poem and the sestet provides some kind of response to it.

The other main kind of sonnet is the Shakespearean or English sonnet. In this kind of sonnet the lines are divided into three quatrains (of four lines each) and end with a couplet (two lines). The rhyme scheme in this kind of sonnet generally follows the pattern of *abab cdcd efef gg*. The theme or idea is developed through the quatrains.

Now read the following two sonnets.

To My Brothers

Small, busy flames play through the fresh laid coals,
  And their faint cracklings o'er our silence creep
   Like whispers of the household gods that keep
A gentle empire o'er fraternal souls.

And while, for rhymes, I search around the poles,
  Your eyes are fix'd, as in poetic sleep,
  Upon the lore so voluble and deep,
That aye at fall of night our care condoles.

This is your birth-day Tom, and I rejoice
  That thus it passes smoothly, quietly.
Many such eves of gently whisp'ring noise
  May we together pass, and calmly try
What are this world's true joys, – ere the great voice,
  From its fair face, shall bid our spirits fly.

John Keats

An Evil Spirit

An evil spirit, your beauty haunts me still,
Wherewith, alas, I have been long possessed,
Which ceaseth not to tempt me to each ill,
Nor gives me once but one poor minute's rest;

In me it speaks, whether I sleep or wake,
And when by means to drive it out I try,
With greater torments then it me doth take,
And tortures me in most extremity;

Before my face it lays down my despairs,
And hastes me on unto a sudden death,
Now tempting me to drown myself in tears,
And then in sighing to give up my breath.

Thus am I still provoked to every evil
By this good wicked spirit, sweet angel-devil.

Michael Drayton

ACTIVITY

1 Examine the form each sonnet is written in and the rhyme scheme each poet has employed.

2 What are the key ideas each sonnet deals with? Examine the language each poet has used to express his ideas.

3 How does the language combine with the structure of each sonnet to fulfil the poets' intentions?

Other forms which you may come across in your studies include the following.

Ballads

Ballads date back to the oral tradition of the late Middle Ages and originally were often set to music. They are poems that tell a story, and therefore the focus tends to be on action and dialogue rather than the contemplative exploration of some kind of theme. The structure of the ballad normally consists of rhyming quatrains, sometimes using dialect forms or repetition to create effects.

Odes

Odes are lyrical poems, often elaborate, addressed to a particular person or thing or an abstract idea. They can present straightforward praise or they can develop complex philosophical ideas, and they can focus on positive or negative feelings with, perhaps, involved arguments. They are complex poems – the language often reflects the complexity of the content and many images may be contained within the poem. Odes are generally organized into fairly long stanzas. In the odes of Keats, for example, the stanzas are usually ten lines long.

Here is Keats's *Ode on a Grecian Urn*. Read it through carefully.

Ode on a Grecian Urn

Thou still unravish'd bride of quietness,
  Thou foster-child of silence and slow time,
Sylvan historian, who canst thus express
  A flowery tale more sweetly than our rhyme:
What leaf-fring'd legend haunts about thy shape
  Of deities or mortals, or of both,
    In Tempe or the dales of Arcady?
  What men or gods are these? What maidens loth?
What mad pursuit? What struggle to escape?
  What pipes and timbrels? What wild ecstasy?

Heard melodies are sweet, but those unheard
  Are sweeter; therefore, ye soft pipes, play on;
Not to the sensual ear, but, more endear'd,
  Pipe to the spirit ditties of no tone:
Fair youth, beneath the trees, thou canst not leave
  Thy song, nor ever can those trees be bare;
    Bold Lover, never, never canst thou kiss,
Though winning near the goal – yet, do not grieve;
  She cannot fade, though thou hast not thy bliss,
  For ever wilt thou love, and she be fair!

Ah, happy, happy boughs! that cannot shed
  Your leaves, nor ever bid the Spring adieu;
And, happy melodist, unwearied,

For ever piping songs for ever new;
More happy love! more happy, happy love!
 For ever warm and still to be enjoy'd,
  For ever panting, and for ever young;
All breathing human passion far above,
 That leaves a heart high-sorrowful and cloy'd,
  A burning forehead, and a parching tongue.

Who are these coming to the sacrifice?
 To what green altar, O mysterious priest,
Lead'st thou that heifer lowing at the skies,
 And all her silken flanks with garlands drest?
What little town by river or sea shore,
 Or mountain-built with peaceful citadel,
  Is emptied of this folk, this pious morn?
And, little town, thy streets for evermore
 Will silent be; and not a soul to tell
  Why thou art desolate, can e'er return.

O Attic shape! Fair attitude! with brede
 Of marble men and maidens overwrought,
With forest branches and the trodden weed;
 Thou, silent form, dost tease us out of thought
As doth eternity: Cold Pastoral!
 When old age shall this generation waste,
  Thou shalt remain, in midst of other woe
Than ours, a friend to man, to whom thou say'st,
 'Beauty is truth, truth beauty,' – that is all
  Ye know on earth, and all ye need to know.

John Keats

ACTIVITY

1 Examine this ode and draw a diagram to show how Keats develops his thoughts throughout the poem.

2 How does this development of ideas relate to the form of the poem?

3 What have you noted about Keats's use of language in this poem?

Free verse

A final form of verse that we should mention at this point is **free verse**. Although modern poets also write in forms which adhere to strict patterns and forms, some of which we have already looked at, it is true that in the Twentieth Century there was a move towards poetry that does not have constraints of form, structure, rhyme or rhythm. Sometimes this type of verse does not even have regular lines, and the flexibility of free verse allows poets to use language in whatever ways seem appropriate to their purpose, and to create the effects they desire in their work.

Here is a poem written in free verse. Read it carefully.

To Women, As Far As I'm Concerned

The feelings I don't have I don't have.
The feelings I don't have I won't say I have.
The feelings you say you have, you don't have.
The feelings you would like us both to have, we neither
  of us have.
The feelings people ought to have, they never have.
If people say they've got feelings, you may be pretty sure
  They haven't got them.
So if you want either of us to feel anything at all
You'd better abandon all ideas of feelings altogether.

D. H. Lawrence

The novelist and poet D. H. Lawrence (1885–1930)

ACTIVITY

1 From the evidence of the way Lawrence uses language here, what do you think are the main features of free verse?

2 How do you think it differs from most other kinds of poetry?

You might have noted some of the following:

❑ Free verse does not follow any regular syllabic, metrical or rhyming pattern.
❑ It tends to follow speech rhythms of language.
❑ The line is the basic unit of rhythm.
❑ Spaces on the page can indicate pauses in the movement of the poem.

Poetic devices

There are a range of poetic devices and techniques of language use that poets can draw upon in writing their poetry. For the most part these techniques, like the use of imagery for example, are common to all kinds of literary writing. However, some devices are found only in poetry. Here are some of the main ones.

Enjambment

Enjambment is the term used to describe an instance where, because of its grammatical structure, verse runs on from one line to another. This can sometimes take the reader by surprise, as the meaning is not complete at the end of the line. Often, punctuation elsewhere in the line reinforces the need to run on at the end of the line.

End stop

End stop, in contrast, describes an instance where the grammatical break coincides with the end of a line. The break is often marked by a punctuation mark, and the meaning of the line is complete in itself.

Caesura

A caesura is simply a break or a pause in a line of verse, but it can be very important in influencing the rhythm of the poem.

> I never had noticed it until
> Twas gone, – the narrow copse,
>
> *Edward Thomas*

Now read *The Flea* by John Donne.

The Flea

Marke but this flea, and marke in this,
How little that which thou deny'st me is;
It suck'd me first, and now sucks thee,
And in this flea, our two bloods mingled bee;
Thou know'st that this cannot be said
A sinne, nor shame, nor losse of maidenhead,
   Yet this enjoyes before it wooe,
   And pamper'd swells with one blood made of two,
   And this, alas, is more than wee would doe.

Oh stay, three lives in one flea spare,
Where wee almost, yea more than maryed are.
This flea is you and I, and this
Our mariage bed, and mariage temple is;
Though parents grudge, and you, w'are met,

➡

And cloistered in these living walls of Jet.
  Though use make you apt to kill mee,
  Let not to that, selfe murder added bee,
  And sacrilege, three sinnes in killing three.

Cruell and sodaine, hast thou since
Purpled thy naile, in blood of innocence?
Wherein could this flea guilty bee,
Except in that drop which it suckt from thee?
Yet thou triumph'st, and saist that thou
Find'st not thy selfe, nor mee the weaker now;
  'Tis true then learne how false, feares bee;
  Just so much honor, when thou yeeld'st to mee,
  Will wast, as this flea's death tooke life from thee.

John Donne

ACTIVITY

> 1 Look at the poem carefully and make a note of where lines are end-stopped and where Donne uses enjambment.
>
> 2 Notice how Donne's punctuation often forces you to pause in the middle of a line rather than at the end. What effect do you think this has?

Rhythm

Rhythm can be an important element in poetry and some of the earliest poems you remember, nursery rhymes such as *Hickory, Dickory Dock* or *Humpty Dumpty Sat on a Wall*, have very strong rhythms. It is these strong rhythms, along with the sounds of the words themselves and the rhymes, that give them such appeal to young children.

However, the influence of rhythm is not something exclusively reserved for nursery rhymes – a sense of rhythm can exert a profound influence on the overall effect of any poem. The rhythm can help to create mood and influence the tone and atmosphere of a poem. It is this rhythm that can give a poem its feeling of 'movement' and life, and the poet can use rhythm to create a whole variety of effects within the poem.

Syllable stress

Poets can create rhythms in poetry in various ways. Language has natural rhythms built into it, which we use automatically every time we pronounce words. For example, with the word 'randomly', we naturally stress the first syllable and not the second. If we did not do this, the word would sound rather strange. Poets, then, use these natural stresses and in-built rhythm patterns to contribute to the overall rhythmic effect.

Emphatic stress

Poets often deliberately place the emphasis on a particular word or part of the word in order to achieve a particular effect. The stress could be shifted to emphasize a particular meaning or reinforce a point, or even change meaning.

Phrasing and punctuation

The rhythm of poetry, along with other kinds of writing, can be influenced by factors such as word order, length of phrases or the choice of punctuation marks, line and stanza breaks and use of repetition.

Metre

Poetic metre is the pattern of stressed and unstressed syllables in a line of poetry, and as such is very closely linked to the idea of rhythm. The concept originated from the principles of classical Greek and Latin verse and was adopted by English poets from early times. These principles stated that each line of verse should follow a precise and regular pattern in terms of how many syllables it contained and the stress pattern used. These regular patterns of stressed and unstressed syllables are called **metres**. By analysing the metre, the reader can see how the poet is using the stress patterns within the language as one of the ways by which the meaning of the poem is conveyed. Variations in the pattern could mark changes in mood or tone, or signify a change of direction in the movement of the poem.

In identifying the metre of a poem, the first thing to do is to establish how the rhythm pattern is created. To help do this, the syllables are divided up into groups of two or three (depending on the particular pattern). Each of these groups is called a **foot**. The number of **feet** in a line can vary.

Here are the main patterns:

One foot	monometer
Two feet	dimeter
Three feet	trimeter
Four feet	tetrameter
Five feet	pentameter
Six feet	hexameter
Seven feet	heptameter
Eight feet	octameter

The process of identifying the metre is called **scansion**. Stressed syllables are marked ′ while unstressed syllables are marked ˘ and the feet are divided up using vertical lines │. A double vertical line ‖ indicates a caesura.

There are five basic patterns of stress. These are:

- Iambic: one unstressed syllable followed by a stressed one.
  (iamb)

> When I | have fears | that I | may cease | to be
>
> Before | my pen | hath gleaned | my teem | ing brain
>
> *Keats*

- Trochaic: one stressed syllable followed by one unstressed.
  (trochee)

> Tyger! | Tyger! | Burning | bright
>
> In the | forests | of the | night
>
> *Blake*

- Dactylic: one stressed syllable followed by two unstressed syllables.
  (dactyl)

> Half a league, | half a league,
>
> Half a league | onward.
>
> *Tennyson*

- Anapaestic: two unstressed syllables followed by one stressed syllable.
  (anapaest)

> Will's | at the dance | in the club | -room below,
>
> Where | the tall liqu | or cups foam:
>
> *Hardy*

- Spondaic: two stressed syllables.
  (spondee)

> One, two
>
> Buckle my shoe.
>
> *Anon.*

For example, look at these lines from Keats's *When I have fears*.

When I have fears

When I have fears that I may cease to be
  Before my pen hath glean'd my teeming brain,
Before high-piled books, in charact'ry,
  Hold like rich garners the full-ripen'd grain:
When behold, upon the night's starr'd face,
  Huge cloudy symbols of a high romance,

And think that I may never live to trace
    Their shadows, with the magic hand of chance;
And when I feel, fair creature of an hour!
    That I shall never look upon thee more,
Never have relish I the faery power
    Of unreflecting love! – then on the shore
Of the wide world I stand alone, and think
    Till love and fame to nothingness do sink

John Keats

ACTIVITY The first two lines were scanned for you on page 40. Now scan the remainder of the stanza. How many metrical feet are there per line? What is the metrical pattern? Look at the stanza again. What effect does the metrical pattern have on the overall effect of the poem?

Lexical choice

The lexical choice (sometimes referred to as **diction**) is the decisions about language that a poet has made when writing his or her poem. The choices that are made will inevitably be influenced by the complex relationship between the reader and the poet. They will depend on the level of formality or informality of the poem, the poet's intentions and the effect that the piece is intended to have on the reader. Abstract or concrete nouns can be chosen depending on the subject matter of the poem, and modifiers can be used to add detail to descriptions of people or places, to create atmosphere, arouse emotions or express opinions and judgements. Verbs will be selected to express actions of various kinds, as well as adding to the message that the poet wishes to convey to the reader.

Of the various aspects considered in lexical choice, probably the most important is a word's connotations, or the associations suggested by a word. This is quite separate from its denotation, or dictionary definition. Words can carry with them many connotations that might bring suggested meanings quite different from the dictionary definition of the word. Connotations are acquired by words depending on how they have been used in the past.

ACTIVITY Look at the following list of words. Although they share a common basic meaning, they have very different connotations. Use each of the words in a sentence, to show the difference in connotation between them.

cunning; sly; devious; crafty; wily; artful; shifty; subtle; guileful.

There are occasions when writers choose words which have the clearest meaning or denotation, without complicating connotations. It all depends on the effects that the writer wishes to achieve – words are chosen to suit the audience and purpose. Sometimes a writer or poet might choose words that are particularly colloquial or particularly formal, according to context. Sometimes archaisms are used to give a sense of the past or add a sense of dignity and solemnity to the language, or dialect words may be used to create a certain social or regional atmosphere – for example, as in this poem by Simon Armitage, written in the Yorkshire dialect:

On an Owd Piktcha
(from tjerman)

Int swelterin eet, mongst birds n tbeez,
side cool watter n rushes n reeds,
tChrahst Chahld sithee, born bath taint,
laikin arahnd on tVirgin's knee.

N poorakin its nooas aht o tleaves n tmoss,
already green, tTree o tCross.

ACTIVITY

Read Armitage's poem carefully.

1 Try writing a 'Standard English' version of it.

2 What are the differences between the two versions?

3 Why do you think Armitage chose to write this in dialect form?

Poets can make their lexis very modern by using **neologisms** (invented words), which can add a sense of individuality to the poem. Sometimes a word may be chosen because it is incongruous and doesn't fit in with the other lexis. It may jar or shock the reader, or defy the reader's expectations.

ACTIVITY

Look at the following extracts from various poems.
Fill each blank with one word from the selection, and explain why you have made your choice.

1 ___a___ the spring onions,
She made this mental note:
You can tell it's love, the real thing,
When you ___b___ of slitting his throat.
Wendy Cope

   a Slicing, decapitating, washing.
   b Think, talk, dream.

2 On shallow straw, in ___a___ glass,
Huddled by empty bowls, they sleep:
No dark, no dam, no ___b___, no grass –
Mam, *get us one of them to keep.*
Philip Larkin

   a transparent, glaring, shadeless
   b water, earth, food

3 It is a beauteous evening, ___a___ and free;
  The holy time quiet as a Nun
  Breathless with ___b___ ; the broad sun
  Is sinking down in its ___c___ .
  William Wordsworth

  a calm, still, fine
  b prayer, devotion, adoration
  c close, tranquillity, stillness

Now let's have a look at a complete poem. This is *Adlestrop* by Edward Thomas:

Adlestrop

Yes, I remember Adlestrop –
The name, because one afternoon
Of heat the express-train drew up there
Unwontedly: It was late June.

The steam hissed. Someone cleared his throat.
No one left and no one came
On the bare platform. What I saw
Was Adlestrop – only the name

And willows, willow-herb, and grass,
And meadowsweet, and haycocks dry,
No whit less still and lovely fair
Than the high cloudlets in the sky.

And for that minute a blackbird sang
Close by, and round him, mistier,
Farther and farther, all the birds
Of Oxfordshire and Gloucestershire.

Edward Thomas

ACTIVITY

Read the poem carefully.

1 Why do you think Thomas has decided to begin the poem with the word 'Yes'? What effect does this have on the poem?

2 Does the nature of the lexis (vocabulary) change as the poem develops? If so, why do you think this is?

3 What unusual words have you noted in the poem? What effect do these have on the poem?

4 What overall effect is produced by Thomas's lexical choices?

Grammar

Many poets use standard forms of grammar, although sometimes the language can be manipulated to fit the restrictions of a particular poetic form.

In the following example, Byron uses standard forms of grammar to create a logical progression that forms the structure of the poem.

So We'll Go No More A-Roving

So we'll go no more a-roving
    So late into the night,
Though the heart be still as loving,
    And the moon be still as bright.

For the sword outwears its sheath,
    And the soul wears out the breast,
And the heart must pause to breathe,
    And love itself have rest.

Though the night was made for loving,
    And the day returns too soon,
Yet we'll go no more a-roving
    By the light of the moon.

Lord Byron

In terms of Byron's use of grammar in this poem, here are some points you might note:

❏ the grammatical relationship between 'So', which opens the poem and 'Yet', which begins the closing sequence – these signal the movement through the poem
❏ in lines 3 and 4, words that link to these appear, giving us, *so, though, still, yet*
❏ these words indicate a state or raise a question
❏ the unspoken question is: though the heart is still as loving, though the moon is still as bright, the roving will stop – why?
❏ the second stanza provides the answer with four parallel examples (sword, soul, heart, love)
❏ the final stanza completes the grammatical and the narrative sequence, repeating the key phrases from the opening – the parallel structure allowing for both the repetition and expansion of the central idea.

Descriptive analysis

Grammatical analysis of a poem can help to shed light on how the text of the poem works. In order to look at the grammar of poetry it is useful to be aware of the various word classes or 'parts of speech', as they are sometimes called. Here is a list of the key ones to be aware of, although it is not exhaustive. They can be used to describe how the language is working and are sometimes referred to as units of structure.

Word class	Examples
Verb	ran, said, eat, served, made, went
Noun	table, window, book, beauty, planet, daughter
Adjective	happy, small, clean, hard, metallic
Adverb	swiftly, harshly, probably, soothingly
Personal pronoun	he, she, they, it, theirs, his, hers
Indefinite pronoun	anyone, someone, everyone, everybody, anything
Preposition	in, on, up, beside, after, at, underneath, towards
Article	the, a, an
Demonstrative	this, that, those, these
Modal	should, could, must, might, can, shall, would
Degree word	how, very, rather, quite
Quantifier	some, every, all

Thinking about what poets are doing with language through describing its grammatical make-up can help you understand just how a particular poem is working.

Some poets might deliberately disrupt our expectations to create their effects, and sometimes they go further still in breaking the conventions of grammar. E. E. Cummings is well known for the unconventional ways in which he uses language in his poems. Here is the first stanza from one of his poems. Some of the words have been removed.

> ___a___ lived in a pretty ___b___ town
> (with ___c___ so floating many bells ___d___)
> spring summer autumn winter
> he sang his ___e___ he danced his ___f___.

ACTIVITY

Fill in the blanks in this stanza choosing words from the appropriate lists.

a	b	c	d	e	f
someone	small	light	din	song	jig
Bill	quiet	gleaming	down	didn't	round
She	how	up	bright	turn	dance
They	hot	down	clamour	notes	did
anyone	slow	chimes	clash	solo	favourite

Now check your version against the original. Here are the words Cummings used:

a anyone **b** how **c** up **d** down **e** didn't **f** did

You probably found some or all of these choices rather surprising – not least because they apparently produce lines that seem nonsensical. This is because Cummings breaks the grammatical rules for combining the parts of speech or units of structure together. In order to see exactly what Cummings has done it is useful to identify each of the parts of speech. In the first line of the poem this works out as –

pronoun	verb	preposition	article	adjective	degree word	noun
anyone	*lived*	*in*	*a*	*pretty*	*how*	*town*

One of the problems with this line is the use of 'how' in the position that it is in. Cummings uses a degree word where we would expect to see another adjective. In fact that word order of article → adjective → degree word → noun is not a combination that is possible under the rules of English grammar.

Apart from the use of the word 'how', the other problem with this opening line is the use of the word 'anyone'. In this context, 'anyone' is an indefinite pronoun. Other indefinite pronouns such as 'someone' or 'it' would fit here, and various personal pronouns such as 'he', 'she', 'they' would also make sense. Cummings has clearly chosen to use none of these but deliberately to use a word that cuts across the rules of grammar. The big question is, why? This is a question that you might be in a better position to answer after you have read the whole poem.

The other words missing from the first stanza pose similar problems. Neither 'up' nor 'down' seem to make sense in the positions they appear in. 'Didn't' and 'did' similarly seem very puzzling, but they also appear deliberately balanced – 'up/down', 'did/didn't' – as if the poet is, in fact, working to a set of rules. It is just that they are not the normal rules of grammar that we recognize and understand.

Now have a look at the whole poem:

anyone lived in a pretty how town

anyone lived in a pretty how town
(with up so floating many bells down)
spring summer autumn winter
he sang his didn't he danced his did.

Women and men(both little and small)
cared for anyone not at all
they sowed their isn't they reaped their same
sun moon stars rain

children guessed(but only a few
and down they forgot as up they grew
autumn winter spring summer)
that noone loved him more by more

➡

when by now and tree and leaf
she laughed his joy she cried his grief
bird by snow and stir by still
anyone's any was all to her

someones married their everyones
laughed their cryings and did their dance
(sleep wake hope and then)they
said their nevers they slept their dream

stars rain sun moon
(and only the snow can begin to explain
how children are apt to forget to remember
with up so floating many bells down)

one day anyone died i guess
(and noone stooped to kiss his face)
busy folk buried them side by side
little by little and was by was

all by all and deep by deep
and more by more they dream their sleep
noone and anyone earth by april
wish by spirit and if by yes.

Women and men(both dong and ding)
summer autumn winter spring
reaped their sowing and went their came
sun moon stars rain

E. E. Cummings

ACTIVITY Now you have read the whole poem, answer the following questions:

1 Does the poet's use of the word 'anyone' mean more to you now in the context of the whole poem? How do you think we are meant to interpret 'anyone' and 'someone'?

2 How does Cummings use pairings of words such as, 'up/down', 'did/ didn't'? Have you found any more such pairings of opposites?

3 How does Cummings make use of repetition in the poem?

4 Now write a brief summary of what the poem is about.

5 The key question is why Cummings chooses to break the conventions of grammar and write his poem in this way. What effects do you think he achieves by this?

When dealing with poems such as this one where the meaning is not necessarily immediately apparent, your initial responses may well be quite tentative. Don't worry about this, and don't worry about putting things down on paper that you feel unsure about. It is all part of the process of unravelling meaning from the text.

Here are the initial, tentative responses of two students as they work towards finding their meaning of 'Anyone lived in a pretty how town.'

Student A

1. *The word 'Anyone' is used to describe the people in the town. It also indicates that it is informal and impersonal, making the poem a story open to interpretation. A trivial tale about two or three people, yet the words indicate he's talking about mankind. 'Anyone' and 'Someone' are opposite words and the poet contrasts these types of words throughout the poem. They are meant to be interpreted as words which create a larger scale to the environment it is set in. The word 'Anyone' throws the poem open to a wider scale of people and 'Someone' is specific to one person. Anyone – male, Someone – female – gives it a universal theme.*

2. *He uses pairs of words such as 'did' and 'didn't', and 'up' and 'down', to describe how objects did things (in place of a adjective). Examples of pairing of words are:*

   did/didn't, down/up, joy/grief, sun/moon, rain/snow – gives a pattern to the words.

3. *He uses repetition to emphasize his points, for example about sleep he says 'all by all' and 'more by more'. The repetition of the seasons indicates people moving on, living and then dying.*

4. *The poem describes what happens to anyone in a certain town. Through the seasons and through the weather how the men and women dance, sleep and live.*

Student B

1. *The poet uses the words 'Anyone' and 'Someone' throughout the poem. This could be to give the poem a more universal and wider meaning than would have been achieved if the characters had been named. 'Anyone' and 'Someone' could mean that the poem would be meant to apply to the reader. It stops stereotyping. Anyone is male + Someone is female.*

2. *Cummings uses pairings of words and opposites throughout the poem such as 'up/down', 'did/didn't', 'joy/grief', 'little/small',*

'dong/ding'. This gives some degree of logic to often illogical sentences. It also means there is some rhyme in the verses. It leaves quite a lot open to interpretation.

3. Some words and lines are repeated throughout the poem. Although in a different order, 'Spring, Summer, Autumn, Winter' and 'Reaped' and 'Sowed' are repeated to show a sense of passing of time. There is also the sense of people moving on and a cyclical element – closely tied in with environment.

4. This poem seems to tell a life story of a person. The fact that there are no names or characters generalizes the story, so it could apply to anyone. The repetition of 'Spring, Summer, Autumn, Winter' suggests that life is the same every year. The inclusion of 'Sun, Moon, Stars' and 'Rain', especially at the end, shows that things go on and everybody is the same, as the sun, moon, stars and rain are a constant for everyone. It seems to trivialize life as everyone is there, they do their thing ('reaped their sowing and went their course') and then die, and it is no big deal.

Examiner's comments

Although these comments are initial and tentative, they are also exploratory. Both students have begun the process of coming to terms with a tricky brief through some of these comments. There are quite a number of points here that could be picked up and examined in more detail – some ideas are very perceptive, and already the students are beginning to identify the effects of such features as word pairings and repetition.

Metaphorical devices

Very often the language of poetry is made more intense through the use of metaphorical devices, which can add layers of meaning to a poem beyond the literal sense of the words on the page. You are likely to encounter several of these linguistic devices in the poetry you study. You may sometimes see these devices referred to as 'figurative language' or see individual examples called **figures of speech**. These are blanket terms used to describe the individual features that we will now look at. This kind of language use, in which the words require an intellectual and/or emotional response beyond their literal meaning, is also called **representational language** and the specific features are called **representational imagery features**.

Old English poets used a device of figurative language called the 'kenning' which consisted of a word or phrase made up to identify a particular object or thing without naming it directly. They had a large selection of kennings for their most frequently used nouns. For example, instead of 'ocean' they could say 'swan's road' or 'foaming field' or 'realm of monsters', for 'ship' they might say 'sea goer' or 'sea wood', for a 'lord' a 'dispenser of rings' or 'treasure giver', for the 'sun', 'candle of the world'.

Look at this poem by John Updike.

Winter Ocean

Many-maned scud-thumper, tub
of male whales, maker of worn wood, shrub-
ruster, sky-mocker, rave!
portly pusher of waves, wind slave.

ACTIVITY

1 How many kennings can you identify here?

2 What is the effect of the use of kennings in this poem?

3 Make up three or four kennings of your own.

In this use of kennings, the Old English poets were using a kind of imagery to describe their particular subject. Images can work in several ways in the mind of the reader. For example, an image can be used literally to describe something, as in Wordsworth's description of taking a boat out on to the lake at night, as the boat moves forward

leaving behind her still, on either side,
small circles glittering idly in the moon,
Until they melted all into one track
of sparkling light . . .

Wordsworth, Prelude Bk 1

This creates a **literal image** as we can picture the scene in our minds from the way in which Wordsworth describes it. Non-literal, figurative or representational images can be created when the thing being described is compared to something else. You will probably already be familiar with the **simile**, in which the comparison is made very clear by the poet using the words 'like' or 'as'. Often the elements being compared are essentially different in nature, but they come together in the poet's perception and ultimately in the reader's perception. Here are some examples of the simile in action:

Her goodly eyes like Sapphires shining bright . . .
Her cheeks like apples which the sun hath redded,
Her lips like cherries charming men to bite.

Edmund Spenser

Saw an iguana once
when I was very small
in our backdam backyard
came rustling across my path

green like moving newleaf sunlight

big like big big lizard
with more legs than centipede
so it seemed to me.

Grace Nichols

The **metaphor** is another representational device that poets often use, and with which you are familiar. In some ways a metaphor is like a simile in that it too creates a comparison. However, the comparison is less direct than the simile in that it does not include the terms 'like' or 'as', but often describes the subject as *being* the thing to which it is compared. For example, in Simon Armitage's poem *The Anaesthetist* he describes the anaesthetist entering the operating theatre:

Hard to believe him when he trundles in,
Scrubbed up and squeaky clean, manoeuvering
A handcart of deep-sea diving gear.

Simon Armitage

Of course, Armitage does not literally mean that the anaesthetist enters pushing a cart piled high with deep-sea diving gear – it is meant metaphorically. The look of the anaesthetist's equipment reminds Armitage of deep-sea diving gear.

Another kind of representational device frequently used by poets is **personification**. This is really a kind of metaphor in which the attributes of a person are given to either abstract or non-human things. In this example from Wilfred Owen's poem *Futility*, the sun is personified:

Futility

Move him into the sun –
Gently its touch awoke him once,
At home, whispering of fields unsown.
Always it woke him, even in France,
Until this morning and this snow.
If anything might rouse him now
The kind old sun will know.

Wilfred Owen

Closely associated with the idea of personification is that of **apostrophe**. This term describes a feature where an inanimate thing is addressed as if it were animate, those absent are addressed as if present, or the dead are addressed as if alive. In this example, John Donne uses apostrophe when he addresses Death as a person:

> Death, be not proud, though some have called thee
> Mighty and dreadful, for thou art not so

Two other representational features that you might encounter in your poetic studies are **metonymy** and **synecdoche**. Metonymy is the figure of speech where the term for one thing is substituted for the term for another thing with which it has become closely associated. For example, if we say 'The pen is mightier than the sword', then 'pen' and 'sword' are metonymies for written, intellectual ideas and military or brute force, respectively. If we use the term 'the Crown' to mean royalty we are similarly using a metonym. A synecdoche is a figure of speech in which part of something is used to represent the whole. For example, Shakespeare uses this device in the following line:

> Nay, if you read this line, remember not
> The hand that writ it

The 'hand' here means the whole person who wrote the line.

Another metaphorical device that poets often use is that of **symbolism**, sometimes drawing in commonly recognized symbols and sometimes inventing their own. In basic terms a symbol is simply a device whereby a word or phrase represents something else – for example the colour white could be used to represent peace. Symbolism in poetry can be very complex, with some poems operating on two levels, the literal and the symbolic. Sometimes in order to fully understand the significance of a poem it is necessary to understand the symbolic importance of some of the ideas or images used.

Now read Keats's *To Autumn*.

To Autumn

> Season of mists and mellow fruitfulness,
>   Close bosom-friend of the maturing sun;
> Conspiring with him how to load and bless
>   With fruit the vines that round the thatch-eves run;
> To bend with apples the moss'd cottage-trees,
>   And fill all fruit with ripeness to the core;
>   To swell the gourd, and plump the hazel shells
> With a sweet kernel; to set budding more,
>   And still more, later flowers for the bees,
>   Until they think warm days will never cease,
>   For Summer has o'er-brimm'd their clammy cells.

Who hath not seen thee oft amid thy store?
  Sometimes whoever seeks abroad may find
Thee sitting careless on a granary floor,
  Thy hair soft-lifted by the winnowing wind;
Or on a half-reap'd furrow sound asleep,
  Drows'd with the fume of poppies while thy hook
    Spares the next swath and all its twined flowers:
And sometimes like a gleaner thou dost keep
  Steady thy laden head across a brook;
  Or by a cyder-press, with patient look,
    Thou watchest the last oozings hours by hours.

Where are the songs of Spring? Ay, where are they?
  Think not of them, thou hast thy music too, –
While barred clouds bloom the soft-dying day,
  And touch the stubble-plains with rosy hue;
Then in a wailful choir the small gnats mourn
  Among the river sallows, borne aloft
    Or sinking as the light wind lives or dies;
And full-grown lambs loud bleat from hilly bourn;
  Hedge-crickets sing; and now with treble soft
  The red-breast whistles from a garden-croft;
    And gathering swallows twitter in the skies.

ACTIVITY Write a short essay (approximately 400–500 words) in which you examine the following aspects:

❏ the imagery
❏ the symbolism
❏ any other representational features

and comment on the effects that Keats achieves through their use.

Rhetorical techniques

Poets use rhetorical techniques to provide extra effects or meanings for their poems. These rhetorical techniques fall into two categories: **phonological patterning**, through such devices as **alliteration**, **onomatopoeia** and **rhyme**, and **structural patterning**, through the use of **parallelism**, **repetition**, **antithesis** and **listing**. Let us have a closer look at these features.

Phonological features

The term 'phonological' will probably have already told you that these kinds of features are to do with sound. Of course, the notion of sound and the repetition of sound is very important in poetry and contributes to what is sometimes called the 'music' of the words. Sometimes a sound or words might be repeated simply because the effect created is pleasing to the ear, but more often the repetition plays an integral part in supporting the sense and overall effect of the poem. Sometimes the repetition might be of a word, a phrase or a whole stanza, as in the case of a refrain, but there are many other smaller units of sound that can be repeated. Here are the key ones that you will come across in your studies.

Rhyme

Rhyme can make an important contribution to the 'musical quality' of a poem and, like rhythm, it affects the sound and the overall effectiveness. The system of rhyme within a poem, or rhyme scheme, can influence this effect in a variety of ways. The rhyme scheme could help to unify the poem and draw it together, it could give it an incantatory quality or add emphasis to particular elements of the lexis (vocabulary). There are various kinds of rhymes and rhyme schemes. The most common rhymes work on the basis of a rhyme occurring at the end of a line and are called 'complete rhymes', as in 'free' rhyming with 'tree', or 'feel' with 'seal'. Sometimes rhymes occur within the line itself. These are called **internal rhymes**. Coleridge makes use of this kind of rhyme in *The Rime of the Ancient Mariner*.

> The fair breeze blew, the white foam flew,
> The furrow followed free;
> We were the first that ever burst
> Into that silent sea.

In this case, the rhyming of 'blew' and 'flew' stresses these words and adds emphasis to the image of the ship's speed and movement.

A rhyme may appear incomplete or inaccurate in various ways. The vowels may not be pronounced in the same way, for example love/move or plough/rough. These are called **eye rhymes** or **sight rhymes**. Some poets choose deliberately to weaken the force of the rhyme by making either the consonant or vowel different. Wilfred Owen frequently uses this technique, as here for example:

> Like twitching agonies of men among its brambles
> Northward, incessantly, the flickering gunnery rumbles

Or:

> We only know war lasts, rain soaks, and clouds sag stormy
> Dawn massing in the east her melancholy army
> Attacks once more in ranks on shivering ranks of gray,

This kind of rhyme is called **half rhyme**, **slant rhyme** or **para-rhyme**.

In the same way that the rhythm in a poem often follows a recognized pattern, so can rhyme. Working out the rhyme scheme is quite a straightforward business and is done by indicating lines that rhyme together through giving them the same letter of the alphabet. For example, look at the first stanza from Thomas Hardy's *The Darkling Thrush*:

I leant upon a coppice gate	**a**
When Frost was spectre-gray	**b**
And Winter's dregs made desolate	**a**
The weakening eye of day.	**b**
The tangled bine-stems scored the sky	**c**
Like strings of broken lyres	**d**
And all mankind that haunted nigh	**c**
Had sought their household fires	**d**

Here Hardy uses a straightforward *abab cdcd* rhyme scheme, where pairs of alternate lines rhyme within the stanza. Various rhyming patterns are described by particular terms. Here are the main ones.

Couplets or rhyming couplets:	pairs of lines that rhyme together – pairs of lines that are written in iambic pentameter (see pages 39–40) are called heroic couplets
Quatrain:	a set of four rhyming lines, usually with a rhyme scheme *abab, abcb, aaaa,* or *abba*
Sestet:	a six-line unit that can rhyme in a variety of ways, eg *ababcc*; this can also refer to the concluding part of an Italian sonnet
Octave:	an eight-line unit which can be constructed in a number of ways. It can be formed by linking two quatrains together (as in Hardy's stanza) or it can have a rhyme scheme which integrates all eight lines. It is also the name given to the first eight lines of an Italian sonnet.

The important thing in looking at the rhyme scheme of a poem, though, is not spotting the rhymes or working out the scheme but being able to identify what effect the rhyme scheme has on the poem. In other words you need to be able to explain why the poet has chosen to use language in this particular way, and what the overall effects of those language choices are. Here are some of the effects that the use of rhyme might have on a poem.

❑ It can make a poem sound musical and pleasing to the ear.
❑ It can create a jarring, discordant effect.
❑ It can add emphasis to certain words and give particular words an added prominence.

❏ It can act as a unifying influence on the poem, drawing it together through the rhyme patterns.
❏ It can give the poem a rhythmic, incantatory or ritualistic feel.
❏ It can influence the rhythm of the verse.
❏ It can provide a sense of finality – the rhyming couplet, for example, is often used to give a sense of 'ending'.
❏ It can exert a subconscious effect on the reader, drawing together certain words or images, affecting the sound, or adding emphasis in some way.

Alliteration

Another phonological feature often used by poets is **alliteration**. This involves the repetition of the same consonant sound, usually at the beginning of each word, over two or more words together, as in Shakespeare's lines from *The Tempest*:

> Fall fathom five thy father lies,
> Of his bones are coral made.

Assonance

Assonance is a feature similar to alliteration but instead of consonants involves the repetition of vowel sounds to achieve a particular effect. An example is the long, drawn-out 'o' sounds in the first line of Sylvia Plath's *Frog Autumn*:

> Summer grows old, cold-blooded mother

This creates an impression of lethargy and lack of life as summer passes and winter approaches.

Onomatopoeia

Onomatopoeia refers to words that, by their sound, reflect their meaning – 'bang' or 'ping' are simple examples that sound like the noises they describe. Here is a more sophisticated example, from Coleridge's *The Rime of the Ancient Mariner*.

> The ice was here, the ice was there,
> The ice was all around;
> It cracked and **growled**, and **roared** and **howled**,
> Like noises in a swound

The words 'cracked', 'growled', 'roared' and 'howled' suggest the sounds of the icebergs grinding around the ship, and therefore make the description more graphic in an aural as well as visual way. It is perhaps worth noting also that Coleridge makes use of repetition here, emphasizing the fact that ice was everywhere.

Structural features

Obviously, the way in which a poem is structured can play an important part in the overall effect it produces. The poet has several devices to draw on to create effects through a poem's structure.

Repetition and listing

The technique of repeating or listing several words with the same or similar meaning (sometimes called cumulation) is often used to add emphasis or a persuasive quality to the poem. Such repetition of a word or words can add force and power to the subject, or it can be used to work towards a dramatic climax. In Gerard Manley Hopkins's poem *God's Grandeur* the simple repetition reinforces the meaning of the line:

> Generations have trod, have trod, have trod

The repetition of 'look' at the opening of *The Starlight Night* creates a sense of excitement as the poet urges us to look at the stars:

> Look at the stars! look, look up at the skies!
> O look at all the fire-folk sitting in the air!

Parallelism

Parallelism is another form of repetition but involves the repetition of larger structural features. It could include the repetition of the same verse form using different words, mirroring the main theme of the poem, or the use of recurring motifs or symbols.

The difference between repetition and parallelism can be seen in these examples:

Repetition: Onward, onward rode the six hundred
Parallelism: Those that I fight I do not hate
  Those that I guard I do not love

Dorothy Parker uses a parallel structure in her poem *Resume*.

Resume

> Razors pain you;
> Rivers are damp;
> Acid stains you;
> And drugs cause cramp.
> Guns aren't lawful;
> Nooses give;
> Gas smells awful;
> You might as well live.
>
> *Dorothy Parker*

Antithesis

Antithesis involves contrasting ideas or words balanced against one another. Usually there are two groups of words with a parallel syntax (or word order) but with a contrasting or opposite meaning, as for example in the phrase:

> to live a sinner or to die a saint

or in Alexander Pope's *Imitations of Horace*:

> 'Tis the first Virtue, Vices to abhor
> and the first Wisdom, to be a fool no more.

Now read *The Windhover* by Gerard Manley Hopkins.

The Windhover

To Christ our Lord

I caught this morning morning's minion, king-
dom of daylight's dauphin, dapple-dawn-drawn Falcon, in his riding
Of the rolling level underneath him steady air, and striding
High there, how he rung upon the rein of a wimpling wing
In his ecstasy! then off, off forth on swing,
As a skate's heel sweeps smooth on a bow-bend: the hurl and gliding
Rebuffed the big wind. My heart in hiding
Stirred for a bird, – the achieve of, the mastery of the thing!

Brute beauty and valour and act, oh, air, pride, plume, here
  Buckle! And the fire that breaks from thee then, a billion
Times told lovelier, more dangerous, O my chevalier!

  No wonder of it: Sheer plod makes plough down sillion
Shine, and blue-bleak embers, ah my dear,
Fall, gall themselves, and gash gold-vermilion.

ACTIVITY Examine the ways in which Hopkins uses language to achieve his effects in *The Windhover*. You should refer to specific details of language use including Hopkins's use of:

❑ imagery and other metaphorical features
❑ phonological features
❑ structural patterning.

Poetic intention

Poets, like other writers, use language to fulfil various intentions. In most poems, of course, there may be elements of a range of poetic intentions, each serving a particular purpose. Here are some key kinds of poetic intentions:

- ❏ to characterize
- ❏ to set the scene
- ❏ to evoke atmosphere
- ❏ to experiment with language.

To characterize

Very often poems focus on the physical description of a character or characters, but sometimes the description moves beyond this surface level to tell you something about the inner person. For example, Chaucer's description of the Miller focuses mainly on the physical aspects of the Miller, but we also learn something about the inner man.

The Portrait of the Miller

(From *The General Prologue to the Canterbury Tales*, Lines 547–568)

The MILLERE was a stout carl for the nones;
Ful big he was of brawn and eek of bones.
That proved wel, for over al ther he cam,
At wrastlinge he wolde have alwey the ram.
He was short-sholdred, brood, a thikke knarre;
Ther was no dore that he nolde heve of harre,
Or breke it at a renning with his heed.
His berd as any sowe or fox was reed,
And therto brood, as though it were a spade.
Upon the cop right of his nose he hade
A werte, and theron stood a toft of heris,
Reed as the brustles of a sowes eris;
His nosethirles blake were and wide.
A swerd and bokeler bar he by his side.
His mouth as greet was as a greet forneys.
He was a janglere and a goliardeys,
And that was moost of sinne and harlotries.
Wel koude he stelen corn and tollen thries;
And yet he hadde a thombe of golde, pardee.
A whit cote and a blew hood wered he.
A baggepipe wel koude he blowe and sowne,
And therwithal he broghte us out of towne.

How does Chaucer use language to:

1 tell you about the Miller's physical appearance?

2 tell you about the Miller's character?

Look particularly at Chaucer's choice of lexis, and the metaphorical and rhetorical features he uses.

To set the scene

Scene setting can be important in poetry, particularly if the poem has a narrative quality to it or the setting is important. The language of the poem may provide specific details about a particular place, or the setting could be created symbolically and changes in the description could signal changes in mood or tone.

Read *The Combe* by Edward Thomas.

The Combe

The combe* was ever dark, ancient and dark,
Its mouth is stopped with bramble, thorn, and briar;
And no one scrambles over the sliding chalk
By beech and yew and perishing juniper
Down the half precipices of its sides, with roots

And rabbit holes for steps. The sun of winter,
The moon of summer, and all the singing birds
Except the missel-thrush that loves juniper,
Are quite shut out. But far more ancient and dark
The combe looks since they killed the badger there,
Dug him out and gave him to the hounds,
That most ancient Briton of English beasts.

*A valley or hollow on the side of a hill.

ACTIVITY The setting is an important element in this poem. Examine the ways in which Thomas uses the language here to set the scene and create a sense of place.

To evoke atmosphere

The creation of atmosphere can be a very important element in poetry. The atmosphere is often linked very closely to the mood and tone of the poem.

Read the poem *Discord in Childhood* by D. H. Lawrence.

Discord in Childhood

Outside the house an ash-tree hung its terrible whips,
And at night when the wind rose, the lash of the tree
Shrieked and slashed the wind, as a ship's
Weird rigging in a storm shrieks hideously.

Within the house two voices arose, a slender lash
Whistling she-delirious rage, and the dreadful sound
Of a male thong booming and bruising, until it had drowned
The other voice in a silence of blood, 'neath the noise of the ash.

ACTIVITY Make notes on the ways in which Lawrence created atmosphere in this poem.
You should refer specifically to the following:

❑ physical description
❑ the use of connotations
❑ metaphorical language
❑ phonological and rhetorical patterning.

To experiment with language

We have already looked at some of the ways in which poets can use language
in all kinds of ways that deviate from normal usage. Poetry as a medium is
very flexible, and poets can effectively convey their ideas in all sorts of ways
using non-standard forms. Look at the following poem by Wendy Cope:

Strugnell in Liverpool

For Allan Ginsberg, Charlie Parker, T. S. Eliot,
Paul McCartney, Marcel Proust and all the
other great men who have influenced my writing

Waking early
listening to
birdsong watching
the curtains brighten
like a shirt
washed in Omo
feeling the empty
space beside me
thinking of you

crawling out of
bed searching
for my glasses
piles of clothing

on the carpet
none of it yours

alone in the toilet
with the Harpic
and the Andrex
thinking of you

eating my cornflakes
plastic flowers on
the windowsill green
formical table lovesong
on the radio bacteria
in the drainpipe
thinking of you

going
up
stairs
again
and
getting
dressed

think-
ing
of
you

thinking
of you your pink
nylon panties
and your blue bra
Body Mist
hairsmell of Silvikrin
shampoo and your white
nylon panties

thinking of you.

ACTIVITY   Why do you think Cope uses language in the way she does here? What
effects do you think she wants to achieve, and how does she use language to
achieve it? How successful do you find the poem?

So far in this chapter we have discussed some aspects of the language of
poetry and you have looked at these features through the examples you have
worked on. It is important to remember, though, that simply identifying
features is meaningless unless you link them to a wider explanation of the
purpose of using language in a particular way to create specific **effects**.

In order to approach an examination question, it can be useful to have a checklist of features of language that you could look for in the poems you study, in order to analyse purpose and effects.

Checklist of language features in poetry

This list may help you to identify key features, but be aware that not every type of poetry will contain all these features.

❑ **Poetic form and structure**
  Form
  Metre
  Rhythm
  Layout
  Structure

❑ **Register**
  Mode
  Manner
  Field

❑ **Lexis**
  Standard / non-standard language
  Connotations
  Modifiers
  Nouns
  Verbs
  Collocations

❑ **Grammar**
  Formal / informal
  Standard
  Modes / archaic
  Dialect form
  Sentence structure

❑ **Metaphorical language**
  Imagery
  Metaphors / similes
  Symbolism
  Other poetic devices

❑ **Rhetorical language**
  Patterning
  Repetition / listing
  Parallelism
  Phonological patterning

❑ **Poetic intention**
  To characterize
  To set the scene
  To evoke atmosphere
  To experiment with language

APPROACHES TO EXAMINATION QUESTIONS

Now let us look at the kinds of questions you will need to deal with in the examination, and apply some of the points we have discussed in order to answer them.

A reminder that the questions test your ability to:

❑ communicate clearly the knowledge, understanding and insights gained from combined literary and linguistic study, using appropriate terminology and accurate written expression

❑ respond to literary texts and distinguish, describe and interpret variation in meaning and form

❑ respond to and analyse texts, using literary and linguistic concepts and approaches.

Remember – you will have your text with you in the examination.

Read *White Christmas* by Simon Armitage.

White Christmas

For once it is a white Christmas,
so white that the roads are impassable
and my wife is snowbound
in a town untroubled by tractor or snowplough.
In bed, awake, alone. She calls

and we pass on our presents by telephone.
Mine is a watch, the very one
I would have chosen. Hers is a song,
the one with the line *Here come the hills of time*
and it sits in its sleeve,

unsung and unopened. But the dog downstairs
is worrying, gnawing, howling,
so I walk her through clean snow
along the tow-path to the boat-house at a steady pace
then to my parents' place

where my mother is Marie Curie, in the kitchen
discovering radium, and my father is Fred Flintstone,
and a guest from the past has a look on her face meaning
lie and I'll have your teeth for a necklace, boy,
your eyeballs for earrings,

your bullshit for breakfast,
and my two-year-old niece is baby Jesus,
passing between us with the fruit of the earth
and the light of the world – Christingle – a blood orange
spiked with a burning candle.

We eat, but the dog begs at the table,
drinks from the toilet, sings in the cellar.
Only baby Jesus wanders with me down the stairs
with a shank of meat to see her, to feed her.
Later, when I stand to leave

➡

my father wants to shake me by the hand
but my arms are heavy, made of a base metal,
and the dog wants to take me down the black lane, back
to an empty house again. A car goes by
with my sister inside

and to wave goodnight
she lifts the arm of the sleeping infant Christ,
but I turn my wrist to notice the time. There and then
I'm the man in the joke, the man in a world of friends
where all the clocks are stopped,

synchronising his own watch.

Discuss Armitage's use of metaphorical, rhetorical and grammatical features in creating his effects in this poem.

Here is Becky's plan for tackling this question:

1. *Isolation/separation*
2. *Presents – static/material goods have no significance*
3. *Dog demanding, insistence on attention – poet feels like an intruder because of upheaval <u>his</u> dog caused.*
4. *Marie Curie + Fred – contrast saviour of others + sacrifice compared with inadequate and lazy Fred.*
5. *Pagan ritualistic – teeth for necklace/ eyeballs for earrings + blood orange spiked with candle → reduces poet to a child and makes Xmas seem barbaric, disguised with religious festival of light and fruit.*
6. *Dog – salvation for the outcast linked with baby Jesus, humanizes acts of God.*
7. *Father handshake – reaction shows separation, no family bond – reality of falsity of Xmas.*
8. *Empty house <u>again</u> isolation.*
9. *'Sleeping infant Christ' metaphor for a helpless non-active Christ.*
10. *Man in the joke – realization of superficiality + same as everyone else. Forced to commit to 'their' time 'synchronizing his own watch'.*

Examiner's comments

These are thorough notes and cover a wide range of points. Becky has obviously found a good deal in this poem and has made her notes on it in the way that she feels most comfortable with. There is a lot of material here – certainly sufficient to form the basis of a good essay on the poem.

Here is how she went on to start her essay:

> *In the poem 'White Christmas', Armitage explores his idea of a family Christmas. The language he uses give the image of a mechanical and ritualistic occasion where there is no excitement, only familiarity with the event. Throughout the poem Armitage introduces the themes of separation and isolation and later contrasts them in that he is the same as everyone else.*
>
> *By entitling the poem 'White Christmas', Armitage gives the impression of an idyllic Christmas which is continued with the poet's description of the snow 'so white that the roads are impassable'. The snow also serves to isolate the poet's wife which introduces the theme of separation, which invariably distances the poet throughout the poem. His wife is described as 'in bed, awake, alone' and Armitage describes how they have to pass on their presents through the telephone, which immediately leaves the poet alone to deal with his family Christmas.*
>
> *The poet describes his dog 'worrying, gnawing, howling' and later he 'begs at the table, drinks from the toilet, sings in the cellar'. The fact that the dog has been banished to the cellar shows the trouble the dog has caused, which reflects on the poet, making him feel like an intruder, which again separates him from the rest of the house.*

Examiner's comments

Although this is just the opening of Becky's essay it does reveal some interesting features. She is clearly following her plan and she focuses closely on the actual language of the poem. She uses some relevant quotations to illustrate her points, although these quotations are not always woven into her essay with complete success. She also has a tendency to adopt a rather 'narrative' approach as she works her way through the poem piece by piece.

There are lots of references to the text, which is obviously a good thing, but as yet little overt attention is paid to 'grammatical features', and explicit reference to 'metaphorical' or 'rhetorical' features is missing, although this may develop later in the essay. Overall, Becky is feeling her way towards an understanding of the poem. A range of relevant points are made and there is implicit reference to the elements suggested by the question.

How this Unit links to other sections of the course

The table below shows the major links between this Unit and others on the course; there are, however, other links that do not carry the same weight.

Question	Skills learned	Links to other parts of the Specification
Poetic Study Question	How to use frameworks for analysis	• Comparative Literary Studies Unit 4 • Dramatic Study Unit 5 Section A • Language in Context Unit 6 Question 1 • Prose Study Unit 3 Section A
	Identifying and analysing literary features	• Prose Study Unit 3 Section A • Comparative Literary Studies Unit 4 • Dramatic Study Unit 5 Section A • Language in Context Unit 6 Question 1
	Using integrated linguistic and literary terminology to provide an insight into literary interpretation	• Prose Study Unit 3 Section A • Comparative Literary Studies Unit 4 • Language in Context Unit 6 Questions 1 and 2

3 The Language of Prose

In this Unit you will focus on the ways in which language is used in prose texts, and at the centre of this study will be the issues of **purpose**, **audience** and **style**. In the examination, this study of prose texts will be closely linked with the study of the Language of Speech, which we will look at in the next chapter. In looking at the language of prose, both linguistic and literary issues will be examined, and you will need to prepare yourself by examining literary issues through the language of the texts you study, noting how writers use language to achieve and enhance literary effects and address issues.

In the examination the section on the Language of Prose will offer you a choice of texts for study (three modern prose texts and three pre-1900 prose texts). In order to meet the requirements of the examination you will need to answer **one** question on **one** of the set texts. We will look at the kinds of questions you might expect later; they will be of the kind that will allow you to employ the frameworks for linguistic and literary analysis that you have studied during your course.

Whatever text you study and whichever question you choose to answer, you will be tested on your ability to:

❑ use literary and linguistic frameworks and approaches to describe, explain and interpret key features of meaning and form in prose works
❑ identify and assess the ways in which attitudes and values are communicated through prose
❑ show understanding of the ways contextual variation and choices of form, style and vocabulary shape prose texts
❑ communicate your insights about the text
❑ write accurately and clearly.

As well as identifying these key objectives, the specification offers the following advice of the possible form of questions.

❑ Candidates will be asked to show how use of language by the writer is used and developed within a text.
❑ Candidates will be asked to refer to a specific section of the text, then widen and contextualize their study and analysis from that section.
❑ Candidates may be asked how literary issues are raised by the writer.

In this Unit we will be looking carefully at exactly how these objectives translate into aspects of study for your chosen text, the kinds of things that you could be asked to do in the examination, and ways of approaching these tasks.

The nature of narrative prose

All the prose text options that you are offered in the specification are of the kind we refer to as **narrative prose** – narrative in the sense that they all 'tell a story' in one way or another.

Narrative prose	Narrative prose consists primarily in the telling of a sequence of connected events, by some kind of narrator.

The events of a narrative are connected in the sense that there is some relationship between these events (such as through cause and effect). Although narrative prose can be difficult to categorize as it can be wide-ranging in style and in terms of the individual writer's intentions, most narrative prose has some features in common.

ACTIVITY Think about the features of the narrative prose you have studied either during your AS course or for work you have done earlier. Make a list of the key features of narrative prose.

Here are some of the key features you might have listed.

- ❑ There is usually a narrator and therefore the story is told from a particular **point of view**.
- ❑ Narrative prose is usually structured so it has a **beginning** and some kind of **ending**.
- ❑ It usually has a point – it is told for some kind of **purpose** – to develop an idea or theme.
- ❑ It usually contains **characters** that are presented in certain kinds of ways by the writer.

Although every novel or short story is different and each writer makes decisions about the **purpose** and **style** of his or her prose, most narrative prose has one function in common. This function is to entertain – although, of course, the vast majority of authors do much more than this. Narrative prose can raise readers' awareness of a particular theme or issue or group of ideas, and thus the prose may educate and inform as well as entertain.

Features of narrative prose

Theories of narrative usually identify two main levels of narrative. These are:

1 the basic events or actions of the narrative, given in the chronological order in which they are supposed to have happened, with the circumstances surrounding them – in basic terms this level is often referred to as the **story** or the **plot**.

2 the techniques and devices used for telling the story. This is sometimes called the **narration**.

The recognition of a distinction between the story itself and the way in which it is told is important because it acknowledges that the same story can be told in different ways depending on the **viewpoint** of the teller.

Point of view

The **point of view** is of central importance to narrative prose because the reader needs to know who is telling the story. The term can be used literally to describe the visual perspective from which the story is presented. It can also be used to indicate the ideological framework from which the story is told, or the bias contained in the text. This is what we are commenting on when, for example, we say that a text presents a 'male perspective', or the story is told from 'the point of view of the working class'.

A third way in which the term can be used is to describe basic types of narration – in other words, the relationship between the narrator of the story and the reader.

At a simple level we can make the distinction between the two basic and most common types of narration: **first-person narration** and **third-person narration**.

Let's have a closer look at these to begin with.

First-person narration

In a first-person narrative, the 'I' narrator tells of the events that he or she experiences. This kind of narration is found in a range of novels and short stories covering a wide variety of styles and periods. For example, Mary Shelley's *Frankenstein* (1818), Charlotte Brontë's *Jane Eyre* (1847), Iain Banks's *The Wasp Factory* (1984) and Eric Lomax's *The Railway Man* (1996). Several features of first-person narrative are worth bearing in mind.

❏ First-person narrative allows the reader directly into the mind of the narrator.
❏ Sometimes the events of the novel can be viewed retrospectively, so the narrator's view of things can change as he or she matures. This is particularly evident in *Jane Eyre* and *Great Expectations*, for example, where the narrators, Jane and Pip, develop and change as they grow into adulthood.
❏ Because this form of narration gives only one person's view of the story, it can present a biased account of events and by its nature seems more subjective than third-person narration.
❏ In some cases, the first-person narrator may not be the central character of the novel. For example in *The Great Gatsby*, the narrator, Nick,

remains very much on the fringes of the events he relates concerning the central character, Jay Gatsby. This has the effect of creating some narrative distance, which is often not present when the narrator is also the central character.

Third-person narration

In a third-person narrative the narrator is often omniscient – he or she 'sees all' and 'knows all' that is going on. There is no 'I' figure and so the story is related directly to the reader. There are two types of **omniscient narrator** – the **intrusive** and the **unintrusive**. The intrusive narrator enters into the novel by explicitly commenting on events and characters. Authors such as Thomas Hardy, Jane Austen and George Eliot do this frequently. On the other hand, the unintrusive narrator tells the story from a distance without the reader being aware that the narrator is making judgements or voicing opinions. Writers such as E. M. Forster and Susan Hill often use this 'invisible narrator' approach.

Third-person narration can also work in other ways. For example, the narrative point of view can be either **internal** or **external**. Third-person narration can simply describe events, characters, and so on as they are observed from the outside, but it can also describe them from the inside. Such a narrator can seem able to see into the minds of the characters and tell us about how they think and feel.

Another distinction that can be made in third-person narration is between **restricted** and **unrestricted** narration. In some novels the narrator apparently has no restrictions on the knowledge he or she possesses concerning the characters and events. On the other hand, some writers deliberately give their narrators restricted knowledge. Such limitations are often signalled by phrases such as *it seemed/appeared/looked as if*.

Sometimes this restricting of the narration reflects the fact that the narrative identifies closely with a single character, while at the same time remaining in the third person. It is important to recognize this as it shows that sometimes third-person narration is not necessarily objective, and it can operate from more subjective and restricted viewpoints.

Other points of view you might come across in your studies do not fit easily into either first- or third-person narration. For example, **interior monologues** can be used to reflect and develop the thoughts in a character's head. You may well be familiar with this form of writing through such works as Alan Bennet's *Talking Heads* and *Talking Heads 2*, but other writers frequently use this approach too, sometimes as a part of a larger narrative. Many Nineteenth-Century novelists use passages of interior monologue to allow the reader to see how a character's thoughts are developing.

Another form of narrative you might come across is **stream of consciousness** writing, in which thoughts are written randomly just as if they have been spilled out of the character's mind on to the page. One of the features of this kind of writing is that it appears unstructured, unpunctuated and chaotic. However, it is important to remember that the writer has deliberately structured it in this way to reflect the complex outpourings of the human mind. Perhaps the best-known writers to experiment with this style of writing are James Joyce and Virginia Woolf.

ACTIVITY

Look carefully at these two short extracts taken from two short stories in *A Bit of Singing and Dancing* by Susan Hill. The first is told in the first person and the second is told in the third person. Try re-writing the first extract in the third person and the second extract in the first person. Make a note of any ways in which you feel your version changes the original. Also note any parts that you found difficult to 'translate' into the other narrative mode, and discuss why difficulties arose.

My work was coming to an end, and I began to think I had had enough of the place. Once or twice, during those last weeks, I felt strongly that all was not as it should be with Mr Proudham and Mr Sleight. Several times I heard raised voices and now and then a loud banging on the floor, as though with a stick.

I came home as it was getting dark one evening, and as I turned from the gate, I caught sight of a pale, still face in the ground floor window. Mr Sleight was propped up on a sofa and he was staring intently at me. The beam, and the rather amusing self-consciousness had quite gone. His face was thin. He did not take his eyes off me and I saw that they had the intense yet oddly blank look of the very mad. He held in his hands one of the wax models: it was unfinished, without clothes and without any features moulded in its smooth, oval face. He held it up a little and, as I stared, began to twist one of the legs. If I had stayed there I should have seen it come away in his hands. I did not, I ran up the path and Mr Sleight watched me, unblinking, unsmiling. That night, the quarrelling began again, one of the voices rose to a scream. In the morning, I saw Mr Proudham go out with the dog, and his face was grey.

(Susan Hill, from 'Mr Proudham and Mr Sleight' in *A Bit of Singing and Dancing*)

At five minutes to three he climbed up the ladder into the loft. He went cautiously, he was always cautious now, moving his limbs warily, and never going out in bad weather without enough warm clothes. For the truth was that he had not expected to survive this winter, he was old, he had been ill for one week, and then the fear had come over him again, that he was going to die. He did not care for his own part, but what would become of the boy? It was only the boy he worried about now, only he who mattered. Therefore, he was careful with himself, for he had lived out this bad winter, it was March, he could look forward to the spring and summer, could cease to worry for a little longer. All the same he had to be careful not to have accidents, though he was steady enough on his feet. He was seventy-one. He knew how easy it would be, for example, to miss his footing on the narrow ladder, to break a limb and lie there, while all the time the child waited, panic welling up inside him, left last at the school. And when the fear of his own dying did not grip him, he was haunted by ideas of some long illness, or incapacitation, and if he had to be taken into hospital, what would happen to the child, then? *What would happen?*

But now it was almost three o'clock, almost time for him to leave the house, his favourite part of the day, now he climbed on hands and knees into the dim, cool loft and felt about among the apples, holding this one and that one up to the beam of light coming through the slats in the roof, wanting the fruit he finally chose to be perfect, ripe and smooth.

(Susan Hill, from 'The Custodian' in *A Bit of Singing and Dancing*)

Narrative voice

Closely associated with the idea of narrative viewpoint is the idea of narrative voice. Different narrators and different narrative techniques change a story, affecting not just how we are told something but what we are told and how we respond to it. The feelings and attitudes of the narrator can be detected through the tone of voice adopted, thus providing the writer with another way of shaping the responses of the reader.

ACTIVITY

Read carefully the two extracts that follow. The first is from Jean Rhys's novel *Wide Sargasso Sea*, which creates an 'early life' of the Mrs Rochester who appears in Charlotte Brontë's novel, *Jane Eyre*. The second extract is taken from *Jane Eyre*.

Compare and contrast the two passages, focusing on the effects achieved by the differing points of view each writer has chosen to adopt. You should consider the following points:

❑ the narrative viewpoint and its effect on the reader
❑ the effect of the narrative voice of each text
❑ the perspectives that the writers create and the ways in which they sustain it.

In this room I wake early and lie shivering for it is very cold. At last Grace Poole, the woman who looks after me, lights a fire with paper and sticks and lumps of coal. She kneels to blow it with bellows. The paper shrivels, the sticks crackle and spit, the coal smoulders and glowers. In the end flames shoot up and they are beautiful. I get out of bed and go close to watch them and to wonder why I have been brought here. For what reason? There must be a reason. What is it that I must do? When I first came I thought it would be for a day, two days, a week perhaps. I thought that when I saw him and spoke to him I would be wise as serpents, harmless as doves. 'I give you all I have freely,' I would say, 'and I will not trouble you again if you will let me go.' But he never came.

The woman Grace sleeps in my room. At night I sometimes see her sitting ➡

at the table counting money. She holds a gold piece in her hand and smiles. Then she puts it all into a little canvas bag with a drawstring and hangs the bag round her neck so that it is hidden in her dress. At first she used to look at me before she did this but I always pretended to be asleep, now she does not trouble about me. She drinks from a bottle on the table then she goes to bed, or puts her arms on the table, her head on her arms, and sleeps. But I lie watching the fire die out. When she is snoring I get up and I have tasted the drink without colour in the bottle. The first time I did this I wanted to spit it out but managed to swallow it. When I got back into bed I could remember more and think again. I was not so cold.

There is one window high up – you cannot see out of it. My bed had doors but they have been taken away. There is not much else in the room. Her bed, a black press, the table in the middle and two black chairs carved with fruit and flowers. They have high backs and no arms. The dressing-room is very small, the room next to this one is hung with tapestry. Looking at the tapestry one day I recognised my mother dressed in an evening gown but with bare feet. She looked away from me, over my head just as she used to do. I wouldn't tell Grace this. Her name oughtn't to be Grace. Names matter, like when he wouldn't call me Antoinette, and I saw Antoinette drifting out of the window with her scents, her pretty clothes and her looking-glass.

There is no looking-glass here and I don't know what I am like now. I remember watching myself brush my hair and how my eyes looked back at me. The girl I saw was myself yet not quite myself. Long ago when I was a child and very lonely I tried to kiss her. But the glass was between us – hard, cold and misted over with my breath. Now they have taken everything away. What am I doing in this place and who am I?

The door of the tapestry room is kept locked. It leads, I know, into a passage. That is where Grace stands and talks to another woman whom I have never seen. Her name is Leah. I listen but I cannot understand what they say. So there is still the sound of whispering that I have heard all my life, but these are different voices.

When night comes, and she has had several drinks and sleeps, it is easy to take the keys. I know now where she keeps them. Then I open the door and walk into their world. It is, as I always knew, made of cardboard. I have seen it before somewhere, this cardboard world where everything is coloured brown or dark red or yellow that has no light in it. As I walk along the passages I wish I could see what is behind the cardboard. They tell me I am in England but I don't believe them. We lost our way to England. When? Where? I don't remember, but we lost it. Was it that evening in the cabin when he found me talking to the young man who brought me my food? I put my arms round his neck and asked him to help me. He said, 'I didn't know what to do, sir.' I smashed the glasses and plates against the porthole. I hoped it would break and the sea come in. A woman came and then an older man who cleared up the broken things on the floor. He did not look at me while he was doing it. The third man said drink this and you will sleep. I drank it and I said, 'It isn't like it seems to be.' – 'I know. It never is,' he said. And then I slept. When I woke it was a different sea. Colder. It was that night, I think, that we changed course and lost our way to England. This cardboard house where I walk at night is not England.

(Jean Rhys, *Wide Sargasso Sea*)

. . . When we left the dining-room, she proposed to show me over the rest of the house; and I followed her upstairs and downstairs, admiring as I went; for all was well-arranged and handsome. The large front chambers I thought especially grand; and some of the third story rooms, though dark and low, were interesting from their air of antiquity. The furniture once appropriated to the lower apartments had from time to time been removed here, as fashions changed; and the imperfect light entering by their narrow casements showed bedsteads of a hundred years old; chests in oak or walnut, looking, with their strange carvings of palm branches and cherubs' heads, like types of the Hebrew ark; rows of venerable chairs, high-backed and narrow; stools still more antiquated, on whose cushioned tops were yet apparent traces of half-effaced embroideries, wrought by fingers that for two generations had been coffin-dust. All these relics gave to the third story of Thornfield Hall the aspect of a home of the past: a shrine of memory. I liked the hush, the gloom, the quaintness of these retreats in the day; but I by no means coveted a night's repose on one of those wide and heavy beds: shut in, some of them, with doors of oak; shaded, others, with wrought old English hangings encrusted with thick work, portraying effigies of strange flowers, and stranger birds, and strangest human beings, – all which would have looked strange, indeed, by the pallid gleam of moonlight.

'Do the servants sleep in these rooms? I asked.

'No: they occupy a range of smaller apartments to the back; no one ever sleeps here: one would almost say that, if there were a ghost at Thornfield Hall, this would be its haunt.'

'So I think: you have no ghost, then?

'None that I ever heard of,' returned Mrs Fairfax, smiling.

'Nor any traditions of one? No legends or ghost stories?'

'I believe not. And yet it is said, the Rochesters have been rather a violent than a quiet race in their time: perhaps, though, that is the reason they rest tranquilly in their graves now.'

'Yes – "after life's fitful fever they sleep well,"' I muttered. 'Where are you going now, Mrs Fairfax?' for she was moving away.

'On to the leads; will you come and see the view from thence?' I followed still, up a very narrow staircase to the attics, and thence by a ladder and through a trap-door to the roof of the hall. I was now on a level with the crow colony, and could see into their nests. Leaning over the battlements and looking far down, I surveyed the grounds laid out like a map: the bright and velvet lawn closely girding the grey base of the mansion; the field, wide as a park, dotted with its ancient timber; the wood, dun and sere, divided by a path visibly overgrown, greener with moss than the trees were with foliage; the church at the gates, the road, the tranquil hills, all reposing in the autumn day's sun; the horizon bounded by a propitious sky, azure, marbled with

➡

pearly white. No feature in the scene was extraordinary, but all was pleasing. When I turned from it and repassed the trap-door, I could scarcely see my way down the ladder: the attic seemed black as a vault compared with that arch of blue air to which I had been looking up, and to that sunlit scene of grove, pasture, and green hill of which the hall was the centre, and over which I had been gazing with delight.

Mrs Fairfax stayed behind a moment to fasten the trap-door. I, by dint of groping, found the outlet from the attic, and proceeded to descend the narrow garret staircase. I lingered in the long passage to which this led, separating the front and back rooms of the third story: narrow, low, and dim, with only one little window at the far end, and looking, with its two rows of small black doors all shut, like a corridor in some Bluebeard's castle.

While I paced softly on, the last sound I expected to hear in so still a region, a laugh, struck my ear. It was a curious laugh; distinct, formal, mirthless. I stopped: the sound ceased, only for an instant; it began again, louder: for at first, though distinct, it was very low. It passed off in a clamorous peal that seemed to wake an echo in every lonely chamber; though it originated but in one, and I could have pointed out the door whence the accents issued.

'Mrs Fairfax!' I called out: for I now heard her descending the garret stairs. 'Did you hear that loud laugh? Who is it?'

'Some of the servants, very likely,' she answered: 'perhaps Grace Poole.'

'Did you hear it?' I again inquired.

'Yes, plainly; I often hear her; she sews in one of these rooms. Sometimes Leah is with her: they are frequently noisy together.'

The laugh was repeated in its low, syllabic tone, and terminated in an odd murmur.

'Grace!' exclaimed Mrs Fairfax.

I really did not expect any Grace to answer; for the laugh was as tragic, as preternatural a laugh as any I ever heard; and, but that it was high noon, and that no circumstance of ghostliness accompanied the curious cachination; but that neither scene nor season favoured fear, I should have been superstitiously afraid. However, the event showed me I was a fool for entertaining a sense even of surprise.

The door nearest me opened, and a servant came out, – a woman of between thirty and forty; a set, square-made figure, red-haired, and with a hard, plain face: any apparition less romantic or less ghostly could scarcely be conceived.

'Too much noise, Grace,' said Mrs Fairfax. 'Remember directions!' Grace curtseyed silently and went in.

'She is a person we have to sew and assist Leah in her housemaid's work,' continued the widow; 'not altogether unobjectionable in some points, but she does well enough. By-the-by, how have you got on with your new pupil this morning?'

The conversations, thus turned to Adèle, continued till we reached the light and cheerful region below. Adèle came running to meet us in the hall, exclaiming –

'Mesdames, vous êtes servies!' adding, 'J'ai bien faim, moi!'
We found dinner ready, and waiting for us in Mrs Fairfax's room.

(Charlotte Brontë, *Jane Eyre*)

Here is how one student responded to this activity. Read her response carefully.

At first, it appears that the person narrating the story in 'Wide Sargasso Sea' is a child as the language is simple and the descriptions of her surroundings are immature in their outlook. She refers to Grace Poole as 'the woman who looks after me', indicating that she herself is not yet a woman and also that she requires supervision. The narration of how the fire is built and how it looks when it has become established adds to this effect in the way it is lit with 'paper and sticks and lumps of coal'. The repetitive use of 'and' here indicates a child's view in the account of the chore. This theme continues to run throughout the piece as Grace is referred to as 'the woman' again and then the narrator 'pretended to be asleep' going on to describe the 'drink without colour'. The language is very matter of fact and logical in a simple way especially when she is negotiating with herself about the importance of having the right name. This simple descriptive language is later repeated when she looks out of her room into 'their world' and sees the corridor as 'made of cardboard' with 'no light in it'. At the same time she flits from subject to subject, never really settling on one object or subject for very long.

However, the reader is informed that the narrator is not a child with the words 'Long ago when I was a child', which gives a new twist to the story. The character of the storyteller takes on a new twist being portrayed as a wistful, trapped and lonely adult. It leads nicely to the correct viewpoint – that of a woman who is in some way retarded, hence the simple language.

The woman comes across as being confused about her situation – especially in the first paragraph with the rush of questions ' . . . why have I been brought here. For what reason? . . . What is it that I must do?' and later on 'What am I doing in this place and who am I?' In the last paragraph, she feels as though they 'lost our way to England' followed by 'When? Where?' and again affirming in the last line 'we lost our way to England'. This all supports the confused tone created at the beginning of the piece.

It is touching the way she refers to the looking-glass and how she would watch herself brush her hair. The hint of loneliness created by the way her mother 'looked away from me, over my head' is affirmed as she saw herself as 'very lonely' and by the way she tried to kiss herself in the mirror. She described it as 'hard, cold and misted over', which is ironically how she now sees England.

There is an air of suspicion held through the writing too as she recounts, 'there is still the sound of whispering that I have heard all my life, but these are different voices.' This prompts the reader to wonder whether she is referring to real or imagined voices in the past, even though they are real at this point in time. However the narrator does not actually question this herself, she just accepts it as though she realizes deep down that she is 'different'.

The whole piece jumps from the past tense to the present tense and as mentioned before uses very basic language. This gives us a clue that perhaps Mrs Rochester was not well educated. All in all though the picture painted is one of a confused and sensitive adult – sensitive, in the way she views the fire as 'beautiful' and reaching out for affection when trying to kiss her reflection in the looking-glass; confused, in the way she does not understand why she is where she is and really cannot remember how she got there.

In contrast, 'Jane Eyre' gives the viewpoint of an educated, well-balanced individual whose prose is far more detailed in its descriptions, using complex rather than simple sentence structure, and having a notably larger range of vocabulary. The writing also flows more fluently as opposed to being stilted and remains in the past tense – hence it does not have the confused childlike qualities of 'Wide Sargasso Sea'. The speech at the end of 'Jane Eyre' also gives credence to the sense that Jane is more educated when Mrs Fairfax asks her about her student who then appears speaking in French.

When looking at the objects and her surroundings, Jane uses many more adjectives and notes numerous intricate details about the different objects as well as metaphors to express her imaginative side. This is very apparent from the first paragraph when admiring the different rooms she passes through with Mrs Fairfax. She appears to be a very fair and kind person, referring to the third-storey rooms as 'interesting from their air of antiquity' despite being 'dark and low'. As a narrator she tries hard to avoid being too critical as shown when realizing the furniture was old yet regarding it as having been 'appropriated' to the upper rooms 'as fashions changed', giving the third storey a 'shrine of memory'. Particular attention is paid to the detail of the furniture and the embroideries. It is as though she could almost see them being sewn when she uses the term 'wrought by fingers'. This imagination rears again later, referring to the attic as 'black as a vault'.

In the centre of the piece there is a break where the viewpoint shifts, as there is some narrative dialogue, but then the viewpoint returns to Jane again, adding to the stable air of the piece.

The non-critical view arises again when Jane sees the beauty of the view from the battlements, using many adjectives such as 'bright . . . velvet . . . tranquil . . . propitious . . . azure' and 'pearly' all within a single sentence. These are punctuated by two metaphors 'the grounds laid out like a map' and 'wide as a park' as well as being complemented by her comparison of the trees and the moss. Her following sentence reads, 'No feature in the scene was extraordinary, but all was pleasing.' How nice to see such detail in a view which is not 'extraordinary'.

The two writings do agree on a couple of points:

One is the appearance of the corridor in which Mrs Rochester is kept. The excerpt from 'Jane Eyre' again shows the imaginative side by use of the metaphor 'like a corridor in some Bluebeard's castle' in contrast to Mrs Rochester's childlike and simple metaphor of 'cardboard'.

The other point is the fact that Grace was perhaps not a suitable name for the woman who 'looked after' Mrs Rochester. Again, Jane Eyre's version is far more descriptive: 'I really did not expect any Grace to answer' calling her laugh 'tragic' and 'preternatural' and her physical appearance as an 'apparition less romantic or less ghostly could scarcely be conceived', whereas Mrs Rochester simply says 'Her name oughtn't to be Grace. Names matter.'

These two examples are typical of the different effects created by the differing points of view the pieces were written from.

Examiner's comments

This is a perceptive and sensitive response to the task. The student has read the passages thoroughly and has employed deductive skills, using the clues to work out what is happening. Note how the student is not thrown but re-assesses the situation when new information is found. For example, the original impression in passage one that the character is a child is re-evaluated when textual clues make it clear that this is not the case.

The student shows a sound understanding of 'narrative voice' and draws contrasts and comparisons between the two extracts. Overall the writing shows a good level of sensitivity to the ways in which writers use language to create their effects, and the importance that 'narrative voice' can have in shaping the readers' perceptions and responses.

Register

The term 'register' is used to describe variation in language according to the way in which it is being used. For example, a solicitor might use a form of language containing many legal words and phrases, while a doctor could use language dominated by medical words and phrases. You might use formal language when attending a job interview, and an informal register when speaking to your friends. When you are asked to analyse a piece of writing containing spoken language it is important to make sure that you note *three* key areas related to register:

The mode	Either spoken or written (although there can be subdivision where a speech is written down, for example).
The manner	The relationship between the creator of the language and the recipient of it. In basic terms this can be either formal or informal.
The field	The way that the words used are linked to the subject matter being dealt with. For example, a writer dealing with a military theme may well use words such as *garrison, sergeant, unexploded, shell, artillery*, etc. The field, therefore, is closely related to lexis, and by examining it conclusions can be drawn about the topic or focus of the language being used.

Lexis

Lexis (also called **lexicon**) is the term used to describe the vocabulary of a novel, poem, speech or other form of language use. You may find this feature referred to as **diction** in some books, particularly those dealing with literary criticism. This is a literary rather than a linguistic term and in a narrow sense it refers to vocabulary that is typically poetic. But more broadly it can mean any use of words thought by the poet to be effective.

Lexis deals with the study of words and the way that they relate to one another, and it can take a variety of forms depending on the choices that writers make to achieve their purposes.

When examining the lexis of narrative prose, certain features are worth watching out for. Here is one way to approach the task:

Nouns	Abstract nouns may focus on describing states of mind, concepts, ideas.
	Concrete nouns are used more to describe solid events, characters, etc.
	Proper nouns are used to establish characters, places, etc.

Verbs	Stative verbs (know, believe) may indicate a writer's interest is in describing states of mind, setting, etc.
	Dynamic verbs place the emphasis on what is currently happening.

Modifiers	Modifiers, such as adverbs and adjectives, can provide a whole range of added detail and writers use them a great deal to influence the reader's perceptions. They can add positive or negative connotations and shape readers' responses.

Here is a checklist of other features to look for when examining the word choice of a writer:

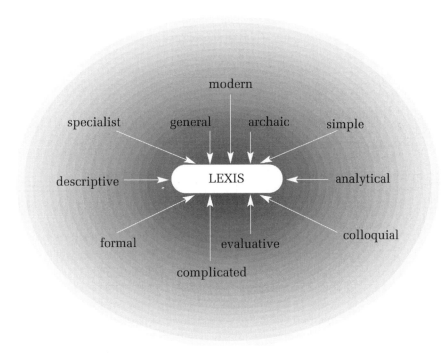

- ❏ levels of formality
- ❏ technical and non-technical vocabulary
- ❏ non-standard vocabulary.

What sorts of vocabulary are being used? Are the words:

- ❏ short or long
- ❏ simple or complex
- ❏ concrete or abstract
- ❏ in everyday use or specialist and relating to a particular area
- ❏ literal or figurative
- ❏ heavily modified or presented with little modification?

Remember, though, that throughout your consideration of lexis you should always bear in mind the time and place in which the narrative is set. The writer's lexical choices will depend very much on the world he or she inhabits and the world he or she creates.

ACTIVITY

Read the following extract carefully. It is taken from an account written by Eric Lomax in which he describes his experiences as a prisoner of the Japanese during the Second World War working on the Burma–Siam Railway. Here he describes his arrival at Catterick to begin training as an officer cadet.

Examine the lexical choices that Lomax has made here and discuss the effects that his choices create. Use specific examples from the text to illustrate your ideas.

I arrived at the Marne Lines and was promptly stripped of my rank. I was now a cadet, my white shoulder tapes and cap bands telling the world that I was neither officer nor man. It had all been too much for one boy: I had barely arrived before I was turned out on parade with the other 250 cadets for a funeral. A cadet on an earlier course had shot himself after being told he was 'RTU'd', the worst humiliation: being returned to your unit.

With this sober beginning, we settled down to seven months of training intended to turn us into effective Royal Signals officers. It was the most demanding and intense period of study I have ever undertaken; the Royal High School seemed child's play by comparison, and of course it was. We learned about radio, telegraphy and telephony to a level beyond the Post Office's dreams, and were taught about military organization, how to use quite heavy machine tools and even about intelligence work.

In June 1940 the British Army was evacuated from Dunkirk, and for the first time the war began to touch us. We were told to expect troops and refugees, and prepared beds and mattresses in halls, gymnasiums and every large building where there was room. After a couple of weeks the emergency passed; the army had retreated in surprisingly good order and it survived. A cloud lifted. Our beds were not needed, the evacuees went elsewhere.

The war then made another stealthy, silent leap in our direction, like a storm threatening to come in off the sea. It was feared that the Germans would follow up their advantage and invade, catching the exhausted troops who were the core of our army at their weakest. That summer, I spent a lot of nights on a little platform at the top of a very high wooden tower, with orders to keep watch for enemy parachute landings. I forced myself to stay awake, looking up at the fields of stars and hoping that I wouldn't be the one to see drifting silk crossing them. But once again the war stayed away, withdrew beyond the coast; nothing happened.

In fact, the worst that happened to me on this marvellous course was pulling an extra drill for my entire class by attempting to poison the company commander. Captain Knowles was a stickler for inspections, and liked to check things in turn; bootlaces, rifle barrels, the insides of hats. One day, he decided to inspect the No.13 course's kit. There we were, shaved and washed, loaded with rifles, gas-masks, haversacks and water-bottles, and he ordered us to present the bottles as we would our firearms. He pulled the cork out of mine and took a deep whiff, and staggered backwards into the arms of the company sergeant-major, who was unfortunately an exceptionally small warrant officer. Dignity was not maintained.

It was not a happy situation, and it resulted from my desire not to leave anything behind that could be useful, a habit that I would have unlearnt then and there if I had known what it could bring down on me. On an exercise out on the moors, I had been appointed cook and at the close of the exercise I had not wanted to waste the leftover milk, so I poured it into my water-bottle. I strongly recommend stale milk, fermented for three weeks in a British Army canteen, as a harmless substitute for gas.

(Eric Lomax, *The Railway Man*)

Speech, dialogue and thought

Narrative prose very often contains speech, through which the characters communicate with the reader or with other characters. If the character is speaking alone, the speech is known as a **monologue**, but if one or more other characters are involved it becomes a **dialogue**. The thoughts of characters are sometimes treated in the same way as speech, as if the character is 'thinking aloud' in order to convey information to the reader.

Writers adopt a number of approaches to convey the speech of their characters through prose. It is worth remembering, though, that these techniques – which present something spoken and heard in the form of writing to be read – are doing something fundamentally artificial with language. Written speech tends to be very much more conventionalized and ordered than speech in real life. Just compare a transcript of a real conversation with a conversation from a novel to convince yourself of this. The writer's talent, however, lies in convincing the reader of the reality of this artificial dialogue, so that disbelief is suspended.

Direct speech

Direct speech presents the reader with an exact copy of the words spoken. They are enclosed within quotation marks and accompanied by a reporting clause such as 'he shouted/said/called/demanded'.

'I am sorry for the rain,' said he. 'But how glad I am to have you here! I am so afraid you will get cold, with nothing upon your arms and shoulders,' he said. 'Creep close to me, and perhaps the drizzle won't hurt you much.'

(Thomas Hardy, *Tess of the D'Urbervilles*)

The use of direct speech gives a prominence and emphasis to the speaker's point of view. It also allows writers to vary spelling, vocabulary, word order and so on in order to give an accurate phonological, lexical and syntactical version to represent a character's accent, dialect or individual manner of speaking.

Indirect speech

Indirect speech presents the material from a slightly different perspective, away from that of the speaker and towards the narrator. For example, if we take the speech from *Tess of the D'Urbervilles*, this could be represented in indirect speech in the following way:

He said that he was afraid that she would get cold with nothing upon her arms and shoulders. He told her to creep close to him so that perhaps the drizzle would not hurt her much.

ACTIVITY   Look carefully at the two versions and identify the changes that have taken place.

Check your points against the following:

1 The quotation marks around the speech, which indicate that direct quotation is taking place, have been dropped.

2 A subordinating conjunction – *that* – is used.

3 There is a change from first- and second-person pronouns (I, you) to third-person (he, she).

4 There is a shift in the tense 'backwards' in time (am → he was).

5 Temporal expressions shift backwards – 'will' becomes 'would'.

6 Demonstratives shift from close to distant ones – *here* becomes *there*.

ACTIVITY   Look at the following extract.

Try re-writing the passage in indirect speech. Make a note of the changes that you need to make to the language in order to convert it. What has changed in your new version? Think about the differences between the two versions.

It was eleven o'clock before the family were all in bed, and two o'clock next morning was the latest hour for starting with the beehives if they were to be delivered to the retailers in Casterbridge before the Saturday market began, the way thither lying by bad roads over a distance of between twenty and thirty miles, and the horse and waggon being of the slowest. At half-past one Mrs Durbeyfield came into the large bedroom where Tess and all her little brothers and sisters slept.

'The poor man can't go,' she said to her eldest daughter, whose great eyes had opened the moment her mother's hand touched the door.

Tess sat up in bed, lost in a vague interspace between a dream and this information.

'But somebody must go,' she replied. 'It is late for the hives already. Swarming will soon be over for the year; and if we put off taking 'em till next week's market the call for 'em will be past, and they'll be thrown on our hands.'

Mrs Durbeyfield looked unequal to the emergency. 'Some young feller, perhaps, would go? One of them who were so much after dancing with 'ee yesterday,' she presently suggested.

'O no – I wouldn't have it for the world!' declared Tess proudly. 'And letting everybody know the reason – such a thing to be ashamed of! I think *I* could go if Abraham could go with me to kip me company.'

(Thomas Hardy, *Tess of the D'Urbervilles*)

Free direct speech

Direct speech has two features, which show evidence of the presence of the narrator:

- ❏ the quotation marks
- ❏ the introductory reporting clause (*she said*, etc.)

In the case of free direct speech the perspective of the narrator is minimized rather than emphasized. Many writers use this approach when creating speech in their narratives. Here is an example from *Beloved* where Morrison uses only the occasional supporting clause.

> Patience, something Denver had never known, overtook her. As long as her mother did not interfere, she was a model of compassion, turning waspish, though, when Sethe tried to help.
> 'Did she take a spoonful of anything today?' Sethe inquired.
> 'She shouldn't eat with cholera.'
> 'You sure that's it? Was just a hunch of Paul D's.'
> 'I don't know, but she shouldn't eat anyway just yet.'
> 'I think cholera people puke all the time.'
> 'That's even more reason, ain't it?'
> 'Well she shouldn't starve to death either, Denvery.'
> 'Leave us alone, Ma'am. I'm taking care of her.'
>
> (Toni Morrison, *Beloved*)

Occasionally some writers remove the quotation marks too. James Joyce, for example, is particularly fond of running speech and narrative together. He uses this method of presenting speech throughout *A Portrait of the Artist as a Young Man*.

Sometimes a writer might use a mixture of direct and free direct speech to create an effect. Dickens adopts this technique in *Bleak House*:

> 'This won't do, gentlemen!' says the Coroner, with a melancholy shake of the head.
> 'Don't you think you can receive his evidence, Sir?' asks an attentive Juryman.
> 'Out of the question,' says the Coroner. 'You have heard the boy. "Can't exactly say" won't do, you know.
> We can't take *that*, in a Court of Justice; gentlemen.
> It's terrible depravity. Put the boy aside.'
> Boy put aside, to the great edification of the audience; –
> Especially of Little Swills, the Comic Vocalist.
> Now. Is there any other witness? No other witness.
> Very well, gentleman! Here's a man unknown,
> proved to have been in the habit of taking opium in large quantities
> for a year and a half, found dead of too much opium. If you think

➡

you have any evidence to lead you to the conclusion that he
committed suicide, you will come to that conclusion.
If you think it is a case of accidental death, you will find a
verdict accordingly.
  Verdict accordingly. Accidental death. No doubt.
Gentlemen, you are discharged. Good afternoon.

(Charles Dickens, *Bleak House*)

ACTIVITY Think about these examples. Why do you think some writers choose to
adopt this free direct speech technique? What effect does it have on the
narrative?

Here are some possible effects:

❏ the removal of the distinction between speech and narrative creates the
   impression that they are inseparable aspects of one unified piece
❏ Dickens's switch to the free direct form allows him to speed up the
   usually lengthy concluding processes of the court. This free direct form
   allows him to focus on the essentials while at the same time retaining
   the narrative line and the sense of the direct voice.

Free indirect speech

This is a form of indirect speech in which the main reporting clause (such
as *She said that . . .*) is missed out, but the tense and pronoun selection are
those associated with indirect speech. The effect of this is to merge the
approach of both direct and indirect speech.

This form of speech is very often associated with third-person narrative –
the third-person narrator apparently filters the speech (or thoughts) of the
characters.

Here, the writer, after a straightforward narrative lead-in, goes into free direct
and then free indirect speech mode:

She scarcely knew Nancy at all, she had gone to the party in place of her
husband, Boris, to whom the invitation was addressed. Boris never went to
parties of any kind, but that did not stop the invitations coming. And she had
gone with this purpose in mind – to meet someone. For she had decided
some weeks beforehand that it ought to be her next experience. I am thirty-
two years old, she told herself, eight years married and childless, what else is
there for me? I am not unattractive, not unintelligent, yet I have never had any
sort of an affair, before marriage or since, there is a whole world about which
my friends talk and people write, and about which I know nothing. There are
emotions, passions, jealousies and anxieties, which I do not understand. It is
time, surely it is time . . .
    Perhaps, after all, it was not as clear-cut, as fully conscious as that, perhaps ➡

there were many doubts and moments of disillusionment. But the decision was in some sort made, and afterwards, she felt herself to be suddenly more vulnerable, more aware, she was receptive to glances and questions and implications. And then, it was only a question of time.

(Susan Hill, from 'In the Conservatory' in *A Bit of Singing and Dancing*)

ACTIVITY

> Think about how this form varies from the others you have looked at. In what ways do you think it differs from the others? What particular effects do you think could be achieved through its use?

Here are some points for you to think about.

- ❏ Free indirect speech blurs the distinction between a character's speech and the narrative voice.
- ❏ It offers a way for writers to present words that seem to come both from inside and outside a character at the same time.
- ❏ It can give speech the emotional power of coming from the character's perspective while at the same time preserving some narrative distance or detachment from the character.
- ❏ It is often used to convey irony because it allows for the introduction of two points of view – the character's and the narrator's – simultaneously.

The presentation of thoughts

In many ways 'thought' can be considered a kind of 'inner speech', and the categories available to a writer in presenting the thoughts of characters are the same as for the presentation of speech. For example:

a He wondered, 'Is the road ahead still clear?' (direct thought)

b Is the road ahead still clear? (free direct thought)

c He wondered if the road ahead was still clear. (indirect thought)

d Was the road ahead still clear? (free indirect thought)

Many narratives use these various methods of telling the reader what is in the minds of characters and many writers, particularly of the Nineteenth and Twentieth Centuries, have experimented with the portrayal of 'internal speech'. One reason for this is the fact that writers have become more and more concerned with ways of presenting vividly the flow of thought through a character's mind. Taken to its extreme this led to the development of what has become known as **stream of consciousness** writing, in which the character's thoughts are poured out in a constant stream, often without punctuation, just as if they were flowing from the character's mind.

ACTIVITY

> Read the following passage carefully. It is from Jane Gardam's 'Stone Trees' and describes the experiences of a bereaved woman.
>
> 1 How does Gardam's use of language here differ from a straightforward description of the scene?
>
> 2 What details do you gather from the text that a straightforward description of the scene would not have given you?
>
> 3 What details are missed out that a straightforward description would have given you?
>
> 4 What effects do you think Gardam wanted to create here?

The boat crosses. Has crossed. Already. Criss-cross deck. Criss-cross water. Splashy sea and look –! Lovely clouds flying (now that you are dead) and here's the pier. A long, long pier into the sea and gulls shouting and children yelling here and there and here's my ticket and there they stand. All in a row – Tom, Anna, the two children solemn. And smiles now – Tom and Anna. Tom and Anna look too large to be quite true. Too good. Anna who never did anything wrong. Arms stretch too far forward for a simple day.

They stretch because they want. They would not stretch to me if you were obvious and not just dead. Then it would have been, hullo, easy crossing? Good. Wonderful day. Let's get back and down on the beach. Great to see you both.

So now that you are dead –
We paced last week. Three.
Tom. Anna. I
And other black figures wood-faced outside the crematorium in blazing sun, examining shiny black-edged tickets on blazing bouquets. 'How good of Marjorie – fancy old Marjorie. I didn't even know she –' There was that woman who ran out of the so-called service with handkerchief at her eyes. But who was there except you my darling and I and the Robertsons and the shiny cards and did they do it then? Were they doing it then as we read the flowers? Do they do it at once or stack it up with other coffins and was it still inside waiting as I paced with portly Tom? Christian Tom – Tom we laughed at so often and oh my darling now that you are dead –

(Jane Gardam, from 'Stone Trees', in *Pangs of Love*)

Overall, we can summarize the presentation of speech and thought in the following points:

- ❏ speech presentation is more than a mere technical feature
- ❏ different modes present different viewpoints and different relationships with the narrator
- ❏ each variation has a different effect, allowing the character to speak as if in his or her 'own words' or filtering them through the perspective of the narrator

❏ different kinds of interplay between the voice of the narrator and the speech of a character are closely connected to the idea of point of view.

Grammar

In narrative prose, the grammar will reflect the kind of world the writer creates and the viewpoint adopted. Analysing the grammar of a text can be useful in establishing how the text works. The writer of narrative prose has a good deal of scope as non-standard grammar and lexis are acceptable.

In examining a piece of prose, look out for these grammatical features:

❏ **Tense** – most narrative is written in the simple past tense but other tenses are sometimes used to create different effects.
❏ **Mood** can be reflected through the use of grammar – the declarative mood is the most common, but the use of imperatives and interrogatives can influence the pace and change the focus.
❏ **Sentence structure** (syntax) can also be used to achieve different effects. Simple sentences are often used to give emphasis, while more complex structures can create various effects. Most writers tend to vary their sentence structure to help give the reader variety and therefore sustain interest.

Syntax

Syntax simply means sentence structure. What is a sentence? There are two answers to this question – a common-sense one and a grammatical one. The common-sense answer is that any group of words that makes sense is a 'sentence', and the visual markers of the sentence are a capital letter at the beginning and a full stop at the end. In spoken language a meaningful utterance may not seem to be a sentence, but could be easily understood. For example, in response to the question 'Where did you find it?' the answer could be 'Over there.' This is perfectly acceptable. The context enables us to supply the missing parts, and so it is unnecessary to say 'I found it over there.' However, in many ways the rules for written and spoken language are different. In grammatical terms a complete sentence must have two things:

a a **subject** – the person or thing the sentence is about

b a **predicate** – describing what the subject is doing.

In some sentences the predicate may consist of a verb only, as in 'James runs.' Or there may be an additional element known as the **adjunct**. This could be an adverb (or modifier) as in 'James runs quickly' or a noun phrase, 'James runs to the house.' All subjects will include a noun or pronoun – 'James' or 'he' – or they can be lengthened by **determiners** (*a*, *the*, *that*, etc.), adjectives (modifiers) and so on.

Sentences can be divided into three basic kinds:

1 Simple sentences have one main clause (one subject and one verb).

2 Compound sentences have two (or more) main clauses, i.e. two subjects and two verbs which are linked by co-ordinating words or conjunctions (*and, but, or, nor, either, neither*).

3 Complex sentences, like compound sentences, consist of two or more clauses but these are linked together by subordination using words such as *because, when, although*. This kind of sentence is the most complicated and in prose usually signals a fairly sophisticated style.

In analysing a writer's stylistic technique, however, it is of no use to simply be able to recognize whether he or she uses single, compound or complex sentences. The real questions are 'What purpose do the sentences serve?' and 'What effect do they have on the piece of writing concerned?'

In answer to this first question, a sentence may perform various **functions**:

For example:

❏ **Declarative** sentences state things (make statements, if you prefer).
❏ **Interrogative** sentences ask questions.
❏ **Imperative** sentences issue commands.
❏ **Exclamatory** sentences always end with an exclamation mark and contain exclamations.

When analysing prose it is important to be able to say something about the syntax, but it is not sufficient to simply say things like 'this piece uses long and short sentences' or 'a lot of hard sentences are used here.' You need to be able to recognize why the writer has chosen to use particular sentence structures, and what effect they have on the tone, mood and impact of the writing overall.

Here are some general pointers:

❏ **Declarative** sentences could be used to create a sense of drama.
❏ **Interrogative** sentences may produce a questioning, probing effect in the prose.
❏ **Imperative** sentences could be used to create an attacking, critical or off-hand effect.
❏ **Exclamatory** sentences could heighten drama, express shock or communicate surprise.
❏ Short, simple sentences could be used to give the sense of action speeding up, or a sense of breathlessness.
❏ Longer, compound sentences could produce a slowing effect on the narrative.
❏ Complex sentences might create a contemplative, philosophical mood.

Remember that these are just some examples of the effects different sentence types can create. In reality, each type of sentence can create a whole variety of different effects, so to determine exactly what effects the syntax has on a piece of prose you must assess it within the context of the individual piece you are examining.

Literal and non-literal language

A piece of writing has potentially two different sorts of meaning:

a a literal meaning

b a non-literal or implied meaning.

Literal meaning is a meaning that is fixed for a particular word or group of words. Many groups of words, however, also have a non-literal meaning or an implied meaning.

Literary devices that are used to create particular effects through non-literal meaning are known collectively as figurative language, and include **metaphors**, **similes** and **symbolism**.

ACTIVITY   Read the following extract from *Hard Times* by Charles Dickens, describing Mr Bounderby. Discuss Dickens's use of non-literal language here, explaining what it contributes to the effect of the description.

Why, Mr Bounderby was as near being Mr Gradgind's bosom friend, as a man perfectly devoid of sentiment can approach that spiritual relationship towards another man perfectly devoid of sentiment. So near was Mr Bounderby – or, if the reader should prefer it, so far off.

He was a rich man: banker, merchant, manufacturer, and what not. A big, loud man, with a stare and a metallic laugh. A man made out of a coarse material, which seemed to have been stretched to make so much of him. A man with a great puffed head and forehead, swelled veins in his temples, and such a strained skin to his face that it seemed to hold his eyes open and lift his eyebrows up. A man with a pervading appearance on him of being inflated like a balloon, and ready to start. A man who could never sufficiently vaunt himself a self-made man. A man who was always proclaiming, through that brassy speaking-trumpet of a voice of his, his old ignorance and his old poverty. A man who was the Bull of humility.

A year or two younger than his eminently practical friend, Mr Bounderby looked older; his seven or eight and forty might have had the seven or eight added to it again, without surprising anybody. He had not much hair. One might have fancied he had talked it off; and that what was left, all standing up in disorder, was in that condition from being constantly blown about by his windy boastfulness.

(Charles Dickens, *Hard Times*)

Rhetorical techniques

Writers can also make use of rhetoric in their writing, to persuade readers and shape their responses in various ways. Various rhetorical devices can be used, and an examination of a particular writer's stylistic techniques should take account of these. The rhetorical techniques of planned speech, which are very similar to those used in writing, are discussed in the next chapter. Here are some of the features you should watch out for:

❏ repetition, of sounds, words, sentence structures, etc.
❏ juxtaposition
❏ listing
❏ parallelism
❏ hyperbole
❏ the rhetorical question.

Coherence and cohesion

Structure is given to prose by **coherence**. There is some form of connectedness in a text in terms of ideas or social action, which holds discourse together. Normally the sentences in a piece of prose do not connect together randomly, but combine in a meaningful way that the reader can interpret.

As with other elements of the language of a piece of prose, the writer can use different means of creating coherence in order to obtain particular effects. An understanding of coherence can help you to develop a better understanding of these effects.

Normally some of the 'connectedness' of a text comes from the topic or subject matter it is concerned with. This prompts a key question: 'How do you know what a text is about?' In some cases the answer to this may be obvious – you understand what a text is about because of the knowledge you already possess about the topic it deals with, and the words used relate to that topic. For example, if we note in the lexis of a piece that words like *desk, teacher, book, homework, bell,* and *assembly* are used, it is likely that the piece is in some way connected to the school. These are **collocations** of words – clusters of words that are likely to occur in the same kinds of text. Words that are generally used less frequently, such as specialist or technical terms, have a stronger tendency to suggest specific contexts than those that are used frequently. Collocations are sometimes referred to as **semantic fields**. They can reflect socially constructed clusters which change between people, periods and societies rather than fixed or natural connections between things in reality. In this way, vocabulary creates links between the forms of the text and the ideas or thoughts within it. Its subject matter is reflected in the patterns of words it is made of.

Besides subject matter and vocabulary, there are other forms of connections between sentences. They can indicate relations of sequence, such as causality (one thing leads to another), exemplification (giving an example), implication (suggesting something) and so on. Other forms simply indicate that sentences are to be taken together and help to avoid duplicating material from one sentence to the next. The text taken together helps the reader to produce connections between its sentences by using various direction signals. These signals act as markers of cohesion in a text. The markers can be of a number of types.

❑ Words and phrases co-refer (i.e. refer to other entities). **Pronouns** such as 'he', 'she', 'they', 'it' refer back to people or things already mentioned.

❑ Words like 'the', 'this', etc. refer to earlier mentions of things.

❑ Verbs that have already been used are repeated in condensed, substitute forms, e.g. *He thought he had missed the train. If <u>so</u>* (missed the train) *he would have to walk.*

❑ Connective words and phrases primarily signal directions, e.g.

consequence:	*therefore, because of this*
ordering:	*firstly, finally*
continuation:	*furthermore, then*
simultaneity:	*meanwhile, in the meantime*
concession:	*admittedly, yet*
opposition:	*nevertheless, in spite of this.*

Taken together, these various elements create what is often known as the texture of a text – presenting it as a unified and connected entity rather than as a random selection of sentences.

ACTIVITY : Examine the following passage and make notes on the writer's use of syntax and the ways in which language give a sense of coherence and texture to the piece.

I rose early the next day and attended to my morning hygiene in a state of small excitation because I had a big day ahead of me. I was going to walk across Windsor Great Park. It is the most splendid park I know. It stretches over 40 enchanted square miles and incorporates into its ancient fabric every manner of sylvan charm: deep primeval woodlands, bosky dells, wandering footpaths and bridleways, formal and informal gardens and a long, deeply fetching lake. Scattered picturesquely about are farms, woodland cottages, forgotten statues, a whole village occupied by estate workers and things that the Queen has brought back from trips abroad and couldn't think of anywhere else to put – obelisks and totem poles and other curious expressions of gratitude from distant outposts of the Commonwealth.

The news had not yet come out there was oil under the park and that it all soon might turn into a new Sullom Voe (but don't be alarmed; the local ➡

authority will make them screen the derricks with shrubs), so I didn't realize that I ought to drink things in carefully in case the next time I came this way it looked like an Oklahoma oilfield. At this time, Windsor Great Park continued to enjoy a merciful obscurity, which I find mystifying in an open space so glorious on the very edge of London. Only once could I remember any reference to the part in the newspapers, a couple of years before when Prince Philip had taken a curious disliking to an avenue of ancient trees and had instructed Her Majesty's Tree-Choppers to remove them from the landscape.

I expect their branches had imperilled the progress through the park of his horses and plus-four, or whatever it is you call those creaking contraptions he so likes to roam around in. You often see him and other members of the royal family in the park, speeding past in assorted vehicles on their way to polo matches or church services in the Queen Mother's private compound, the Royal Lodge. Indeed, because the public aren't allowed to drive on the park roads, a significant portion of the little traffic that passes is generated by royals. Once, on Boxing Day when I was ambling along in a paternal fashion beside an offspring on a shiny new tricycle, I became aware with a kind of sixth sense that we were holding up the progress of a car and turned to find that it was being driven by Princess Diana. As I hastened myself and my child out of the way, she gave me a smile that melted my heart, and since that time I have never said a word against the dear sweet girl, however pressed by those who think that she is a bit off her head because she spends £28,000 a year on leotards and makes occasional crank phone calls to hunky military men. (And who among us hasn't? is my unanswerable reply.)

(Bill Bryson, *Notes from a Small Island*)

Authorial intentions

In your examination of narrative prose it is important that you are able to identify what the writer is trying to achieve at various points in the narrative. Authorial intention can take various forms but here are the key ideas:

❑ to characterize
❑ to set the scene
❑ to evoke atmosphere
❑ to experiment with the language.

To characterize

We have already looked at ways in which writers can use first- or third-person narrative to reveal character. In both these types of narrative, other linguistic and stylistic techniques also have a part to play in the creation of the overall effect.

The most obvious way a character can be created is through physical description. In analysing such description, it is important to establish from the outset whose view is being given, the writer's, another character's, or the narrator's, in order to make some assessment of its reliability.

ACTIVITY

Read this description carefully.

How does Proulx use language to make her description effective here? You should pay particular attention to her use of nouns and modifiers, syntax, the connotations of the lexis and any symbolic value you might find in the physical details listed.

A great damp loaf of a body. At six he weighed eighty pounds. At sixteen he was buried under a casement of flesh. Head shaped like a crenshaw, no neck, reddish hair ruched back. Features as bunched as kissed fingertips. Eyes the color of plastic. The monstrous chin, a freakish shelf jutting from the lower face.

    Some anomalous gene had fired up at the moment of his begetting as a single spark sometimes leaps from banked coals, had given him a giant's chin. As a child he invented stratagems to deflect stares; a smile, downcast gaze, the right hand darting up to cover the chin.

(E. Annie Proulx: *The Shipping News*)

To set the scene

Scene setting is obviously very important to narrative prose if the writer wants to convince the reader of the fictional world created. Physical details of time and place can help to enable the reader to visualize the background against which the action takes place. Although separate from atmosphere, the setting could be closely linked to the atmosphere and mood the writer wishes to create.

To evoke atmosphere

The creation of different atmospheres can be very important to the overall impact of a novel. If readers are to be convinced of the fictional world created it is important that the writer successfully arouses the reader's emotions. By creating various atmospheres and moods the writer can persuade the reader to feel things in certain ways, perhaps evoking a sympathy for one of the characters or anger at a particular situation.

ACTIVITY

Read the following extract carefully and analyse the techniques the writer uses to set the scene and evoke atmosphere. You should pay particular attention to the following: the ways in which the writer conveys a feeling of the place; the effects of such features of language as lexical, grammatical and phonological aspects.

Coketown, to which Messrs Bounderby and Gradgrind now walked, was a triumph of fact; it had no greater taint of fancy in it than Mrs Gradgrind herself. Let us strike the key-note, Coketown, before pursuing our tune.

It was a town of red brick, or of brick that would have been red if the smoke and ashes had allowed it; but, as matters stood it was a town of unnatural red and black like the painted face of a savage. It was a town of machinery and tall chimneys, out of which interminable serpents of smoke trailed themselves for ever and ever, and never got uncoiled. It had a black canal in it, and a river that ran purple with ill-smelling dye, and vast piles of buildings full of windows where there was a rattling and a trembling all day long, and where the piston of the steam-engine worked monotonously up and down, like the head of an elephant in a state of melancholy madness. It contained several large streets all very like one another, and many small streets still more like one another, inhabited by people equally like one another, who all went in and out at the same hours, with the same sound upon the same pavements, to do the same work, and to whom every day was the same as yesterday and tomorrow, and every year the counterpart of the last and the next.

These attributes of Coketown were in the main inseparable from the work by which it was sustained; against them were to be set off, comforts of life which found their way all over the world, and elegancies of life which made, we will not ask how much of the fine lady, who could scarcely bear to hear the place mentioned. The rest of its features were voluntary, and they were these.

You saw nothing in Coketown but what was severely workful. If the members of a religious persuasion built a chapel there – they made it a pious warehouse of red brick, with sometimes (but this only in highly ornamented examples) a bell in a bird-cage on the top of it. The solitary exception was the New Church; a stuccoed edifice with a square steeple over the door, terminating in four short pinnacles like florid wooden legs. All the public inscriptions in the town were painted alike, in severe characters of black and white. The jail might have been the infirmary, the infirmary might have been the jail, the town-hall might have been either, or both, or anything else, for anything that appeared to the contrary in the graces of their construction.

(Charles Dickens, *Hard Times*)

To experiment with language

Writers often experiment with non-standard language in order to intensify a particular aspect or aspects of the fictional world that they have created. By using variations of language for different characters, the writer can make them seem more realistic and individual and can place them more specifically in a time or place. Often this is a technique that can be seen in the writer's use of dialogue, reflecting the accents and dialects of characters.

ACTIVITY Read the following extract. How does Walker use language here to achieve her effects? What is the impact of this non-standard use of language?

Dear God,

Harpo ast his daddy why he beat me. Mr ⎯⎯ say,
Cause she my wife. Plus, she stubborn. All women good for – he don't finish.
He just tuck his chin over the paper like he do. Remind me of Pa.

Harpo ast me, How come you stubborn? He don't ast How come you his wife? Nobody ast that.

I say, Just born that way, I reckon.

He beat me like he beat the children. Cept he don't never hardly beat them. He say, Celie, git the belt. The children be outside the room peeking through the cracks. It all I can do not to cry. I make myself wood. I say to myself, Celie, you a tree. That's how come I know trees fear man.

Harpo say, I love Somebody.

I say, Huh?

He say, A Girl.

I say, You do?

He say, Yeah. Us plan to marry.

Marry, I say. You not old enough to marry.

I is, he say. I'm seventeen. She fifteen. Old enough.

What her mama say, I ast.

Ain't talk to her mama.

What her daddy say?

Ain't talk to him neither.

Well, what *she* say?

Us ain't never spoke. He duck his head. He ain't so bad looking. Tall and skinny, black like his mama, with great big bug eyes.

Where yall see each other? I ask. I see her in church, he say. She see me outdoors.

She like you?

I don't know. I wink at her. She act like she scared to look.

Where her daddy at while all this going on?

Amen corner, he say.

(Alice Walker, *The Color Purple*)

The novelist Alice Walker uses non-standard language to achieve her effects

So far in this chapter we have suggested some aspects of language present in prose writing and you have looked at some examples of these features in the extracts you have worked on. However, the question is how this will help you in the analysis of the texts you have studied. Merely being able to identify features of language is meaningless unless you link it to a wider explanation of the **purpose** for using language in a particular kind of way to create specific **effects**.

In order to approach an examination question, it can be useful to have a checklist of features of language that you could look for in the piece of writing in order to analyse its purpose and effects.

Checklist of language features of prose

This may help you to identify key features, but be aware that not every example of prose will contain all these features.

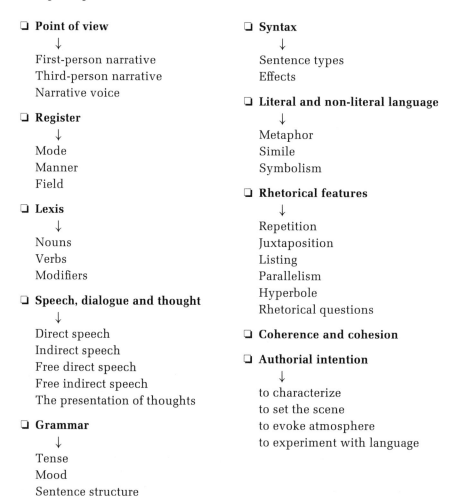

❑ **Point of view**
   ↓
   First-person narrative
   Third-person narrative
   Narrative voice

❑ **Register**
   ↓
   Mode
   Manner
   Field

❑ **Lexis**
   ↓
   Nouns
   Verbs
   Modifiers

❑ **Speech, dialogue and thought**
   ↓
   Direct speech
   Indirect speech
   Free direct speech
   Free indirect speech
   The presentation of thoughts

❑ **Grammar**
   ↓
   Tense
   Mood
   Sentence structure

❑ **Syntax**
   ↓
   Sentence types
   Effects

❑ **Literal and non-literal language**
   ↓
   Metaphor
   Simile
   Symbolism

❑ **Rhetorical features**
   ↓
   Repetition
   Juxtaposition
   Listing
   Parallelism
   Hyperbole
   Rhetorical questions

❑ **Coherence and cohesion**

❑ **Authorial intention**
   ↓
   to characterize
   to set the scene
   to evoke atmosphere
   to experiment with language

APPROACHES TO EXAMINATION QUESTIONS

We are now ready to look at the kinds of questions you will need to deal with in the examination, and to apply some of the points we have discussed in order to answer them.

A reminder that the questions test your ability to:

❏ respond to literary texts and distinguish, describe and interpret variation in meaning and form
❏ respond to and analyse texts, using literary and linguistic concepts and approaches
❏ show understanding of the ways contextual variation and choices of form, style and vocabulary shape the meanings of texts
❏ identify and consider the ways attitudes and values are created and conveyed in speech and writing.

Don't forget – you will *not* have the text with you in the examination.

Read the extract printed below. How does Lomax use language here to convey to the reader the full horror of his treatment, both here and elsewhere in the book? In your answer you should consider:

❏ the ways in which the writer's attitudes and values are conveyed to the reader
❏ features of language such as lexical, grammatical and phonological aspects.

The gang came back out of the night. My special friend Morton Mackay was called forward. I was next in line. As they started on Mackay and the rain of fearful blows commenced I saw to the side another group of guards pushing a stumbling and shattered figure back towards the guardhouse. Smith was still alive; he was allowed to drop in a heap in the ditch beside the entrance.

Mackay went down roaring like a lion, only to be kicked up again; within a matter of minutes he was driven into the semi-darkness and out of the range of the lights, surrounded by the flailing pick-helves which rose and fell ceaselessly. I remember thinking that in the bad light they looked like the blades of a windmill, so relentless was their action. In due course Mackay's body was dragged along and dumped beside Smith's in the ditch.

The moments while I was waiting my turn were the worst of my life. The expectation is indescribable; a childhood story of Protestant martyrs watching friends die in agony on the rack flashed through my mind. To have to witness the torture of others and to see the preparations for the attack on one's own body is a punishment in itself, especially when there is no escape. This experience is the beginning of a form of insanity.

Then me. It must have been about midnight. I took off my spectacles and my watch carefully, turned and laid them down on the table behind me in the guardroom. It was almost as if I was preparing to go into a swimming-pool, so careful was the gesture of folding them and laying them down. I must have　➡

had to take a couple of steps backward to perform this neat unconscious manoeuvre. None of the guards made a move or said a word. Perhaps they were too surprised.

I was called forward. I stood to attention. They stood facing me, breathing heavily. There was a pause. It seemed to drag on for minutes. Then I went down with a blow that shook every bone, and which released a sensation of scorching liquid pain which seared through my entire body. Sudden blows struck me all over. I felt myself plunging downwards into an abyss with tremendous flashes of solid light which burned and agonized. I could identify the periodic stamping of boots on the back of my head, crunching my face into the gravel; the crack of bones snapping; my teeth breaking; and my own involuntary attempts to respond to deep vicious kicks and to regain an upright position, only to be thrown to the ground once more.

At one point I realized that my hips were being damaged and I remember looking up and seeing the pick-helves coming down towards my hips, and putting my arms in the way to deflect the blows. This seemed only to focus the clubs on my arms and hands. I remember the actual blow that broke my wrist. It fell right across it, with a terrible pain of delicate bones being crushed. Yet the worst pain came from the pounding on my pelvic bones and the base of my spine. I think they tried to smash my hips. My whole trunk was brutally defined for me, like having my skeleton etched out in pain.

It went on and on. I could not measure the time it took. There are some things that you cannot measure in time, and this is one of them. Absurdly, the comparison that often comes to my mind is that torture was indeed like an awful job interview: it compresses time strangely, and at the end of it you cannot tell whether it has lasted five minutes or an hour.

I do know that I thought I was dying. I have never forgotten, from that moment onwards, crying out 'Jesus', crying out for help, the utter despair of helplessness. I rolled into a deep ditch of foul stagnant water which, in the second or two before consciousness was finally extinguished, flowed over me with the freshness of a pure and sweet spring.

I awoke and found myself standing on my feet. I do not recall crawling out of that ditch but the sun was already up. I was an erect mass of pain, of bloody contusions and damaged bones, the sun playing harshly on inflamed nerves. Smith and Slater were lying on the ground beside me, blackened, covered in blood and barely conscious. Mac and Knight were in a like state a few yards further away. We were only a few feet from the guardroom, close to the point where we had been standing the previous night. Slater was nearly naked; a pair of shorts and some torn clothing lay on the ground behind him, mud-stained and blood-stained.

The guards simply ignored us. The stood in front of a barely moving, battered pile of human beings under the fierce sun and acted as though we were not there.

By the middle of the morning I must have felt brighter because I began to wonder why I should stay standing up when the other four were lying down. I sagged at the knees and sprawled out beside Smith and Slater. There was still no response from the guards.

About noon, the large American-speaking Japanese interpreter sauntered over from the camp offices, squatted down beside us and inspected us with a critical eye. He sent a guard for a bucket of tea, which he offered to each of us from a mess-tin. Vague stirrings of life from the others; bodies in various horizontal postures managed to drink quite a quantity of tea. I was sitting up. I tried to take the tin, only to find that my wrists and hands were so swollen and useless that they couldn't hold it. The Japanese interpreter solved the problem by pouring warm tea down my throat. I gagged on the acid lukewarm liquid, but it was a huge relief to my dreadful thirst.

(Eric Lomax, *The Railway Man*)

Here is how one student responded to this question. Read the response through carefully and make a note of what you think its strengths and weaknesses are.

Lomax describes his torture in three different stages. The first part, where he is waiting his turn, has a clear and even tone, which is surprising considering the awful feelings he is describing. By describing the torture of one of his friends and the feelings he has, he is giving the reader a clear sense of what it was like to go through it. Lomax's syntax leaves you in no doubt about his story. It is the preciseness and severity of an army report. The language is, however, more emotive with words like 'fearful', 'stumbling' and 'shattered' used alongside colourful imagery like 'roaring like a lion'. There isn't really a sense of place in this part of the extract, there doesn't really need to be one. All Lomax wants us to concentrate on is empathizing with him and the others who were tortured.

The second section describes Lomax's torture. Where before we were watching from a viewpoint outside the attack and got an idea of the bigger picture, this section retreats entirely into Lomax's head. This is particularly effective, as it shows the way the pain cuts you off from the world. The mood is definitely more tense than before and as you read on, there is an increase of tension all the way through until the attack is over. Lomax's use of language goes through a definite change in this section. He uses short sentences to imply a sense that he is beyond fear, and knows the inevitability of his situation. The three sentences beginning, 'I was called forward' show Lomax's attitude towards his captors. He says that he 'stood to attention' which makes him sound smart, honest and human, where they are breathing heavily like animals on a hunt or something.

Then the attack comes suddenly as if it was a surprise, and launches into a long section of imagery. Lomax's use of mis-matching adjectives and concepts work very well. The ideas of 'liquid pain' and 'solid light' give the impression that Lomax is describing something the human brain was not supposed to have to cope with.

The fact that Lomax knows exactly what they are doing to him is very frightening. It is slightly uncomfortable to read, 'I realized my hips were being damaged', or 'I remember the actual blow that broke my wrist'. The formal brutal analogy of the attack, it was 'like having my skeleton etched out in pain' is horrifying and yet calm. The comparisons with the job interview in the next paragraph are oddly light-hearted. It is definitely strange to read an account of horrible torture followed by a strange little aside on the way it affects the perception of time.

The last section, starting from where the attack ends and Lomax is pushed into the ditch, is where the pace drops off. In the last two sections the pace was fairly fast and non-stop, but in this it slows to a fairly domestic pace which like most of Lomax's style, sits strangely with the actual events he is describing. He does not describe himself as a person but as 'an erect mass of pain', which describes the dehumanization the POWs must have felt when they were treated with such cruelty. Lomax later insists that the pile of broken bodies are human beings when he is speaking with disgust of the guards' business-like manner.

The ordinary event of drinking tea is turned into a display of suffering at the end of the extract. Bringing the tea in a bucket and force-feeding the tattered Lomax is a perfect example of the disgusting treatment they were given. It sounds like the Japanese are feeding animals and not humans. This extract is very effective at showing suffering as it works from different angles, such as watching suffering, experiencing suffering and the aftermath of suffering.

Examiner's comments

This is a good response, and gives comprehensive coverage to all elements of the question. There is a clear focus on the ways that Lomax uses language and on the effects that this use of language have on the reader. The comments that the student makes are specific and detailed and throughout there is an awareness of the writer consciously shaping his material and shaping the responses of the reader. There are a number of insights into the complexity of language use here, together with a significant exploration of the lexical, grammatical and phonological patterns that emerge through the text.

What the response does not do is to broaden the discussion to look at Lomax's uses of language elsewhere in the text, which is something that the question asked for. Also, a final paragraph to sum up and pull all the ideas together would have been useful. Nevertheless, as an examination of the given passage this is a very good response.

How this Unit links to other sections of the course

The table below shows the major links between this Unit and others on the course; there are, however, other links that do not carry the same weight.

Question	Skills learned	Links to other parts of the Specification
Prose Study Question	Using frameworks for analysis	• Comparative Literary Studies Unit 4 • Dramatic Study Unit 5 Section A • Language in Context Unit 6 Question 1 • The Language of Speech Unit 3 Section B
	Identifying attitudes and values	• The Language of Speech Unit 3 Section B • Dramatic Study Unit 5 Section A • Language in Context Unit 6 Question 1
	Using integrated linguistic and literary terminology to provide an insight into literary interpretation	• Comparative Literary Studies Unit 4 • Language in Context Unit 6 Questions 1 and 2

4 The Study of Speech

Whichever specification you study at AS- and A2-level in English Language and Literature, you will have to examine speech and the way it is represented in a variety of situations. This is a new departure for students of English Literature, although English Language students may well be familiar with the conventions of speech and discourse. However, by studying speech you will be in a much stronger position to understand the part that speech plays in literature and what writers are doing when they represent speech within certain types of text, such as dramatic works and interchanges between characters in novels. For the purposes of both AS and A2 study, you must also be able to recognize, deconstruct and comment upon spontaneous speech or natural conversation. Your ability to do this, by examining different types of speech acts and the constituent parts of these acts, will enable you to analyse and, ultimately, compare the ways writers adapt or choose to represent speech in their works.

The differences between speech and writing

Linguistically, there are many differences between speech and writing and we must take a number of factors into account when studying the differences between the two. These two types of communication are often distinguished by use of the term **mode**.

Mode	Modes are the two methodologies that we choose between when we communicate with each other; that is, we either use the **spoken mode** (speech) or produce the **written mode** (writing).

When a speaker or writer chooses a particular mode, he or she has often made intuitive if sometimes unconscious decisions as to why speech or writing has been adopted as a means or mode of communication. Before we look at some of the reasons why we choose a certain mode, let us examine two pieces of language that highlight some of the differences between speech and writing. The following two extracts show that the writers have explicit purposes and audiences in mind, by virtue of the mode they choose and what they do with their language within that mode.

ACTIVITY Look closely at the following two pieces of language. The first extract is from the opening pages of a novel and the second is from a recording of a student speaking. Both pieces have a similar purpose, in that they are introductions to the speaker/writer.

❏ What differences can you see between the two pieces?
❏ For what reasons are these particular modes adopted?
❏ Who do you think is the target audience for each piece?

For each question, use textual evidence to support your answer.

Extract 1 *Skin* by Joanna Briscoe

I have very pale skin, very red lips. The lips are a fleshy cushion of pink, but I colour them dark scarlet. The skin is naturally pale, that prized magnolia of lovers, the skin of fairy tales and calves, and it is dusted with Shiseido, a white powder. The journalists have always talked about my skin.

Today I'm walking through the Jardin du Luxembourg on my own. It's April, there's a sore yellow light teasing the shadows between the trees, and the young English nannies push babies along the paths and stop at the sandpit.

The shaded section soothes me. I must protect my face from the divings of sunlight because I am using Retin-A, a vitamin A based cream that sheds layers of skin like sheaves of paper. If the sun reaches my face, it will burn. So I use sun block all over, that gives me a greased sheen when I first step out, but which is later absorbed, and will protect me from second degree burning. I am Adele Meier, something of a celebrity, and I must protect my skin.

Extract 2 Joanne

My name's Joanne (0.5) I'm eighteen years old (1.0) an' I live in a small village (0.5) called Castleton (0.5) near Whitby (.) on in the middle o'the North Yorkshire Moors (0.5) with m'mum 'n dad (1.0) an' ma brother Simon (0.5) who's twenty-three a:::nd (0.5) erm (0.5) ma sister Emma (1.0) who's (1.0) fourteen (1.0) thirteen (1.0) fourteen (1.5) er (0.5) fourteen (0.5) [laughs] also and erm (0.5) I'm at (0.5) studyin' at the moment (1.0) I'm at uni Leeds University (0.5) erm (0.5) which I'm enjoyin' very much (1.0) I've made some really good fr (.) I've bin there since September (0.5) an' I've made some really good friends (.) and (0.5) having a bri::lliant time (0.5) erm (1.0) I'm quite small (3.0) errr (1.0) I like to think I'm quite thin (0.5) but er (0.5) I'm not sure if (0.5) if that's the case at the moment (2.5) um (1.0) I've got long blonde hair (1.0) blue eyes (1.5) a::nd (1.0) big feet (1.0) er:: (1.0) er I've bin home fer a coupla weeks (1.0) an' I went out with ma cousins ter do (.) at a party at a nearby pub (1.0) where we dressed up (0.5) as Reservoir Dogs (1.0) [quietly laughs] an' then this mornin' (1.5) I didn't feel too good [laughs]

Key
(.)   micropause
(1.0)   pause in seconds
::   elongation of sound
[italics] non-verbal sounds

There are many differences between speech and writing, and you will have only touched the tip of the iceberg by focusing on the two passages above. Let us look at some of these differences in much more detail. We can best see the main differences between modes through the following distinctions:

1 the differences of **channel** or the way in which each mode is transmitted

2 the different **uses** of each mode, including the kinds of message each sends and the situations or contexts where each is used

3 the differences in **form**; this is the section that will outline the major characteristics of speech and will provide the basis of your understanding of how spontaneous speech operates.

Channel differences

The most obvious differences between speech and writing arise through the way each mode is produced; speech is formed through sound waves, from the mouth and voice box, and is transmitted to the ears. There are also usually other people present when we talk, but not always. Writing, on the other hand, is produced manually and is read, usually by eye, but in the case of blind people by touch. Writing is often undertaken for other people who are not present at the time of writing. These fairly transparent differences lead to another major distinguishing feature between the two: that is, speech, because it is transmitted orally at a certain point in time, is bound by time, whereas writing is produced for readers who are not present and is as such space-bound or spatial. This also results in the fact that the former is essentially temporary (although it can be given permanency through recording) and the latter is more permanent.

When considering channel, it is necessary to consider how the **forms** of each mode supplement the linguistic content, although the specific linguistic forms will be dealt with in much more detail later in the chapter.

In brief, speech includes what are known as **paralinguistic features**, those characteristics that transcend the language. These include:

❏ intonation, pitch and stress
❏ volume
❏ pace and rhythm
❏ pauses, gaps and silences
❏ laughter, coughing and other non-verbal sounds
❏ quality of voice.

On the other hand, the paralinguistic features of writing include:

❏ paragraphing
❏ punctuation including the spacing between words
❏ capitalization.

A sub-set of paralinguistic features is **kinesics**, which can be applied only to speech as it includes all those bodily features that go towards helping us communicate meaning. These include:

❏ body language, such as use of the hands (pointing) and head (nodding)
❏ facial expression including use of the eyes, the mouth (smiling) and the forehead (frowning).

If there is an equivalent of kinesics in writing, it is **graphology**, which would include:

❏ the design of specific graphemes (individual letters) or the font
❏ the point size in lettering
❏ use of colour
❏ use of white space and margins
❏ use of illustrations and pictures
❏ columning and layout.

All of the above are, in many ways, incidental differences, but they do help to underpin your understanding of the more concrete differences between speech and writing. Therefore, your understanding of why communicators choose a certain mode, and by implication a certain channel with all its attendant characteristics, should be heightened, especially when in the next section we consider the uses or functions of each mode. Here is a tabular representation of the differences we have considered so far.

Channel characteristics: permanent, dynamic and temporal differences		
	Speech	**Writing**
1	When people speak to each other, they do so in the knowledge that there will be no record of the conversation (except in their minds or memories) and that when the conversation ends it ceases to exist. When they speak they use sounds to communicate.	When people write, they do so to make a record of their thoughts or ideas and they know that their writing will be permanent (as long as the text is kept). When people write, they use handwriting or some mechanical means to represent writing.
E.g.	*a conversation between two sixth-form students on the way to their next lesson*	hand-written (not permanent): *a shopping list* hand-written (permanent): lecture notes printed: *a novel or play-script*
2	Speech is most often an interactive process, where there are one or more other persons present. Thus, it can be seen as an active or dynamic process.	Writing is an activity where the audience is distant and very often not known. Thus, writing can be seen as a non-dynamic process.
E.g.	*any face-to-face conversation between two or more people*	audience unknown: *a magazine article* audience known: *a letter to a friend*

3	Speech is bound by time in that it is produced during a certain finite period of time where the participants are present during the interaction. Thus it is temporally bound.	Writing is bound by space as it is produced for readers who are not present at the time of writing; only the writer is usually present at the time of production, although there are exceptions. Thus it is spatially bound.
E.g.	*any verbal interaction that takes place*	space bound: *an essay for a teacher* space bound with participants: *minutes of a meeting*
4	Paralinguistic features and kinesics supplement meaning within speech.	Graphological features supplement the appearance of writing. Conventions of writing aid our understanding of its meaning.
E.g.	*someone telling a dramatic story using intonation and the hands to add to the effect he or she intends*	*the use of capitalization, sentence boundary markers, headlines, columns and photographs in a newspaper article*

Differences in mode usage

Speech

In the previous section on channel characteristics, we discovered that speech has the unique quality of being dynamic and that it is often temporary, in that it is 'lost' as soon as it has been said. However, speech can be made permanent through recording, transcription or a combination of the two. **Transcriptions** enable us to study various speech acts and events in this book, and it is the method you will become most familiar with when you study speech in an examination situation.

Transcription A method of writing down exactly what is said in a systematic way. The style of transcription used in the English Language and Literature specification is phonemic, with additional symbols to aid understanding of what is said. This style of transcription is sometimes called an impressionistic transcription. A second style of transcription is phonetic which uses symbols for sounds, the most widely known symbols being the International Phonetic Alphabet.

Speech can be seen as falling into the following categories, depending upon the intended degree of permanency:

❏ face-to-face interaction such as conversations or interviews
❏ non face-to-face interactions such as telephone conversations
❏ broadcast materials such as live radio or television programmes
❏ recordings such as audio books or 'teach yourself' tapes.

Even though speech in all of the above situations can be either temporary or permanent, it does have the unique quality of being 'live' in all of them because, as listeners, we hear the voices of the speakers, whether they are recorded or not, and the voice has the ability, through the paralinguistic features we have already outlined, to convey a unique personality which makes the communication more special.

Beyond the categories listed above, speech covers a range of specific functions that are dependent upon the situation, or are bound by the **context**.

Context	The social circumstances and situation in which speech takes place; the context influences the nature of what is said and how it is communicated. External contexts must be considered and commented upon when you analyse any speech act.

The definition given above is to draw your attention to the importance of context in speech, which is slightly different from the contexts we have examined so far. To highlight its importance, the following activity focuses solely on context.

ACTIVITY

Look closely at the following examples of speech from a range of situations. The context is vital for our understanding of each speech act, but can be guessed from these particular examples.

- ❑ What is the context for each of the following pieces of speech?
- ❑ What information can you give about each of the people speaking?
- ❑ What function does each piece of speech have?

1 Young girl: Can you tell me the way to the bus station, please?
   Man: Take the next right and follow the road for about half a mile and it's on your left. You can't miss it.

2 George: How are yer Fred?
   Fred: Mustn't grumble y'know, although t'missus in't too well.

3 So what yer need ter do (.) er is (0.5) er click on the bl (.) the tab (.) which says blank publications an' (0.5) er find cust (.) erm (1.0) the custom page button.

4 What a great song that is. Well, it's almost half past eight and it's time for our regular look at the papers. Hmm. Some interesting stories to catch the eye this morning.

5 Today we meet in the aftermath of the Falklands Battle. Our country has won a great victory and we are entitled to be proud. This nation had the resolution to do what it knew had to be done – to do what it knew was right.

These examples all show that the context or situation in which speech has been produced is integral to our understanding of what is being said. We can now look at the range of situations where speech is used.

The functions of speech

The situation or context of speech helps us to understand its function more clearly and to distinguish the nuances of certain speech acts. The functions of speech are as follows, starting with the most obvious and most common.

1 Conversation This includes any spoken situation where speech is exchanged between participants, although they are not necessarily face-to-face. For instance, we often have telephone conversations without looking at the person we are talking to (with the advent of videophones and video conferencing, this is now not always the case). We can say that conversation is interactional in that it involves two or more participants. However, utterances within conversations have a number of sub-functions, which are outlined below:

- ❏ Making propositions. When we make conversation, we establish relationships with others, we co-operate and we keep channels open for further conversations. In order to facilitate these, we make propositions to each other where the things we talk about and discuss are linked to real or possible events in our own world, and where what we say can be either true or false. These are called **constative** (or **representative**) **utterances** since they are capable of being analysed as to their veracity or truthfulness. All of the following are examples of constative utterances:

  A: I've had a terrible day at school, Mum.
  B: It was lovely on Saturday.
  C: Coronation Street's on!

- ❏ Exchanging pleasantries. When we engage people in conversation, we do not launch straight into what we have to say without signalling that we want to open up a route of communication. These indicators, such as 'Excuse me' or 'Hello' are called **phatic utterances**, and usually precede the content of our conversations. We may also engage in phatic communion when it is not what is said that is important, more the fact that we are talking. When we meet one another and comment on the weather or ask how the other person is, it could be viewed as an exchange of simple pleasantries and nothing more; in other words, it is linguistically vacuous and serves only a social function.

- ❏ Expressing feelings. Another function of speech is to convey our feelings and emotions. Obviously, this depends upon how comfortable we feel about articulating our feelings and how confident we are as people. However, with people we know or are close to, we often use **expressive utterances** to transmit our innermost feelings.

A: I feel dreadful about it.
B: I really hate Cliff Richard.
C: Oh, I do love you so much!

❏ Doing something. There are certain times where we want someone to do something for us, so we will order, suggest or request a particular thing. This kind of utterance is a **directive**.

A: A pint of beer and give me a bag of crisps, too.
B: Will you shut the window for me?
C: Don't speak with your mouth full.

2 Pedagogic talk It is sometimes difficult to draw the line between conversation and the kind of talk that takes place in the classroom. It is often said that educational talk is not only interactional but also **transactional**, since its function is to get something done. The formality of the classroom has, to some extent, disappeared as teachers embrace the advantages of learning through informal means and differing teaching styles. Nonetheless, the classroom does not always allow the same degree of feedback in exchanges as everyday conversation, and the teacher often controls who can feed back. Similarly, when parents are talking to their children about appropriate behaviour, they adopt a position akin to a teacher and control the number of turns and amount of feedback from the child they are addressing.

Sub-functions of pedagogic talk are as follows:

❏ Conveying information. Speech is frequently used to communicate information and facts, as teachers do in many different ways. The talk is often informal, participatory and includes turn-taking and feedback. However, some aspects of conversational 'rules' are flagrantly ignored in teaching – this will be addressed later in this section. This type of conversation or speech produces **referential utterances** having factual information as their basis; they can also be constative or representative in their nature, since they are based on truth.

A: The Normans invaded England in 1066.
B: There are a number of different types of noun: common, proper, abstract, collective and so on.
C: Copenhagen is the capital of Denmark.

❏ Ethical transmission. There is also an aspect of teaching and parenting that embraces the transmission of morality and ethics. This results in **ethical propositions**, that is behavioural guides that usually embed values or moral codes within their main content. These types of utterance often have their foundation in civil law.

A: You should not kill other people.
B: Nice girls don't swear.
C: Do not urinate in public places.

3 Accompanying performance When people accompany certain actions in the real world with speech, a unique type of speech act takes place: the **performative** (or **declarational**) **utterance**. This includes ceremonies where certain procedures are followed, and formalized events that require certain accompanying actions. Events such as religious observances, marriage ceremonies and legal procedures can all be included here.

> **A:** By the power invested in me in this court, I sentence you to sixty days of community service.
> **B:** I take this woman to be my lawful wedded wife.
> **C:** I name this child Finlay Thomas Burnie.

This type of speech could also include those speech acts that require the speaker to undertake some future action. These are known as **commissive utterances** and include threats, promises, pledges and refusals.

> **A:** I promise to meet you next week.
> **B:** I'll come right back.
> **C:** We will not be going to the cinema today.

4 Entertainment This includes talk on television, radio and the stage. These media all use speech in quite special ways. For instance, television and radio can include spontaneous, unscripted speech, as seen in interviews and chat shows, although these will usually have some kind of agenda or topic to guide the discussion. Obviously, the former is supplemented by visual elements yet both base much of what is seen or heard on speech. Scripted speech plays a massive part in such programmes as news bulletins (through the use of autocues), soap operas and documentaries. Scripted speech as seen in dramas and theatrical productions is another area that deserves separate consideration.

5 Rhetorical speech Again this is a unique type of speech in that it is (usually) scripted and relies, to a great extent, on the use of rhetorical and persuasive devices, in order to influence listeners. Politicians are very adept at using rhetoric; advertisers often use persuasive techniques to boost sales of their products. Rhetoric and scripted speech will be examined later in the chapter.

6 Egocentric speech When we are alone we sometimes talk to ourselves, children more so than adults perhaps. The purpose of this is unclear: are we articulating our thoughts, and if we are, then aren't thoughts a kind of silent speech in themselves? Whatever the purpose, we are certainly able to talk to ourselves and many of us do it, even if we might not admit it! Perhaps we should view egocentric speech as a kind of personal monologue for our own benefit.

ACTIVITY Using the following table, collect examples of your own that show:

❏ different usages of the range of utterances listed above
❏ the context of each utterance.

Utterance type	Your example	Context
Constative utterance		
Phatic utterance		
Expressive utterance		
Referential utterance		
Directive utterance		
Commissive utterance		
Ethical proposition		
Performative utterance		

Writing

We noted at the start of this section that modern technology allows us to make speech permanent through recordings. Writing has always had the quality of permanency, as seen in the vast corpus of printed matter. So much printed matter is produced today that much of it is in fact disposed of as soon as (or even before) it is read: good examples of this are the tabloid culture or the plethora of junk mail everyone receives! It is an interesting fact that the amount of printed matter in just one copy of today's *Sunday Times* would represent the average reading for a year of an educated man in the Seventeenth Century. This is a good indicator of how adept we have become at coping with printed matter as well as revealing our reliance upon it in day-to-day life. Until very recently, it was difficult to keep or store such vast amounts of literature. The advent of microfiche, CD ROMs and the Internet has aided the process enormously and has certainly helped those people whose occupation requires access to large amounts of material on a regular basis for reference purposes.

To illustrate the variety of different materials we read on a daily basis, complete the following activity.

ACTIVITY   Use the table below to collect names and details for the reading you do in a week. You could also collect examples of different types of writing to keep as a selection of different styles: this will help you to appreciate the range of materials a course such as this will draw on. Use the last blank rows in the table to put in written materials of your own which are not listed below.

Type of written material	Name or title	Details e.g. genre, whether printed, handwritten, permanent, bought, etc.
Newspapers		
Magazines		
Periodicals		
Leaflets		
Literature		
Comics		
Catalogues		
Advertisements		
Application forms		
Manuals or instructions		
Menus or recipes		
Reference materials		
Computer materials		
Televisual materials		
Letters and correspondence		

The functions of writing

Having examined the variety and range of written matter that is available to us, let us briefly examine the different functions of writing. This will allow you to see some of the more obvious differences between the two modes, before we look at details of the characteristics of speech.

1 **Cultural transmission** Writing allows us the opportunity to accumulate a huge amount of information and to pass it on generation after generation. This is how some of our greatest literature has been passed down to us. We must also remember that the written mode allows one person to communicate with potentially millions of other people, thus allowing the sharing of experience. It is this aspect of the written mode that makes it so culturally important. In direct contrast to the oral tradition, writing helps to preserve historical details that can be referred to at a later date. This definition accounts for such written material as novels, newspapers, magazines and other non-literary forms.

2 **Reference and lists** This function is a direct result of cultural transmission, in that it is possible for the brain to store only a finite amount of factual information, and we need to access reference material fairly often. Writing down lists allows our brains to be engaged in more important activities, and we can refer back when necessary to something that is written down; how many of us have forgotten to buy a vital item when we have not made a shopping list! It is also a reflection of the nature of our lives today that many electronic personal organizers have a list function as part of their software . . . and that many people rely on them massively!

3 **Prose forms** Because of the difficulty in remembering long tracts of language, written prose has developed as the major literary form, used in the widest sense of the word. Fictional stories, biographies, news stories, history and religion all use the prose medium for recording details that could not be stored in the memory or transmitted orally with accuracy.

4 **Dictionaries and thesauri** The dictionary developed out of the opulence of the language associated with literature and prose writing, and allows a formalized recording of the lexicon with an alphabetical, defined list. A thesaurus groups sets of words according to their meaning.

5 **Legal documentation** Writing has given society the ability to record laws and thus promote consistency of interpretation and application. Consider the difference between slander and libel, for instance, and the difficulty of proving the former.

6 **Education** Books and written material are vital in terms of our education. They supplement and verify the information passed on through educators and teachers; they can also lessen the role of teachers and in theory allow everyone (who can read) access to information that at one time was the privilege of a tiny proportion of the population.

7 **Cognitive development** Written material and the vast amount of printed matter has, again theoretically, enabled the human race to become more educated. In other words, our cognitive skills have become more highly developed and consequently so has our intelligence. This would certainly account for the rapid expansion of technology during the past century.

8 Exploration of theories and views The written word often formalizes theories and ideas that have developed through discussion and informal debate. Once they are written down, a more formal debate can occur, with a theory being either propounded or disputed. This is very important in the development of science and medicine as well as other fields such as philosophy.

The above divisions of the functions of writing are in many ways artificial, and certainly more areas could be considered, such as advertising, which has a unique and vital place in our present culture. However, the purpose of this section is to underline the differences between the functions of the two modes, of speech and writing, so let us finish by tabulating these.

Differences in function		
	Speech	**Writing**
1	Speech is essentially a social activity. We use it for many different ends, from passing the time of day to the more formalized rituals of ceremony.	Writing is more suited to the recording of factual material, giving an accurate account of what has happened in printed form.
E.g.	*talking to a friend about what we did last night*	*an account of what happened at a political summit in the newspaper*
2	Speech is suited to the 'here and now', where we do not need to make records. It is more immediate and temporary.	Writing allows us to record more facts and material than we could remember for future reference. It is less immediate but has the advantage of permanency.
E.g.	*any conversation which is purely informal and not recorded in any way*	*a diary that is written every day over a sustained period of time*
3	Speech allows us to tell someone how we feel, how to behave or what should be done in certain situations. We can access these perceptions instantly.	Writing tends to give us the opportunity to explore the possibilities of ideas and theories. It also records laws formally, rather than suggest codes of behaviour.
E.g.	*telling someone what you believe they should do, after they have asked you for advice*	*scientific theories as seen in periodicals, written local by-laws*
4	Since the brain allows retention of only a certain number of facts, speech allows us to verbalize only what we can recall; it can therefore be subject to inaccuracy.	Writing allows us access to reference material when we do not know something or are uncertain of facts. It often allows us to ascertain the truth about matters.
E.g.	*retelling a story where certain facts are misreported or muddled up*	*any reference book e.g. an encyclopaedia or dictionary*

Differences of form

Speech

Some of the major characteristics of speech arise out of the fact that much speech is **unplanned** or **spontaneous**. Because a lot of speech is not thought out preceding its expression, we find that a number of unique features occur that give spontaneous speech its special quality.

One of the characteristics we have already noted is that we do not speak in the carefully constructed, standard sentences which make up the prose of written English; we speak in non-sentences or **utterances**. This is a much more accurate way to describe units of speech, since it reflects what we utter or say, and it would be quite misleading to say we speak in sentences. Indeed, if we did speak in sentences, we would find conversation boring and a trial to listen to and take part in. It is the fact that we use non-sentences, part-sentences, paralinguistics and kinesics that gives speech its distinctiveness and makes it such a useful tool in everyday life.

When we examine the form of spoken language, it is helpful to break down the component parts of the speech act itself: the relationship of the speakers, the manner of the speech, the topic or subject matter and, finally, the structure of the conversation. Many of the examples of spontaneous speech you have looked at so far in this book have been self-contained speeches (such as Joanne's piece of speech at the start of this section) or snippets of longer conversations where the full effect of the whole conversation cannot be seen. In practice, you will rarely have to work on full conversations, since they are often very lengthy and it can be difficult to determine where one conversation ends and another begins.

Examine carefully the following piece of spontaneous speech, which occurred at the start of a conversation between three young men in a student common room: Bill (B), Andrew (A) and Jamie (J).

B: All right (.) good time last night
A: Er:::m (1.0) {*laughs*} pretty good (.) yer
                                    [
B: What d'yer do
A: Yer shoulda bin there (.) ma::n (0.5) it were (.) well (.) coo::l
B: Really (.) w (.) what (.)
A: God we (.) didn't half (1.0) really went for it (.) later
B: Oo was there
A: Er:::m (.) everyone
                    [
J: Now then
A: Yer know that (.) Hiya Jay (.) that lass (1.0) er (.) the one who went (.) to Stereophonics (0.5) with Gray n' Luce
                    [

→

J: Julie (.) Huh (0.5) God wa'
                                                    [
A: Yeah Julie (0.5) thas 'er
                                                        [
J: she (.) disgrace (.) las night
A: Shockin wan she
B: Wha (.) er (.) she do
J: She went wi Pete
B: Pete
A: Yeah (0.5) Christ (1.0) wait till Beccy finds out

This is a typical example of any opening section to a conversation between youngsters who see each other on a regular basis (and where their social life is very important!) Let us look at some of the evidence that helps us to unlock the secrets of this exchange.

1 Relationship We can see immediately that the participants in the conversation are known to each other:

❑ the participants rarely use each other's names
❑ they have common friends (Pete, Julie)
❑ they have knowledge of shared experiences (whatever went on last night, the Stereophonics concert).

2 Formality The conversation is quite informal, despite having a structure to it:

❑ the participants use many contracted forms ('thas 'er' for 'that's her')
❑ they also employ terms which are fairly exclusive to their peer group ('cool' and 'went with')
❑ there are very few external constraints in terms of context, and it is obviously possible for other students to join in (Jamie joins the conversation without any apparent difficulty).

3 Topicality Since this is the opening of the conversation, theoretically any subject could be opened up; as it is, the topic that is taken up is what happened the previous night. The reasons for this appear to be:

❑ that Bill was not there and wants to know what happened (he broaches the subject first)
❑ Andrew eventually decides to give Bill some details about the evening (about Julie and her apparent fling with Pete, who seems to be a mutual friend)
❑ Jamie was also out with Andrew and has the same shared experience and effortlessly picks up the topic of conversation when he comes in.

Once the topic has been exhausted, a new topic can be introduced and explored (this does not really happen here, although the sub-topic of Julie and Pete is introduced at the end); if a new topic is introduced before the present topic has worked out its natural course, then the new topic may be rejected or picked up later.

4 Structure Since this is the start of a conversation, it is easy to pick up the thread of what is happening and what the participants are talking about. It can be more difficult to tune into the middle of a conversation, as you have no doubt experienced yourself when you have come into a room to find a conversation in full flow. It takes a little while to work out what the parameters of the conversation are and what subject is being discussed; sometimes we pick up the wrong subject, and this can result in mis-understandings or confusions.

Let us look in more detail at some of the strategies we use to make conversations progress, through the piece of conversation we have examined above.

Adjacency pairs

One vital organizational device we employ all the time in conversation, whether it be formal or informal, is the adjacency pair. This is where one type of utterance leads to another, always with a distinctive pattern that we have intuitively come to recognize through conversational practice. Adjacency pairs:

❏ are spoken by different people
❏ always have a rational link
❏ are characterized by the second utterance following on from the first utterance.

The conversation above starts with an adjacency pair.

Utterance number	Utterance	Commentary
1 B:	All right (.) good time last night {*Question*}	*Bill opens with a phatic utterance (All right) and then asks a question that obviously requires an answer from the person he has phatically greeted, in this case Andrew.*
2 A:	Er:::m (1.0) {*laughs*} pretty good (.) yer {*Answer*}	*Perhaps because Andrew is a little worse for wear from the previous evening, he does not initially respond. When he does, it is a fairly direct informal response (pretty good), prefaced by a laugh as he presumably remembers the details of what happened during the course of the evening. Andrew could also be understating his enjoyment of the evening to spare Bill's feelings, since he wasn't there.*

Adjacency pairs allow conversation to progress in a structured, if **unplanned** way. They are unplanned in the sense that we don't know what is going to be said next, even though the topicality has already been decided upon. We can see this structure in the conversation by examining the way that the pairings are linked; here, conjoining arrows mark the main pairings. The linking of these adjacency pairs is called **chaining**, since each pair is attached to the previous one, usually in a linear fashion and rather like the links in a chain. This enables the participants to explore topics and work them out to their natural conclusion.

Adjacency pairings can include the following, although this is not an exhaustive list:

❏ greeting and returned greeting
❏ question and answer
❏ request and acceptance or refusal
❏ statement and corroboration
❏ compliment and reply (not necessarily accepted)
❏ complaint and apology
❏ leave-taking and farewell.

ACTIVITY   Break down the conversation into its component adjacency pairs (the arrows will help you do this) and comment on what is happening in each utterance of each adjacency pair, modelling your answer on the table above.

B: All right (.) good time last night

A: Er:::m (1.0) {*laughs*} pretty good (.) yer

[

B: What d'yer do

A: Yer shoulda bin there (.) ma::n (0.5) it were (.) well (.) coo::l

B: Really (.) w (.) what (.)

A: God we (.) didn't half (1.0) really went for it (.) later

B: Oo was there

A: Er:::m (.) everyone

[

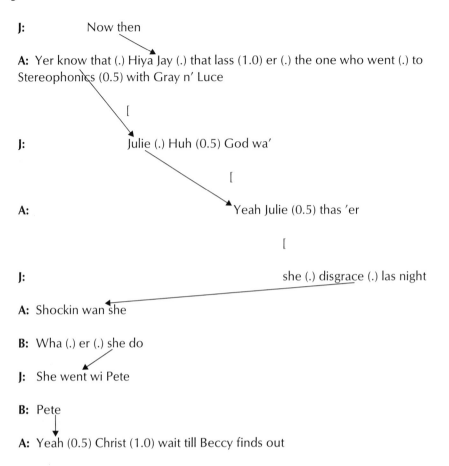

J: Now then

A: Yer know that (.) Hiya Jay (.) that lass (1.0) er (.) the one who went (.) to Stereophonics (0.5) with Gray n' Luce

                                 [

J: Julie (.) Huh (0.5) God wa'

                                        [

A: Yeah Julie (0.5) thas 'er

                                              [

J: she (.) disgrace (.) las night

A: Shockin wan she

B: Wha (.) er (.) she do

J: She went wi Pete

B: Pete

A: Yeah (0.5) Christ (1.0) wait till Beccy finds out

As you can see from the example you have just looked at, we are fairly dependent on the notion of conversational chaining through adjacency pairs, as they allow conversation to flow unimpeded. When we violate the unspoken rules of adjacency pairing, conversation tends to break down. For instance, if we persistently fail to respond to a question we have been asked, then the questioner will assume that something is wrong and will either ask what is the matter or end the conversation!

A development of the adjacency pair is what Michael Stubbs has called the **three-part exchange**. This is the idea that any piece of conversation requires three distinct, ordered sections:

❏ an initiation or beginning utterance
❏ a reply
❏ a response to the reply or **feedback**.

| **Feedback** | The process of receiving a reply to a piece of speech, which shows that the listener has understood the nature of the message sent by the speaker; a tool to show that the effectiveness of a piece of communication can be verified. |

The three-part exchange can in fact help us to track conversation more accurately, and it can assist us in seeing how new adjacency pairs are 'born'.

ACTIVITY

Use the piece of conversation you have already worked on above.

❑ Divide it into three-part exchanges, commenting on how each part relates to the other two parts.
❑ Does this method help you to follow the structure of the conversation more easily compared to the previous method you used? Why or why not?

Turn-taking

One of the skills we possess as conversational participants is taking turns when we talk. We 'pass' the conversation over to other group members, and it is taken up or refused by other participants as they see fit. Conversations are characterized by the fact that only one person speaks at a time: each is taking a turn, as it were. However, that turn may be relinquished, may be passed on to someone else or may even be 'stolen', especially if one speaker is monopolizing the conversation. As participants in a conversation, we are fairly certain that we will get a turn to say something at some point. But how do we know when a turn is 'up for grabs', or whether a certain person will speak as opposed to someone else? A number of signals occur in utterances to help us here. They include the following.

❑ The speaker **elongates** or **stresses** the final word of the utterance; there is a good example of this in the fourth utterance of the conversation, where Andrew says to Bill that the evening out was 'coo::l', the elongation of the vowel sound signalling the end of his utterance. This is the part of the utterance that Andrew wants to stress, so he does this by placing the adjective at the end of his utterance and by elongating the final sound.
❑ The speaker may also indicate that his or her turn is ending by dropping the sound level, coupled with less emphasis. A good example of this in the conversation is where Andrew corroborates the identity of the mystery girl by saying, 'Yeah Julie (0.5) thas 'er.' We can see that the second part of the utterance is less important, as the name of the girl has already been articulated and the second part is merely a confirmatory statement. The fact that it also includes an abbreviated form of both the words 'that' and 'her' also signals the fall in sound.
❑ Phrases such as 'you know', 'like' and 'or something' can sometimes indicate the end of a turn as these words are being used like **fillers**, thus showing that the speaker is running out of steam and it is time for someone else to take up the turn.
❑ Speakers may designate that their turn is over by making their utterance complete grammatically and syntactically. Questions are good examples of this although the fact that they require an answer makes it doubly obvious that the turn is being handed over. Completed statements such as 'And that's the end of it' or 'That's all I have to say on the matter' are

examples of syntactically complete utterances which show the speaker has finished.

❏ Finally, there are those signals that cannot be seen on the page, which are paralinguistic in nature: eye contact with another listener, sitting back in a chair or another similar relaxation of the posture, and use of the hands or head (nodding) could all signal it is another person's turn to speak.

Turn-taking is a vital part of conversational management and, in conjunction with adjacency pairings, it is one of the two major structures of spoken interaction. There are other features that are less frequent, but nonetheless important.

Insertion and side sequences

Once a conversation has been initiated, there can be interruptions from unexpected sources. People can come into the room or something might happen that requires the speaker's immediate attention such as a knock at the door or a telephone ringing. The consequence of this is a **conversational insertion** or **insertion sequence**, where the original conversation is suspended and then resumes once the interruption has been dealt with. There is an example of this in the conversation we have already looked at:

Utterance number	Utterance	Commentary
7 B: **8 A:**	Oo was there Er:::m (.) everyone	*This part of the conversation has already had the topicality decided and Bill is keen to find out who was at the function. By looking at utterance 10, we can see that Andrew is keen to embellish his assertion of everyone being there by picking out a specific person to discuss.*
9 J:	[Now then {**Adjacency pair:** **Phatic utterance**}	*It is at this point that Andrew has to deal with an outside interruption in the form of Jamie coming into the conversation, as he overlaps with Andrew's 'everyone' in utterance 8.*
10 A:	Yer know that (.) Hiya Jay (.) {**Insertion sequence**} that lass (1.0) er (.) the one who went (.) to Stereophonics (0.5) with Gray n' Luce	*Andrew's 'Hiya Jay' is the insertion sequence here as it interrupts the topic, which is then effortlessly resumed with the words 'that lass'. Jamie is left to make his own interpretation of what they are discussing.*

As can be seen by the example given above, the second part of the adjacency pair is inserted into Andrew's speech with his original topic hardly being interrupted at all. The conversation certainly does not break down in any way, so we can see that insertion sequences help us to manage our conversations without affecting the topic. **Side sequences**, however, are much more obvious and sometimes last for a number of utterances. They act as an elucidation or explanation of something that has previously been uttered:

X: Let's go to the pub.
Y: Will Mike be there?
X: Nah.   *Side sequence*
Y: What about Alan?
X: Don't think so.
Y: Oh all right then.

In the snippet of conversation given above, we see that Y wants clarification of who will be in the pub prior to giving his affirmation in the final utterance that he will go; note that the first and last utterance form an adjacency pairing within which the side sequence is embedded.

Closing sequences

When we draw towards the end of a conversation, especially if we are standing talking in the street or some other place, we signal that we wish the conversation to come to an end by a variety of methods. This is another form of conversational management; it can often take a number of utterances to achieve, and repetition is frequently used to sum up and then close the exchange. Look at this example, taken from the end of the conversation between the three young men Andrew, Bill and Jamie:

A: So yer off to Art then
B: Yeah
A: Right (.) I'll come wi' yer
J: See yer then
A: Yeah (.) see yer Jay (.) Going down town (.) fer lunch
J: Could do (.) yeah
                    [
A: 'Kay (.) see yer
J: Out front (.) of school
A: Yeah
J: Right (0.5) see yer
A: Bye
  [
B: See yer
J: Bye

This sequence has a number of distinctive features to it, including pre-closing signals which tell other people in the group that the closing ritual is about to commence. If we break down the sequence into three distinct parts, we can see how this works.

Utterance number	Utterance	Commentary
1 A:	So yer off to Art then	*Andrew indicates that he is ready to leave (or perhaps has to?) and wonders if Bill will come with him; this is a pre-closing statement.*
2 B:	Yeah	*Bill replies to the question that is then confirmed by Andrew as he states he is going to accompany his friend there. It also signals the break up of the group, which is why Jamie responds.*
3 A:	Right (.) I'll come wi' yer	
4 J:	See yer then	*Jamie is obviously not going their way (or perhaps sees he is not wanted?) so he closes his own part of the conversation.*

This first section seems to close the conversation, but a new topic is introduced and so the end of the conversation is deferred while they discuss this.

Utterance number	Utterance	Commentary
5 A:	Yeah (.) see yer Jay (.) Going down town (.) fer lunch	*Andrew replies to Jamie's 'Bye' and then indicates that there is more to say: perhaps he feels awkward at leaving Jamie and going off to Art with Bill.*
6 J:	Could do (.) yeah	*Jamie replies to Andrew's question by hedging slightly before deciding in the affirmative.*
7 A:	['Kay (.) see yer	*Andrew's 'Kay' indicates that he is keen to get going as it overlaps Jamie's added 'yeah' and he once more signals he is going.*
8 J:	Out front (.) of school	*Jamie, however, wants clarification of where they are going to meet and asks Andrew this.*
9 A:	Yeah	*Andrew replies in the affirmative and brings this topic to a close.*

The final section of the conversation then enters its closing sequence and completion, after a pre-closing sequence and a topic clarification.

Utterance number	Utterance	Commentary
10 J:	Right (0.5) see yer	*Jamie is now satisfied as to where they will meet: 'Right', and he can bid them good-bye.*
11 A: **12 B:**	Bye [See yer	*Andrew and Bill both utter their goodbyes at the same time, presumably while go-ing off together since they do not repeat themselves again.*
13 J:	Bye	*It is left to Jamie to repeat his final goodbye or perhaps he is saying this to Bill in particular whom he has not directly addressed in this sequence.*

In much the same way that phatic utterances signal the opening of a conversation and open up avenues for discourse, closing sequences round off a conversation in a co-operative manner, and also allow those conversational avenues to be re-opened at a later date.

Some other features of conversation

Elision, ellipsis and other shortened forms

Because speech is often quick and characterized by informality among friends, elision often occurs. **Elision** is a characteristic of connected speech and often occurs when we put certain words together to make well-used phrases. A good example would be *fish 'n chips* where the 'and' is contracted to 'n and the whole phrase sounds like one word. Examples from the conversation we studied earlier are 'shoulda' for 'should've' which itself is a **contraction** of 'should have'; there is also the phrase 'thas 'er' which is an elided form of 'that's her'. This last phrase also highlights some people's predilection for dropping h's and t's in speech.

Whereas elision refers to the omission of certain letters in words and phrases, **ellipsis** refers to missing whole words, which are generally understood from the context of the speech. This can take a variety of forms:

❏ pronouns: Hope you can come   *for*   I hope you can come
❏ verb phrases: Wanna beer?   *for*   Do you wanna beer?
❏ full phrase: Q: Where you off to?
                          A: To town.   *for*   I am off to town

In the conversation above, a good example of an elliptical sentence is the opening one: 'good time last night' where the words 'did you have a' are redundant in such an informal exchange.

Other contractions include shortened versions of such things as:

❏ names: shortening of names is often seen as an indicator of informality; in the conversation 'Jamie' is shortened to 'Jay', 'Lucy' to 'Luce' and 'Graham' to 'Gray'
❏ verbs: in speech we often shorten negated verbs, so 'cannot' becomes 'can't', 'shall not' becomes 'shan't' and 'is not' becomes 'isn't'
❏ pronouns and verbs: as with the forms we have seen in the previous section, when some verbs are placed with pronouns, contraction occurs in speech: 'I will' becomes 'I'll', 'you will' becomes 'you'll' and so on.

Liaison

Liaison is another feature of speech that occurs when two words are spoken at speed and the running together or **liaison** of these two words produces a new sound. For instance, when a word starts with a vowel, there is sometimes a carry-over sound, which is a direct result of the previous word ending in a consonant.

'There is someone over there' might be heard as 'There ris someone', where the r is sounded at the start of the verb 'is', resulting in a word that sounds like 'ris'.

Juncture

As we have already seen, when we speak we can meld words together so they become virtually indistinguishable. **Juncture** is the almost imperceptible gap that appears between words so we can distinguish them; it is most often characterized by silence, but it is not always clear in spontaneous speech. This can result in some interesting, and occasionally amusing, misunderstandings, which *The Two Ronnies* used in a famous sketch set in a hardware shop. A man enters the shop and asks for various items but the shopkeeper misinterprets his request, simply because of the juncture (or lack of it) between the shopper's words. For instance the shopper asks for 'fork 'andles' (his accent drops the 'h' at the start of the word 'handles') and the shopkeeper returns to the counter with four candles, as the juncture between the shopper's words (as well as his accent) allow for this misinterpretation.

Non-standard forms and slang

The standard forms that are used in writing are often flouted in speech; no doubt those of you who use **non-standard forms** will have had some of your written English corrected before now! In the conversation we have been examining, a couple of non-standard forms are used: Andrew says, 'it were (.) well (.) coo::l'. Here the third-person plural verb form is used instead of the standard English singular form, 'was'. Later on in the conversation Bill asks, 'Wha (.) er (.) she do' where the sentence is elliptical, resulting in a non-standard form of the more acceptable 'What **did** she do?'

Informal speech is also characterized by use of **slang** terms, words that are acceptable in casual speech and understood by everyone; in writing, they would often be deemed inappropriate unless they were part of reported speech. Slang terms are often short-lived and sometimes recognizable only to the peer group who use them. An example within the conversation we have studied is 'well cool' meaning 'great' or 'brilliant'.

Non-verbal aspects

We have already mentioned, and seen in the transcriptions, **overlaps** where two people speak at once; this is marked by a [in the transcriptions, with the overlapping speech being printed side by side. They occur for various reasons: an end of turn may have been misjudged, someone may be keen to add to a point and wish to steal a turn, or there may be many participants who all hold equal status within the conversational group.

Pauses are self-explanatory – they indicate a gap in something said, and are marked by a parenthesis with a number inside, to indicate the number of seconds of time that elapsed between speech: (1.5) would indicate a pause of one-and-a-half seconds. Pauses allow thinking time, obviously quite important in spontaneous speech. Micropauses (.) are sometimes seen as the punctuation of speech, as they can indicate the boundaries of clauses and unitary pieces of information; at other times, they exist solely to allow the speaker the opportunity of taking a breath or considering the next utterance.

Voice-filled pauses are gaps that are filled. Examples of voice-filled pauses from the piece of conversation we have been exploring are 'erm' and 'er'; 'um' and 'ah' are two other well-used examples. They help to indicate that the speaker's turn is not over yet and so prevent interruption. If they are words in their own right but carry no apparent meaning, they are called **fillers**, because they fill a gap. Frequently used fillers include:

- ❏ you know
- ❏ sort of
- ❏ you see
- ❏ I mean
- ❏ kind of
- ❏ well.

Repetitions can often be found in conversations: it is as if the speaker is searching for the right word and is unsure as to whether he or she has found it. It may be only a letter that is repeated, as in the conversation when Bill says: 'Really (.) w (.) what (.)' where he seems to be uncertain of how he is going to start his question.

False starts also occur periodically, especially if the speaker becomes muddled or has so much to say that he or she loses track of speech constructions. Andrew says in the conversation above, 'God we (.) didn't half (1.0) really went for it (.) later' Here the phrase 'didn't half' is unfinished and he starts again, using a slightly different construction 'really went for it', which follows on more neatly and logically from the pronoun 'we' at the start of the utterance. Sometimes, if we start an utterance and realize we have made a mistake and need to correct ourselves, we use a conversational **repair**, which can often be prefaced or coupled with the filler 'I mean'.

Remember that girl (.) er Stacey (.) er no (0.5) Tracy I mean

---

ACTIVITY

Look at the following piece of conversation; it is part of an interview that was conducted on television by Michael Parkinson (P), with the Scottish comedian, Billy Connolly (C).

Examine this interview transcript closely, and comment on the ways in which each speaker conveys his feelings and thoughts, by looking at:

❑ the context of the conversation
❑ the words and constructions they choose
❑ any features of speech that help to explain their attitudes and feelings.

P: There's a there's a (.) kind of sense of vocation isn't there in a comic (.) I think I mean (.) you are driven to it aren't you

　　　　　　　　　　　[

C: 　　　　　　　　　　　It's vocational
P: It not (0.5) er really

　　[

C: Witho::ut (.) question
P: It has to be doesn't it
C: Aye (1.5) an' I think most k (.) things are (0.5) yours is vocational obvious (.) you've a great love of what you do (0.5) I have a love of what I do (.) an' we're very lucky because you find it (0.5) I think it's a question of bein' (0.5) try to be honest with yourself (0.5) what you a:ctually want to be (1.0) an be (.) eve even if its embarrassin' (.) like yer wanna be a comedian (.) an' you say to yer dad (.) I'd like to be a comedian an he goes (.) you're no funny (0.5) you're no very funny (0.5) w w what t d'y'wanna be a comedian for (0.5) are you daft (1.5) an' I became (0.5) a welder to escape the worst excesses of homosexuality actually (1.0) I
P: Wha'
C: I wanted (.) ter go to drama school (0.5) an' an' ma father said (.) O:::::h they're all homosexuals (.) you don't wanna go there (1.0) an I said I'd like to be in the merchant navy (1.0) O:::::h for God's sake (1.0) they're all homosexuals (2.0) so I I became (.) this this welder guy
P: And this
C: an' it haunted me you know (1.0) u until (.) I er got

➡

P: What what (.) er haunted you
C: Bein bein (.) what I thought I should be
P: Yes

Writing

This chapter concentrates on the features of speech and we have now examined its major characteristics, so we need not go into great detail about writing, as many of the differences are obvious. However, a brief outline of some of the features of writing will help you to understand speech more fully.

When we write, we have the opportunity to develop and organize our work, making amendments and revisions as necessary. We also have the ability to plan out documents prior to writing them; this enables us to use complex sentence structures, with subordination and intricacy of syntax. In speech, especially spontaneous unplanned speech, we do not often use intricacy and we tend to keep our utterances syntactically and grammatically simple.

Similarly, because writing does not have the visual clues that speech often does, the former tends to use unambiguous expressions and descriptions and avoid **deixis**, that is the use of terms and expressions that rely on the context to give their meaning, such as 'that one', 'over there' and 'here'.

When we study literature, as you have already found in the prose section, we often see sophisticated patterning and elaborate use of literary techniques; these are, in many ways, characteristic of the written mode and allow the reader to reflect upon how construction and meaning both contribute to the overall effect intended by the writer. In speech, we are rarely faced with such complexity and we often find speech is shot through with vagueness and ambiguity.

Certain words, phrases and sentences are hardly ever spoken. For instance, the language of the legal system requires such precision and organization that sentences alone often run to hundreds of words. Other words that are rarely spoken are full names: we seldom, when we speak to each other, use full names, preferring instead to use one name which is frequently contracted, such as Michael into Mike or Elizabeth into Lizzie. However, we often have occasion to write down our full names, when we are filling out official forms, for instance. Similarly, scientists would never refer in speech to some chemicals by their full name, preferring to use the chemical symbol, a more common name, or a contraction or abbreviation:

HCl	for	hydrochloric acid
Vinegar	for	acetic acid
Salt	for	sodium chloride
TNT	for	trinitrotoluene
HMD	for	hexamethylenediamine

However, in a paper for a scientific journal or periodical, the full name of the chemical would more likely be used, especially if it was obscure.

As we have already seen, speech is immediate and unplanned, and it can be quite difficult to recall the exact nature of what has been said, especially as time goes by. However, writing allows us to keep a record of events or data, if needed, and then we have the opportunity to refer back to it at a later date. Similarly, it is easy and more convenient to keep records through writing, rather than committing them to memory. It is also much less demanding to read text at your own speed, when it comes to learning something, than being told or taught something by another person through the mode of speech, where you have to follow at the speaker's pace, which is dictated by the speed of speech and delivery.

Mistakes, revisions, and shortfalls in writing can all be rectified or removed, either immediately or at a later time; in the intervening period, no one need see the document, so once the mistakes have been corrected, only the writer is aware that they were present in the first instance. In speech, however, once a mistake is made it cannot be undone.

Finally, writing does not share the prosodic or auditory properties of speech; intonation, pace, rhythm and volume are all characteristics of spoken discourse and will be discussed in the next section on rhetoric and the art of planned speech. Perhaps the only features writing does have that relate to prosody are elements such as emboldening or underlining for emphasis, and exclamation or question marks to indicate degrees of astonishment or inquiry.

As with the other sections in this chapter, we will end by summarizing the differences between forms in a table.

Differences in form and features		
	Speech	**Writing**
1	Speech is unplanned, with much repetition, hesitation and non-standard forms.	Writing can be planned and revised and it conforms to standard English usage.
2	Pauses, fillers and simple syntactical constructions often mark out where utterances begin and end. However, this still does not ensure that all boundaries are clear.	Sentence boundaries are marked by the conventions of punctuation. Sentences often vary in their simplicity and complexity in a way that speech utterances do not.
3	Speech is more immediate and quicker, but it is less easy to learn through listening to someone else talking to you, since you need to work at the speaker's speed.	Writing is less immediate and has to be searched out, and is slower to access than speech, but it does allow the reader to work at his or her own pace.
4	Once a mistake in speech is uttered it cannot be erased or withdrawn, although it can be qualified – but the audience may well be suspicious of these qualifications.	Mistakes in writing can be altered at the writer's own convenience prior to the written matter being seen by its audience.

5	Speech relies heavily on deictic expressions and the knowledge of immediate context	Writing can often be free of context and needs to use detail and sub-ordination for the sake of clarity.
6	Speech is enhanced by our ability to manipulate speed, volume and stress in what we say to facilitate meaning; this is difficult to replicate in the written mode.	In writing, if we wish to include prosodic features we need to resort to complex description or use punctuation to help us. This is not very efficient and can be cumbersome.
7	Speech is not conducive to recording and it is usually a matter of memory as to what has occurred in a conversation; it is therefore not a useful reference tool.	Writing allows easy and accurate reference to be made; it also allows easy recording of facts and data to enable us to have access to them at a later date; we do not need to rely on our own memory.

The language and features of planned speech

Planned speech differs from spontaneous speech, in that it is thought out, considered, and perhaps scripted in some form prior to its delivery. We hear many examples of this on a daily basis, ranging from the broadly planned but unscripted delivery of a teacher or lecturer, to the formulaic **rhetoric** of political speeches.

Rhetoric	The art of speech making, with the express purpose of altering or affecting the listener's emotions, by conveying the individual viewpoint of the speaker and/or the speaker's logic or reasoning

In planned speech, the speaker often makes use of an assortment of devices that are specifically intended to convey his or her message. In many instances, this is inextricably linked to the purpose of persuading the audience to adopt, or at least consider, the speaker's point of view. The devices are often supplemented by skilful use of phonological features such as sound and rhythm, thus enhancing the impact of what is articulated. It can be quite difficult to represent such features on the page, although we will make brief reference to these in this section as they play such a vital part in the art of rhetoric.

Look closely at the following piece of rhetoric. The Prime Minister, Tony Blair, made this speech in September 1999, at the Labour Party Conference. The following extract is from the beginning of the speech and it allows us to examine the use of a number of rhetorical devices at first hand.

Today at the frontier of the new Millennium I set out for you how, as a nation, we renew British strength and confidence for the Twenty-First Century; and how, as a party reborn, we make it a century of progressive politics after one dominated by Conservatives.

➡

A New Britain where the extraordinary talent of the British people is liberated from the forces of conservatism that so long have held them back, to create a model Twenty-First Century nation, based not on privilege, class or background, but on the equal worth of all.

And New Labour, confident at having modernized itself, now the new progressive force in British politics which can modernize the nation, sweep away those forces of conservatism to set the people free. One hundred years in existence, twenty-two in power, we have never, ever won a full second term. That is our unfinished business. Let us now finish, and with it finish the Tory Party's chances of doing as much damage in the next century as they've done in this one.

Today's Tory Party – the party of fox hunting, Pinochet and hereditary peers: the uneatable, the unspeakable and the unelectable.

There's only one thing you need to know about today's Tory Party. Clarke and Heseltine: outcasts. Hague, Widdecombe, Redwood and Portillo: in charge.

The only Party that spent two years in hibernation in search of a new image and came back as the Addams family.

Under John Major, it was weak, weak, weak! Under William Hague, it's weird, weird, weird! Far right, far out!

There is no doubt that this piece of speech is going to tell us much about the speaker's views and his reasoning: he refers to his purpose in the first sentence, underpins it by the use of the first-person singular pronominative form, 'I', and continues by including the audience in what he asserts, with a shift to the first-person plural pronominative form, 'we'. There is also little doubt that there is going to be much appeal to the emotions. It is here that we can begin to examine specific rhetorical features.

Emotive language

Rhetorical speech-making uses emotive language to appeal to the audience. The following techniques are used in Tony Blair's speech.

Giving opinions

Tony Blair offers his opinion on the Tory Party by concentrating on three emotive issues that the Conservatives championed: fox hunting, the opposition to the extradition of General Pinochet, and the retention of hereditary peerage. By naming these three issues, Blair gives his opinion of what the Tory Party stands for and consequently diminishes its credibility. At the end of this section of the speech, Blair calls John Major, the former leader of the Conservative Party, 'weak' three times. He again impresses his opinion upon his audience through use of an emotive adjective. At various points throughout the address, Blair continues to pepper his speech with his opinions.

Mocking opponents

Blair cannot resist the opportunity to disparage his opponents (indeed, what politician can!) and he pokes fun at the Conservative Party by making a comparison between the new Tory leadership and the fictional family of monsters, *The Addams Family*. This evokes an image of, amongst other things:

❑ their grotesqueness
❑ their dysfunctional nature
❑ the artificial nature of their relationships
❑ the comical way that they behave
❑ the reaction of horror they provoke in some people.

Along with the opinions given earlier, this helps to disparage and belittle the Tory Party, which is all part of Blair's agenda in this address.

Threatening disaster

This is a tool often used in planned speeches, akin to saying, 'if you don't do this then something earth-shattering will happen that will have dreadful consequences for all!' Blair alludes to this in the opening sentences, although he does not overtly say it; he hints at the possibility of the new Millennium being stifled by the politics of conservatism and that the British people should embrace the idea of the 'progressive politics' of the Labour Party.

Using exclamations

We can see Blair using exclamations at the end of this particular section, when he states that the conservatives were 'weak' under John Major and are now 'weird' under William Hague; but it is the use of adjectival repetition that enforces the exclamatory nature of his message. He concludes by a play on the word 'far', first with its associations of extremity ('far right') then with its link to hippy culture and eccentricity ('far out').

Exaggeration or understatement (respectively, **hyperbole** and **litotes**) may also be used to help add vigour to exclamatory statements.

Giving personal guarantees and surety

Later in this same speech, Tony Blair offers his personal, political guarantee that he will put a stop to child poverty: 'So when I pledge to end child poverty in 20 years, I do so not just as a politician, but as a father.' He endorses his political assurance by backing it up with his role as a father: this effectively doubles the force of his words and compels the listener to take note. Obviously, the use of the first-person pronominative form adds further power.

Use of summary

In rhetoric, one of the most effective devices is the use of a conclusive sentence that draws the whole of the speech together, while also leaving the listener with something memorable to take away, ponder on and digest. Here are a couple of very famous examples.

Winston Churchill: 'Let us therefore brace ourselves to our duties and so bear ourselves that, if the British Empire and its Commonwealth last for a thousand years, men will still say, This was their finest hour.'

Martin Luther King: 'When we let freedom ring, when we let it ring from every village and every hamlet, from every state and every city, we will be able to speed up that day when all of God's children, black men and white men, Jews and Gentiles, protestants and Catholics, will be able to join hands and sing in the words of the old Negro spiritual, Free at last! Free at last! Thank God almighty, we are free at last!'

In the speech we have studied, Tony Blair's ending is perhaps not as strong as these two, now famous, examples, but it still has a certain resonance and conclusiveness about it:

On our side, the forces of modernity and justice. Those who believe in a Britain for all the people. Those who fight social injustice, because they know it harms our nation. Those who believe in a society of equality, of opportunity and responsibility. Those who have the courage to change. Those who have confidence in the future. The battleground, the new Millennium. Our values are our guide. Our job is to serve. Our workplace, the future. Let us step up the pace. Be confident. Be radical. To every nation a purpose. To every Party a cause.

And now, at last, Party and nation joined in the same cause for the same purpose: to set our people free

Notice that many of Blair's sentences are in very fragmentary form, and that this adds to the increasing pace of the piece; however, his final sentence is longer and slightly more complex, and draws on the notion of the country being united with his party in a common goal.

Structural techniques

Some of the structural techniques of rhetorical speech are described below.

Patterning

Various types of pattern are often employed during planned speech: in the speech of Tony Blair, we can see a very common use, **patterns of three**. There is certain cohesion to ideas packaged in threes, and the rhythm and completeness of the ordering can be clearly seen.

'Today's Tory Party –

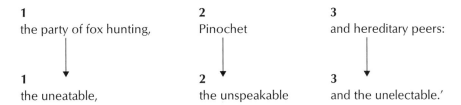

1	**2**	**3**
the party of fox hunting,	Pinochet	and hereditary peers:
1	**2**	**3**
the uneatable,	the unspeakable	and the unelectable.'

Not only does the opening clause 'Today's Tory Party' – contain three words with alliterative qualities, showing Blair's contemptuous feelings about the party (you can almost hear the plosive 't' sounds), the first part of the sentence is tripartite. The three nouns or noun phrases are mirrored in the final part of the sentence, with the added value of repetition of the first and last syllable for each word. This gives the whole sentence clear cohesive qualities, which help to communicate the attitude of the speaker.

Repetition

Any repetition of words or phrases can highlight the central ideas of a speech, and has the cumulative effect of driving home the message. Many orators use this technique simply to emphasize a point; Tony Blair does so at the start of his speech.

'Under John Major, it was <u>weak, weak, weak</u>!
Under William Hague, it's <u>weird, weird, weird</u>!'

At the end of the speech, he uses the same method, this time repeating the same word at the beginning of each new sentence. Once more, this helps the overall cohesive effect.

<u>Our</u> values are <u>our</u> guide. <u>Our</u> job is to serve. <u>Our</u> workplace, the future.

Lists

The effect of listing is similar to that of using repetition, as the message is further emphasized simply through the accumulation of the list of words.

In the middle of his speech, Tony Blair says: 'I was lucky. A good education, a loving home, a great family, strong beliefs, a great Party in which to give them expression.' This type of listing, which makes use of commas to link the ideas together, is called **asyndetic listing**. Sometimes, conjunctions such as 'and' are used to link ideas into lists, again having a cumulative effect. This technique, which is called **syndetic listing**, is not used by Tony Blair in this particular speech.

Questions

The use of **rhetorical questions**, those that do not require an answer or where the answer is obvious from the context, is another feature of planned speech. It has the effect of adding weight to the point being made, by implicitly providing an answer, but it can also help to move an argument on. Again, in Tony Blair's speech, he rarely uses questions, but when he does, the effect is clear in terms of supporting his opinion: 'And if a Headteacher transforms a school and so transforms the life chances of our children, aren't they worth as much as a good doctor, banker or lawyer?'

Opposites

Use of **antithesis**, or balancing of opposite ideas, can also have a powerful effect when coupled with other devices. Blair does not use it in this speech but you will find plenty in the exercise at the end of this section.

Literary techniques

Metaphor (and imagery and simile) are terms you will be familiar with from your literary studies and they need no glossing here. At the start of his speech, Tony Blair talks of being '. . . at the frontier of the new Millennium'. This metaphorical use of the noun 'frontier' carries with it all kinds of connotations:

❏ discovery of uncharted territory
❏ new beginnings
❏ a boundary between one era and another.

The noun 'Millennium' has the following connotations:

❏ a new country (denoted by the capital letter)
❏ a place that holds promise and hope
❏ a boundary that has to be crossed physically.

This metaphor allows the speaker to gain maximum effect from what is essentially a simple idea or image. Since it appears at the start of the speech, it carries extra weight and provides the metaphorical backdrop for the rest of Blair's imagery.

Similes carry similar effects but seek to gain them by comparing one thing to another. Blair consciously steers away from these in his speech, in order to keep his examples rooted in the factual.

There may also be examples of **personification**, **symbolism** and **irony** in planned speech, all terms you will have already been introduced to in your literary studies. Any effect they have will be largely similar to the effect gained when used in literature.

Phonological techniques

Phonological techniques use the sound qualities of language to enhance its effects.

Alliteration and assonance

These are literary devices that you will have already come across: **alliteration**, the repeated use of the same consonant sounds, and **assonance**, the repeated use of the same vowel sounds, both have the effect of making the words and phrases stand out and consequently help us to remember them later. Naturally, these techniques are often used in advertising and other forms of persuasive writing.

Consonance

This technique is perhaps one that is often overlooked in planned speech but has, when used, a similar strength to alliteration and assonance – it helps us to remember a phrase, because of a consonant repetition in the middle or at the end of words: 'the uneatable, the unspeakable and the unelectable.' This is a type of repetition, but it has the added effect of drawing attention to the words through the repeated sound.

Rhyme

This is a subject you have already studied in Chapter 2, Poetic Study. As with all other phonological techniques, the use of rhyme enhances the sound of the words and adds to the structural cohesion of the speech, particularly at the end of phrases or sentences.

Intonation and stress

The way in which words are intoned and the stress they are given can often help to convey the attitude of the speaker.

'One hundred years in existence, twenty-two in power, we have never, ever won a full second term. That is our unfinished business.'

The stress on the three words here gives a special force to them and reinforces the primary point that Blair is making here, the need to win a second term of office.

Sometimes words are elongated to accentuate their importance; you have already seen examples of this in the section on unplanned speech.

Volume and speed

Changes in volume can have a radical effect on any speech, whether planned or unplanned. The effect of raising one's voice is obvious: it carries with it associations of power, commitment, certainty, passion and possibly anger. It can also be used for dramatic effect, especially after a period of quiet and calm speech. This can help shock the audience and have the effect of waking them up to listen more intently to the speaker!

Speech can also be slowed down or speeded up. When speech is made more deliberate and slowed down, individual words are given special enunciation: 'Under John Major (0.5) it was weak (0.5) weak (0.5) weak!' The pauses add to the strength of the repetition here, with the dramatic effect resulting from the tripartite crescendo. It is both stylized and rhythmical in its delivery.

Putting theory into practice

Now that we have examined the different features of planned speech, here is an example of a text showing many of these features in action.

ACTIVITY

The following piece of writing began life as a speech by the animal rights activist and one-time actress Brigitte Bardot. Printed below is the written text, but it contains many of the techniques that are characteristic of its rhetorical genesis.

What techniques does the speaker use to convey her feelings and attitudes about cruelty to animals?

In your answer you should consider:

❏ use of rhetorical devices
❏ semantic choices
❏ grammatical and phonological features.

Who has given Man (a word which has tragically lost all its humanity) the right to exterminate, to dismember, to cut up, to slaughter, to hunt, to chase, to trap, to lock up, to martyr, to enslave and to torture the animals? Who has given legal sanction for his power, backed by every modern means, to be used against their helpless innocence? Who authorizes the genocides, the atrocities, which lead to the extinction of whole species? Why is there so much carnage, so much suffering, so much inhumanity, on this earth where men rule?

We must be reminded that every second of every day an animal dies in an experimental laboratory; a slow death and, for the most part, a useless death, a hellish death, a death endured in terror at the hand of sadistic evil (for our survival . . .).

We must be reminded that each morning as dawn breaks, millions upon millions of animals are slaughtered for food in town and village the world over: death on production lines, death en masse, industrial death; they see it, they smell it, they know it is coming. Neither their sight nor their instincts

➡

deceive them. They *know*. More horrible still is death by ritual slaughter, drawn out to last as long as the prayers said over them! What God could want that (for our survival . . .)?

We must be reminded what transportation means for them – by sea, by road or by train. Destined for the slaughterhouse, crammed together without food or water, they trample each other in the pounding vehicles or heaving seas. Hooves broken, eyes blinded, they die for lack of air, freeze to death or expire from the heat. What does it matter? . . . they are to die in any case (for our survival . . .)!

We must be reminded of the shameful traffic in exotic animals: for each one which survives, a hundred others are left dead. Animals traumatized, uprooted, often smuggled in crates with false compartments, left in customs so long that they die and no one knows (for our survival . . .).

We must be reminded about the hunters, stalkers and beaters who turn our forests, our countryside, into battlefields. These men, dressed for combat, armed to the teeth with the latest weapons, slaughter everything that moves, kill anything that lives. For these people, the death of one small animal is a victory. We must be reminded about the persistence of those who live by killing animals for their fur: those who set traps and snares for the smaller animals, lay poisoned meat, use helicopters and machine-guns to kill wolves, smoke foxes from their earths – the females emerge unable to breathe, their little ones still clinging to their teats, to be killed at point-blank range by these greedy men. And then the mass murder of the baby seals, the only babies in the world to have the privilege of being killed for their beautiful white fur (and all for our vanity).

We must be reminded of the battery animals whose universe is a concentration camp, forced to live an intolerable, mechanized existence. The unbearable lives of those who, like machines, eat, lay, give birth, excrete and sleep to order; worn out, fattened in spaces so small that they cannot move. They know neither the sweetness of straw, nor the colour of the sun, nor the fragrance of the meadowland. They live to die an economically quick death (for our survival . . .).

We must be reminded of the distress of the animals condemned forever in zoos, in menageries, behind bars, for us to take pleasure in their pain. And, finally, we must be reminded of the massacre of the whales for oil which goes into beauty products. The wholesale killing of the elephants for ivory, the kangaroos for tinned meat. We know what has caused all this extermination, incarceration and injustice. But we do not know where it will end. Because there is no end. Who justifies, who permits, who allows, who suggests, who promotes that collective indifference, which will lead sooner or later to the complete destruction of the animal kingdom? Greed, cruelty, violence, sadism: these qualities, alas, are all too typical of present-day human behaviour.

It is time to act, high time – if we want to regain the dignity the animals have never lost. If we really wish that the world might become once more what it was at the beginning of time: a shared Paradise.

How to tackle this type of question

When you come to write about speech, whether it is spontaneous or planned, you will need to adopt a framework around which to build your answer. This will help ensure that you have covered all the required areas and that you have commented on the effects of the type of speech you are analysing.

Here is one framework for approaching speech questions.

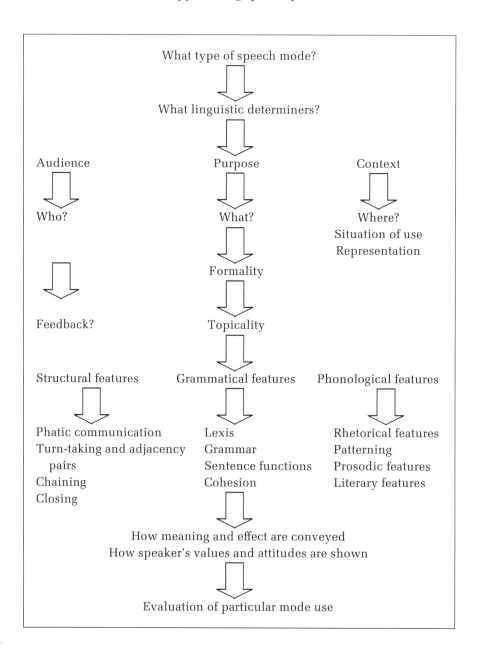

APPROACHES TO EXAMINATION QUESTIONS

Here is a specimen question and a student response on a piece of planned speech.

Evaluate the effect of Stalin's speech style in his radio broadcast to the Russian people, explaining how he conveys his attitudes and values in the context of this speech.

In your answer you should comment on the effectiveness of the following features of language:

- ❏ rhetorical devices
- ❏ semantic choices
- ❏ grammatical and phonological features
- ❏ any other issues you consider important.

Joseph Stalin

Moscow, 3 July 1941

'A grave danger hangs over our country'

Stalin was taken by surprise in 1941 when Hitler tore up the Nazi-Soviet pact and invaded Russia. Initially he suffered some kind of mental breakdown, especially when he realized the speed of the German advance. Only after establishing a state defence committee under his chairmanship did Stalin come to recover his self-confidence and emerge once again as the indispensable leader. On 3 July he spoke to the people over the radio appealing to Russian patriotism and asking them to destroy everything if forced to retreat.

Comrades! Citizens! Brothers and Sisters! Men of our Army and Navy!

I am addressing you, my friends!

The perfidious military attack on our fatherland, begun on 22 June by Hitler's Germany, is continuing.

In spite of heroic resistance of the Red Army, and although the enemy's finest divisions and finest air-force units have already been smashed and have met their doom on the field of battle, the enemy continues to push forward, hurling fresh forces into the attack.

Hitler's troops have succeeded in capturing Lithuania, a considerable part of Latvia, the western part of White Russia, and a part of the western Ukraine.

The Fascist air-force is extending the range of operations of its bombers and is bombing Murmansk, Orsha, Mogilev, Smolensk, Kiev, Odessa, and Sevastopol.

➡

A grave danger hangs over our country.

How could it have happened that our glorious Red Army surrendered a number of our cities and districts to the Fascist armies?

Is it really true that German Fascist troops are invincible, as is ceaselessly trumpeted by boastful Fascist propagandists? Of course not! History shows that there are no invincible armies, and never have been. Napoleon's army was considered invincible, but it was beaten successively by Russian, English, and German armies. Kaiser Wilhelm's German army in the period of the first imperialist war was also considered invincible, but it was beaten several times by Russian and Anglo-French forces, and was finally smashed by Anglo-French forces.

The same must be said of Hitler's German Fascist army today. This army has not yet met with serious resistance on the Continent of Europe. Only on our territory has it met serious resistance, and if as a result of this resistance the finest divisions of Hitler's German Fascist army have been defeated by our Red Army, it means that this army, too, can be smashed and will be smashed as were the armies of Napoleon and Wilhelm.

There can be no doubt that this short-lived military gain for Germany is only an episode, while the tremendous political gain of the USSR is a serious and lasting factor that is bound to form the basis for development of decisive military successes of the Red Army in the war with Fascist Germany ...

In case of a forced retreat of Red Army units, all rolling stock must be evacuated; to the enemy must not be left a single engine, a single railway car, not a single pound of grain or a gallon of fuel.

Collective farmers must drive off all their cattle and turn over their grain to the safekeeping of state authorities for transportation to the rear. All valuable property including nonferrous metals, grain, and fuel which cannot be withdrawn must without fail be destroyed.

In areas occupied by the enemy, guerrilla units, mounted and foot, must be formed, diversionist groups must he organized to combat enemy troops, to foment guerrilla warfare everywhere, to blow up bridges, roads, damage telephone and telegraph lines, and to set fire to forests, stores, and transports.

In occupied regions conditions must be made unbearable for the enemy and all his accomplices. They must he hounded and annihilated at every step and all their measures frustrated.

This war with Fascist Germany cannot be considered an ordinary war. It is not only a war between two armies, it is also a great war of the entire Soviet people against the German Fascist forces.

The aim of this national war in defence of our country against the Fascist oppressors is not only elimination of the danger hanging over our country, but also aid to all European peoples groaning under the yoke of German Fascism.

➡

The Soviet leader Joseph Stalin (1879–1953)

In this war of liberation we shall not be alone.

In this great war we shall have loyal allies in the peoples of Europe and America, including German people who are enslaved by Hitlerite despots.

Our war for the freedom of our country will merge with the struggle of the peoples of Europe and America for their independence, for democratic liberties. It will be a united front of peoples standing for freedom and against enslavement and threats of enslavement by Hitler's Fascist armies.

Comrades, our forces are numberless. The overweening enemy will soon learn this to his cost. Side by side with the Red Army and Navy thousands of workers, collective farmers, and intellectuals are rising to fight the enemy aggressor. The masses of our people will rise up in their millions. The working people of Moscow and Leningrad already have commenced to form vast popular levies in support of the Red Army.

Such popular levies must be raised in every city that is in danger of an enemy invasion; all working people must be roused to defend our freedom, our honour, our country – in our patriotic war against German Fascism.

In order to insure a rapid mobilization of all forces of the peoples of the USSR, and to repulse the enemy who treacherously attacked our country, a State Committee of Defence has been formed in whose hands the entire power of the state has been vested.

The State Committee of Defence has entered into its functions and calls upon all our people to rally around the party of Lenin-Stalin and around the Soviet government so as self-denyingly to support the Red Army and Navy, demolish the enemy, and secure victory.

All our forces for the support of our heroic Red Army and our glorious Red Navy!

All the forces of the people – for the demolition of the enemy!

Forward, to our victory!

Here is one student's response to the question.

In order to evaluate the effectiveness of this speech, given by Joseph Stalin, we must first identify what the purpose of the speech is – what Stalin is hoping to achieve by saying what he does.

This process is relatively simple because Stalin states his intentions and hopes at numerous times throughout the speech. The speech is a radio broadcast given by the Russian leader, at a time when the German armed forces, once allies to Russia, had turned against the pact Hitler had made with Stalin, and were beginning to invade the areas surrounding Russia. Stalin, knowing that his weakening army would never be enough to counter the trained and equipped German army, is appealing to ordinary Russian civilians to rise up and fight against the 'Fascist forces'.

The aim of the speech then, given this scenario, is not to lay down any concrete political plans or policies, but to inspire. He wants to motivate the people, perhaps to inspire them to fight an almost impossible battle against the Germans. This is not a simple task. In order to provoke such a response, Stalin tries to tailor his language to appeal to the patriotic and proud side of the Russian people.

We can measure the success of the speech with this aim in mind by looking at various aspects of its linguistic content including the semantic choices Stalin makes, grammatical and phonological features of the speech and various literary and rhetorical devices. Once we have considered these areas individually, we can then assess the overall impact of the speech as an inspirational, motivating piece.

The decisions Stalin makes regarding the vocabulary of the piece will undoubtedly have a strong bearing on the ultimate success of the speech. In my opinion, he does make stirring linguistic choices when selecting his lexis. As I have already identified, the speech is meant to inspire, and so Stalin must use rousing, powerful language to provoke the response he wants from the audience.

In the opening lines of his speech he captures his intended mood by addressing the audience as 'Comrades! Citizens! Brothers and Sisters! Men of our Army and Navy!' He immediately recognizes that he must attempt to present and address a united Russia, he must call on everyone, anywhere, in any walk of life to fight against the Germans. He goes on to say: 'I am addressing you, my friends!' It is important that Stalin tries to get the listeners on his side, and to do so, he maintains an air of familiarity towards his audience. 'Comrades', 'Brothers and Sisters', 'my friends' are all terms Stalin purposefully uses to try to endear himself to his audience.

Stalin is also very conscious of the fact that he is addressing an audience which is not approaching the war with its eyes shut. They know the reality of the war, the suffering and death. He realizes their understandable reluctance to go to battle against the Germans. Because of this, he adopts an 'us-against-the-world' approach, whereby he implies that the Russian people are the final resistance against the tyranny that is the German army, and without their 'heroic' efforts, the world will perish at the hands of the Germans. Though this is not quite true, it is important that Stalin exaggerates the situation as much as possible – the more drastic the people see it to be, the more likely they are to do something about it.

He furthers this approach throughout his speech. He describes a 'grave danger hanging over our country', and goes on to demand that grain and cattle be turned over to the authorities so that the 'Fascist Germans' can't get hold of them. These measures are extreme, and Stalin recognizes this. He must make the situation sound as serious as possible to provoke an extreme response from the people.

Stalin is also very aware that he must highlight the evil of the Germans as much as possible. The people must never doubt that they are the true enemy, even though Stalin signed a pact with Hitler, a pact which would still be in place had Hitler not attacked Russia. Stalin, therefore, refers to the Germans repeatedly as Fascists. 'German Fascism', 'Fascist Germany', 'The German Fascist forces' are all terms he uses so the audience is left with no doubts about who the enemy is.

Stalin also uses the kind of elevated language that is commonly found in political speeches. Descriptions such as 'the perfidious military attack on our fatherland' are a prime example of this. The use of the premodifying adjective 'perfidious' highlights his elevated status as leader, but while using language of this kind, he recognizes the requirement to be able to move between the rhetorical polarities of this type of speech and more accessible, everyday language. He is the leader of the people and the country; he needs to prove to his people and the rest of the world that he and his country will fight to the end, die if they have to.

So, I believe that Stalin makes quite appropriate decisions regarding the lexis he uses in this speech. He uses powerful and rousing concepts (pride, patriotism, honour) mixed with language that seeks to unite everyone behind him, while simultaneously appearing a genuine and intelligent leader to his audience by including some elevated language.

The grammar of the piece is relatively straightforward. It is important that we remember at this point, however, that we are dealing with a speech, not a written piece of literature. It is intended to be performed, so the grammatical structures will not be of any great complexity. This said, I think that Stalin makes a conscious effort to use a majority of simple declaratives because he does not want to lose his audience and detract from the message he is trying to convey to them. The success of the speech lies entirely with his audience – if they get lost or confused, the speech is a failure, so he needs to maintain their concentration and focus, and the simple statements aid this goal.

Stalin also makes very good use of fragmentary sentences for impact. This can be seen most clearly in his concluding passage:

> *All the forces of the people – for the demolition of the enemy! Forward, to our victory!*

The two sentences in this section are very dramatic and provide impact. 'All the forces of the people' sums up what Stalin has said continuously throughout his speech, and would prove quite inspiring. He is at this point speaking almost in slogans as he is drawing to the climax of his speech. He also includes a patriotic 'Forward, to our victory' to appeal to the audience's pride, or instill some if it had perhaps waned in the times during the war. He also maintains his united front with 'our victory'. Victory for the country, for everyone together.

The most significant grammatical feature, however, is the way that Stalin addresses the audience. I have touched on this point earlier in the analysis. Right from the very start, Stalin uses the first person plural pronominative forms of 'we' and 'us' to address the audience. He is, as mentioned, very conscious of including and uniting everybody – as he did with the lexis – so as to inspire a united effort against the Germans. He wants to create an inspired Russia and so he needs people to feel united, to feel a part of the 'numberless' Russian force, so it is imperative he addresses the audience in this way.

So, as I have briefly outlined, there are certain grammatical features which have significance in this piece, even though it is a speech and not a piece of written literature.

Finally, Stalin uses a number of literary devices to make his speech more vivid and add a little interest to how he describes his ideas. He makes use of the pattern of three commonly found in political speech. For example, he describes Napoleon being defeated by 'the Russian, English and German armies' to try to highlight how the Germans are not invincible. He tells them to burn 'forest, stores and transports'. This three-part list is an ancient rhetorical structure, which in political speech gives maximum opportunity for the audience to react. If supported by a strong rhythm, list structures like these provide invaluable rhetorical and structural control and possess a sense of completeness, leaving the listener satisfied with what has been said. The third item in the list often provides a climax to which the audience can respond with cheering or applause, for example – ideal for motivating and inspiring the listener. Stalin uses this a number of times in his speech which serves to engage the listener and draws focus to important issues or points.

In conclusion, I feel I have demonstrated that this is indeed an effective and successful speech by Joseph Stalin. His words are purposeful and have impact and meaning and the linguistic choices he makes allow him to maintain the focus and attention of the audience, which results in a stirring, inspiring yet simple address.

Examiner's comments

This answer shows that there are many routes into such a question and that there is absolutely no need to cover all possible points under each of the subheadings of the question. Indeed, this student uses a framework that allows him to cover the main points of his essay through an examination of purpose, audience, context, and lexical, grammatical and cohesive choices. In examining these four areas, the student integrates comment on the way Stalin conveys his attitudes and values through detailed analysis of a few carefully chosen examples which substantiate his points.

The student could have made any number of other points about Stalin's speech that would also be quite acceptable in an answer of this kind. Some of these areas are:

1 An analysis of the patterning and differentiated use of sentence construction.

2 Use of other rhetorical devices such as repetition, his different patterns of listing, the use of exclamations, use of contrasts.

3 There are issues of lexis that could be highlighted: emotive adjectives, use of connectives, the pronominative forms of the piece (first- and third-person usage, both singular and plural), the use of statement and declaratives.

4 There is also much to say about the cohesion of the piece and its chronology.

If there is a weakness in the answer, it is that text quotation is rarely deconstructed and analysed. But this candidate has a clear overview of the text, interesting ideas, and seamlessly moves from one section of the question to the next, so this answer would have to be placed securely in the upper bands.

How this Unit links to other sections of the course

This particular section of the specification, the second part of Unit 3, links specifically to Unit 6, the synoptic Unit – on this paper, you will compare speech with other literary and linguistic forms. However, other parts of the course also have overlaps with this particular Unit. Unit 1, for instance, may give a springboard text that is a piece of planned or unplanned speech, and your knowledge of how speech works should help you to appreciate and understand more deeply how speech works in Prose (this Unit), in the literature you study as part of the comparative unit (Unit 4) and in the study of drama (Unit 5).

The table below shows the major links between this part of the Unit and others on the course.

Question	Skills learned	Links to other parts of the Specification
Language of Speech	Understanding how speech works; knowledge of functions of speech	• Production question Unit 1 Question 1 • Synoptic question Unit 6 Question 1
	The importance of audience	• Dramatic question Unit 5 Section A • Recasting question Unit 5 Section B • Synoptic question Unit 6 Questions 1 and 2
	How attitudes and values are highlighted by lexical choice and grammatical structures	• Dramatic question Unit 5 Section A • Synoptic question Unit 6 Question 1
	Reflecting on how language is used to help target an audience	• Recasting question Unit 5 Section B • Synoptic question Unit 6 Question 1
	Reflecting on context and form	• Recasting question Unit 5 Section B • Synoptic question Unit 6 Question 1

SECTION II: A2-LEVEL

Developing and Extending Your Skills and Knowledge

As you have found from your studies of the Advanced Subsidiary part of this course, certain aspects of integrated literary and linguistic studies need to be highlighted before your learning takes place. This helps you to contextualize the modules of the course. At AS-level, emphasis is given to the interrelationship of such issues as audience, purpose and context – the key determinants of textual study, analysis and interpretation. A certain body of knowledge has to be learned and used in the different kinds of analysis that need to be undertaken, and there are certain procedures and frameworks that should be followed when producing texts of your own and when engaging in textual analysis.

At A2-level, your study of texts will be wider and the tasks linked to their study are more demanding, requiring more of your analytical skills. At AS-level, the textual study you were engaged in was largely limited to single texts; at A2 your textual analyses will be characterized by the need for **comparison**. This skill is tested on all three of the A2 units, and you therefore need to make good use of any opportunities to practise the comparison of any texts.

You will also study two or three further literary set texts: one pairing will be the basis for your studies in Unit 4, Comparative Literary Studies. You will note that it is possible to carry one of your texts forward from AS into this Unit. This may help ease the transition between AS and A2 for you. However, if you wish to widen your studies and have the time to do so, then the study of two new texts in Unit 4 is recommended. The other set text you will study is a pre-1770 dramatic text as part of Unit 5, Texts and Audience. You will also continue to learn how to use and apply frameworks for analysis, which will be vital for both of these units but will also be important for the final Unit, Language in Context.

One of the skills you will need is the adaptation and recasting of material for a new purpose and audience. This is linked to Unit 5, Texts and Audience, and will provide you with the opportunity of taking forward the skills you learned during Unit 1, Language Production, at AS-level. You will have the opportunity of contrasting or comparing parts of your new text with one or both of the original texts, to highlight the ways in which you have made your adaptations and changes. This will afford you a new angle on textual analysis, since it allows you to reflect on your choices through comparison with 'live' texts.

The final, and perhaps most important, paper of both AS and A2 is the synoptic paper. This Unit is the culmination of your studies – it tests your ability to draw together all you have learned about literary and linguistic study and apply it through comparison of three unseen texts, covering literary, non-literary and spoken texts.

Your analysis will be more penetrating because of the comparative element of A2 study, and it will also go further because of the **evaluative** aspect of all the papers. If comparison is the tool through which analysis is delivered, the evaluation of textual, authorial and analytical success becomes the other key feature in A2 study of English Language and Literature. In consequence, you are expected to become much more autonomous in your studies, your analyses, and your construction and application of frameworks. You should be more searching and evaluative in your analysis, particularly of the unseen texts that appear in both Units 5 and 6. It is also necessary for you to study the part that historical and social contexts play in the literature you read.

In Unit 4 you will be asked to make evaluative comments on the nature of the textual comparison you have undertaken; in Unit 5, Section B you will be asked to formulate an evaluation of your own text's success in comparison to the original texts used for adaptation. Finally, you will be asked in the synoptic paper to evaluate the success of your own method of comparative analysis of unseen texts, reflecting the importance of the construction and use of analytical frameworks at this level.

You will have noted that the time allowed for examination is longer than that at AS-level; this reflects the increasing demands of the tasks, as well as the nature of comparative and evaluative analysis.

In summary, you will have to undertake the following at this level in the subject:

❑ comparative analytical studies with evaluation of textual and authorial success
❑ study of the impact of audience on texts
❑ adaptation of different texts
❑ use of personal frameworks for analysis and evaluation of those frameworks
❑ detailed study of two or three further set texts.

At the end of each section of AS-level, we pointed out ways of carrying forward what you had learned at that level into the A2 section of the course. We are now in a position to draw these strands together and formalize the connections between the two parts of the course, by showing the ways in which the foundation studies of AS are explored and embellished at A2-level.

	Advanced Subsidiary Level skills	**Advanced Level skills**
All Units	Integrated literary and linguistic study of single set texts	*Integrated literary and linguistic study of two or more texts*
All Units	Use of analytical frameworks to aid personal responses	*Evaluation of analytical frameworks after personal response*
Units 1 and 5	Consideration of audience through creative writing	*Consideration of audience through textual adaptation and recasting*
Units 1 and 5	Exploration of audience and purpose through textual production	*Exploration of audience and purpose through textual recasting*
Units 1 and 5	Commentary on production work	*Comparative commentary on recasting work*
Units 2, 3, 4 and 5	Analysis of prepared poetry and prose texts	*Analysis of prepared and unprepared poetry, prose and drama texts.*
Units 3 and 6	Study of speech as single text	*Comparison of speech with other modes*
Units 3, 5 and 6	Integrated literary and linguistic study of single texts	*Comparative integrated literary and linguistic study of two or more unseen texts*
Units 3, 5 and 6	Consideration of audience through the study of speech	*Consideration of audience through literary and non-literary writing*
Units 1, 3, 5 and 6	Consideration of purpose through creative writing and study of speech	*Consideration of purpose through literary and non-literary writing and textual recasting*

As you can see, there are many ways in which you can build on those foundations laid at AS level; it is up to you to use them in a constructive manner and mesh them into the key aspects of the study of language and literature at A2 level:

❏ comparison
❏ evaluation
❏ construction and use of personal frameworks to aid analysis.

We wish you good luck with the second part of your course and studies.

5 Comparative Literary Studies

In this Unit you will make full use of the skills you have developed so far in the course. You will be looking at the issues raised in some literary texts and the ways these issues are explored through the language used by the writer.

In the specification there will be a choice of six pairings of texts. You will study one pair and the questions in the examination will focus on a comparison of some aspects of these two texts. The texts themselves will be drawn from a range of historical settings, differing cultures and varying genres, including non-literary texts. You will be able to take the texts into the examination room with you.

The Unit will test your ability to:

❏ communicate clearly the knowledge, understanding and insights gained from combined literary and linguistic study
❏ use literary and linguistic frameworks to distinguish, describe and explain key linguistic features in specific sections of the texts
❏ show an understanding of how language is used in literary/non-literary texts
❏ make valid and informed comparisons and connections between texts by showing understanding of the ways contextual variation shapes the meanings of texts.

As well as identifying these key objectives, the examination board's specification offers the following advice on the possible form of questions:

❏ candidates should be prepared to comment on specific sections of text and widen their comments to the whole of both texts with reference to the way language is used
❏ candidates should be prepared to answer on thematic, generic, developmental and stylistic links and comparisons in the texts.

This Unit therefore focuses on the central areas you have already studied through the prose, poetry and drama units of this book. You will need to use the skills you have developed through your study of texts at AS level. The pairing you study will probably be dependent on which your teacher or lecturer chooses or which texts have been selected for your study modules. Pairings can be made in various ways:

❏ same genre; same period
❏ different genre; different period
❏ different genre; same period
❏ same genre; different period.

For example:

The Ghost Road: Pat Barker (prose fiction/Twentieth Century)
The Railway Man: Eric Lomax (prose non-fiction/Twentieth Century)

This is an example of a comparison of texts of different genres but written in a similar period.

The Miller's Tale: Geoffrey Chaucer (poetry/Middle Ages)
Talking Heads 2: Alan Bennett (prose/Twentieth Century)

This is an example of a comparison of texts of different genres and different periods.

Approaching the comparison

Before you can really get to grips with the comparison, of course, you must study each of the texts carefully, looking at all the relevant features that we have discussed in earlier Units. However, when you have developed a sound knowledge of the two texts you are studying you will need to begin to think carefully about them as a pair. Of course, as you have been reading and studying them it is likely that you will have been noting links, similarities or differences between them, but in order to fully compare them it is useful to have some kind of framework to help structure you thoughts and your work.

The following model is one way in which you could approach your comparative study.

Framework

❏ Identification of comparative areas and issues in the texts

Analysis and explanation

❏ Identification and exemplification of central features of the texts, using contextual and structural frameworks
❏ Description and comparison of the features of the text, e.g. exploration of ideas, themes, character, linguistic issues
❏ Consideration and comparison of meanings and effects created in each text
❏ Consideration of different levels of analysis

Evaluation

❏ Consideration and comparison of texts' success with reference to explanatory frameworks

---

It should be noted that not all these points will apply equally to all texts. Which particular areas are the main focus of interest will depend on the nature of the texts under discussion.

Now we will have a closer look at how this approach could be used in practice in comparing two texts. For this example we will look at how an initial comparison of *Murmuring Judges* by David Hare and *Measure for Measure* by Shakespeare could be made using the above approach. It doesn't matter if you are not familiar with these texts, as it is the general approach to making comparisons that we are looking at. Bear in mind that not all the areas will apply to the same extent with the texts you are studying, but some of the features certainly will. The main thing is to develop an understanding of the basic way in which you can approach your two texts and the kinds of things you could look for in them.

Frameworks

Begin by establishing the **frameworks** which will provide the structure to your comparative work. In order to do this you need to identify the **areas** and **issues** within the two texts that you are going to compare. In *Murmuring Judges* and *Measure for Measure* this could look something like this:

Comparative areas and issues:

❏ Characters
❏ Themes
❏ Linguistic features
❏ Dramatic techniques
❏ Historical context
❏ Social context.

Analysis and explanation

Identification of central contextual frameworks and structural features:

❏ General historical context within which each play was written
❏ Social structure within which each play is set
❏ Comparison of the overall dramatic structure of each play

Description and comparison of the features of each text:

❏ Comparison of the **characters** in each text – their roles, their significance within the scheme of the play, their function in relationship with other areas such as the development of theme.

Measure for Measure	*Murmuring Judges*
Angelo	Barry
Claudio	Gerard

The Duke   Sir Peter
Isabella   Irina
Mariana   Sandra

(and others as appropriate)

❑ **Thematic** links within the plays:

Justice
Appearance and reality
Power
Corruption
Sexual attitudes

Linguistic features – a comparison of the ways in which the language is used in each play:

❑ The soliloquy
❑ 'Comic' scenes
❑ Metaphorical features
❑ Rhetorical features
❑ Pace
❑ Tone

Dramatic techniques, effects and meanings:

❑ Effects created in each play
❑ The dramatic techniques used to create these effects
❑ Relationships between effects, themes and characters
❑ The creation of 'meaning'

Different levels of analysis:

❑ Different views of the plays
❑ Different interpretations of characters, themes and meanings
❑ Audience response

Evaluation

Consideration of the success of each text:

❑ In terms of the various ideas and frameworks described above
❑ As a piece of 'theatre'
❑ As a comment on the themes presented.

ACTIVITY   Think about the pair of texts you are studying. Using the methods described above, draw up a plan of how to approach your comparative study of these texts. Make sure that you think about details such as which themes you are to deal with, the characters, the linguistic elements, etc.

The methods discussed above will give you a framework within which to plan your comparative study. We will now look at some specific comparisons between texts. These are not meant to replicate the kinds of questions that you will meet in the exam, because it is unlikely that you will have studied the texts from which the passages are taken. The activities are to give you practice in comparing the ways that different writers use language to achieve their effects.

Read the following two extracts carefully. The first is from *Frankenstein* by Mary Shelley, and in it the creature that Victor Frankenstein has created is described.

Extract A

It was on a dreary night of November that I beheld the accomplishment of my toils. With an anxiety that almost amounted to agony, I collected the instruments of life around me, that I might infuse a spark of being into the lifeless thing that lay at my feet. It was already one in the morning; the rain pattered dismally against the panes, and my candle was nearly burnt out, when, by the glimmer of the half-extinguished light, I saw the dull yellow eye of the creature open; it breathed hard, and a convulsive motion agitated its limbs.

How can I describe my emotions at this catastrophe, or how delineate the wretch whom with such infinite pains and care I had endeavoured to form? His limbs were in proportion, and I had selected his features as beautiful. Beautiful! Great God! His yellow skin scarcely covered the work of muscles and arteries beneath; his hair was of a lustrous black, and flowing; his teeth of pearly whiteness; but these luxuriances only formed a more horrid contrast with his watery eyes, that seemed almost of the same colour as the dun-white sockets in which they were set, his shrivelled complexion and straight black lips.

The different accidents of life are not so changeable as the feelings of human nature. I had worked hard for nearly two years, for the sole purpose of infusing life into an inanimate body. For this I had deprived myself of rest and health. I had desired it with an ardour that far exceeded moderation; but now that I had finished, the beauty of the dream vanished, and breathless horror and disgust filled my heart. Unable to endure the aspect of the being I had created, I rushed out of the room and continued a long time traversing my bedchamber, unable to compose my mind to sleep. At length lassitude succeeded to the tumult I had before endured, and I threw myself on the bed in my clothes, endeavouring to seek a few moments of forgetfulness. But it was in vain: I slept, indeed, but I was disturbed by the wildest dreams. I thought I saw Elizabeth, in the bloom of health, walking in the streets of Ingolstadt. Delighted and surprised, I embraced her, but as I imprinted the first kiss on her lips, they became livid with the hue of death; her features appeared to change, and I thought that I held the corpse of my dead mother in my arms; a shroud enveloped her form, and I saw the grave-worms

➡

crawling in the folds of the flannel. I started from my sleep with horror; a cold dew covered my forehead, my teeth chattered, and every limb became convulsed; when, by the dim and yellow light of the moon, as it forced its way through the window shutters, I beheld the wretch – the miserable monster whom I had created. He held up the curtain of the bed; and his eyes, if eyes they may be called, were fixed on me. His jaws opened, and he muttered some inarticulate sounds, while a grin wrinkled his cheeks. He might have spoken, but I did not hear; one hand was stretched out, seemingly to detain me, but I escaped and rushed downstairs. I took refuge in the courtyard belonging to the house which I inhabited, where I remained during the rest of the night, walking up and down in the greatest agitation, listening attentively, catching and fearing each sound as if it were to announce the approach of the daemoniacal corpse to which I had so miserably given life.

Oh! No mortal could support the horror of that countenance. A mummy again endued with animation could not be so hideous as that wretch. I had gazed on him while unfinished; he was ugly then, but when those muscles and joints were rendered capable of motion, it became a thing such as even Dante could not have conceived.

(Mary Shelley, *Frankenstein*)

The second extract is from *Dracula* by Bram Stoker. Here we meet the Count as he makes his guest feel at home!

Extract B

The Count himself came forward and took off the cover of a dish, and I fell to at once on an excellent roast chicken. This, with some cheese and a salad and a bottle of old Tokay, of which I had two glasses, was my supper. During the time I was eating it the Count asked me many questions as to my journey, and I told him by degrees all I had experienced.

By this time I had finished my supper, and by my host's desire had drawn up a chair by the fire and begun to smoke a cigar which he offered me, at the same time excusing himself that he did not smoke. I had now an opportunity of observing him, and found him of a very marked physiognomy.

His face was a strong – a very strong – aquiline with high bridge of the thin nose and peculiarly arched nostrils; with lofty domed forehead, and hair growing scantily round the temples but profusely elsewhere. His eyebrows were very massive, almost meeting over the nose, and with bushy hair that seemed to curl in its own profusion The mouth, so far as I could see it under the heavy moustache, was fixed and rather cruel looking, with peculiarly sharp white teeth; these protruded over the lips whose remarkable ruddiness showed astonishing vitality in a man of his years. For the rest his ears were pale and at the tops extremely pointed; the chin was broad and strong, and the cheeks firm though thin. The general effect was one of extraordinary pallor.

Hitherto I had noticed the backs of his hands as they lay on his knees in the firelight, and they had seemed rather white and fine, but seeing them now   ➡

close to me, I could not but notice that they were rather coarse – broad, with squat fingers. Strange to say, there were hairs in the centre of the palm. The nails were long and fine and cut to a sharp point. As the Count leaned over me and his hands touched me, I could not repress a shudder. It may have been that his breath was rank, but a horrible feeling of nausea came over me, which do what I would, I could not conceal. The Count, evidently noticing it, drew back; and with a grim sort of smile, which showed more than he had yet done his protuberant teeth, sat himself down again on his own side of the fireplace. We were both silent for a while; and as I looked towards the window I saw the first dim streak of the coming dawn. There seemed a strange stillness over everything; but as I listened I heard, as if from down below in the valley, the howling of many wolves. The Count's eyes gleamed, and he said: –

'Listen to them – the children of the night. What music they make!' Seeing, I suppose, some expression in my face strange to him, he added: –

'Ah, sir, you dwellers in the city cannot enter into the feelings of the hunter.' Then he rose and said: –

'But you must be tired. Your bedroom is all ready, and to-morrow you shall sleep as late as you will. I have to be away till the afternoon; so sleep well and dream well!' and, with a courteous bow, he opened for me himself the door to the octagonal room, and I entered my bedroom . . .

(Bram Stoker, *Dracula*)

Count Dracula, created in Bram Stoker's 1897 novel, has featured in many horror films

ACTIVITY Compare the ways in which Shelley and Stoker use language to create an impression of the Creature and the Count respectively. You may wish to consider such features as lexis, syntax and various aspects of descriptive language in your response as well as any other features that strike you as effective.

Here are two student responses to this task. Read the responses through carefully.

Student A

The first paragraph in the extract conveys a sense of anticipation. Victor is waiting for his toil to be rewarded.

> 'The rain pattered dismally against the panes, and my candle was nearly burnt out.'

This seems symbolic of the mood of Frankenstein – he is tired and reaching the end of his work. This sentence also embodies the mood of the first paragraph. It does this because it moves very slowly. The anticipation is building up and reaches its peak when the creature opens its eye and is infused with life.

The second paragraph is rich with descriptions of the creature.

> 'Beautiful! Great God!'

This quote illustrates the contempt that Victor feels toward his creation. The use of the descriptions in this paragraph creates a sense of panic. The lack of full stops in this section causes the reader to increase the speed in which the piece is read, which results in the formation of this panic-stricken atmosphere.

The phrase 'few moments of forgetfulness' is used to describe sleep and this suggests that Victor will suffer for his mistakes. It suggests that sleep will be his only escape from the torment that he has unleashed. Even this, it seems, does not completely release him from what he has done.

In the same paragraph a dream is described. Elizabeth, his adopted sister, becomes the creature. This is symbolic of the future as Victor's life becomes taken over by the creature. It is almost as if Victor is having a premonition about his future. This creates atmosphere. His use of language when describing this dream is very graphic, and this creates a very vivid picture in the mind of the reader.

> 'I saw the grave-worms crawling in the folds of the flannel.'

Victor is woken from his sleep by the creature.

> 'I beheld the wretch – the miserable monster.'

The clash in this quote illustrates the emotional state of Victor. The alliteration used, 'miserable monster' also displays a deep contempt that is continued throughout the remainder of the novel.

In the *Dracula* extract the vocabulary used is, for the most part, simple and self-explanatory. The extract is made interesting by the atmosphere that is maintained throughout which is ominous and warns of things to come in the future. There is a particularly interesting section in the extract, which describes in great detail the Count.

> 'The general effect was one of extraordinary pallor.'

This is said with almost comical calmness and creates irony. The whole description is written with an objective tone, and there is no feeling in it – it is just a simple description. This seems symbolic as Jonathan has much to learn about the Count and his secrets. Therefore, superficial description is all that he is capable of at this time.

> 'Strange to say, there were hairs in the centre of his palm.'

This quote illustrates the conversational tone that is being used in this extract. It is effective in that the reader knows more than Jonathan. To the reader his observations stimulate a reaction.

> '"Listen to them – the children of the night. What music they make!"'

This quote also adds to the atmosphere as it contrasts with the calm, sane writing of Jonathan.

'I entered my bedroom . . .' this is how the extract concludes. The ellipsis at the end of the extract suggests that the writer has broken off and therefore creates atmosphere. The reader is left to wonder why the extract was broken off and encouraged to read on.

Student B

In the extract from *Frankenstein* there is very vivid description and an effective use of language, which creates atmosphere and tension throughout the passage. In the second line alone, 'an anxiety that almost amounted to agony', alliteration is applied by Mary Shelley. This creates a sense of anticipation and anxiety on behalf of Victor as he is awaiting the birth of his creation. The use of the alliteration here slows the piece down and so the reader has to wait for the creature's birth similarly to Victor. The whole of the first paragraph is devoted to creating an atmosphere, and this is done through describing the situation and nature of the night, which results in imagery.

> 'The rain pattered dismally against the panes, and my candle was nearly burnt out, when by the glimmer of the half-extinguished light' . . .

This adds to the anticipation as an aura of tension is created, as the scene has been set for expectation of something great to occur.

Through description of the creature's introduction to life, strong words are used which builds up a rather revolting picture of what the creature looks like.

'His yellow skin scarcely covered the work of muscles and arteries . . . hair was of lustrous black.' Here, Shelley has described the features in such detail that images are built up rapidly. The creature seems highly unpleasant with its 'watery eyes' and 'shrivelled complexion and straight black lips'. This creates a sense of horror through the use of descriptive words.

The word 'infusing' creates a sense and image of Victor 'injecting' life into this creation, which is rather a vivid image. After the building up of this description and tension, the atmosphere changes as Victor sleeps. Yet, the atmosphere is not lost as Victor is 'disturbed by the wildest dreams'. This also creates an atmosphere of horror as it is implied that Victor cannot escape this, even through dreams. The horror is enhanced further as Victor pictures holding the 'corpse of his dead mother in his arms'. Even later the use of the word 'ugly', although a very simplistic word to use, creates the sense of the revoltingness of this creation. 'Daemoniacal corpse' implies that the creature is already dead. Even Shelley's sentence structure adds to the success of the piece. In the first paragraphs, the use of commas and semi-colons adds to the slowness and anticipation of the creature's wake.

In the extract from Bram Stoker's *Dracula*, very strong description is used when referring to the features. This, similarly to the description used in *Frankenstein*, creates a sense of horror as the reader is able to build up pictures of the appearance, learnt through the very intricate details.

'High bridge of the thin nose . . . peculiarly arched nostrils with lofty domed forehead.' This is high detail of such simplistic features. The description is rather plain with an intense lack of feeling. This bland monotony adds to the tension and creates a feeling of expectation of what to come.

'A grim sort of smile' is a paradox as 'smile' is meant to emphasize joy, but 'grim' emphasizes misery. The use of the ellipsis at the end of the description of the entrance into the room also indicates expectation and a sense of anticipation.

ACTIVITY Look carefully at these responses. How closely do they agree with what you thought about the extracts? Write down what you think are the strengths and weaknesses of each response.

Examiner's comments

Student A begins well by identifying the mood of the extract and the way in which the slow-moving quality of the language reflects the mood of the opening. The image of the candle being nearly burnt out, symbolizing Frankenstein's tiredness is a point well made. The student is also sensitive to the sense of anticipation that is built up here and focuses well on the connotations of the language. For example, the implications of 'few moments of forgetfulness' are well observed.

As Student A moves on to the extract from *Dracula* she immediately identifies a difference in the way in which language is used by Stoker as compared with Shelley. The point is made that the vocabulary is simple and self-explanatory. She rightly makes the point it is the atmosphere created by Stoker that adds interest here. The description is simple and straightforward when compared to that in the *Frankenstein* extract. Overall this is a sound response, which makes a number of interesting and valid comparisons. However, a more detailed analysis of the language used and the effects created by it across both extracts would have been useful.

Student B also picks up on the vivid description and creation of atmosphere in the *Frankenstein* extract. The point about Shelley's use of alliteration is perceptive and it is backed up by a sensible comment on the effect it creates. There is also a good use of quotation to support the point about the creation of atmosphere. The student is sensitive to the way in which tension is created so that there is an expectation something momentous will happen. The close attention to the vocabulary used is a strength of this response, and the point about the 'horror' effect created is a good one. The links between the build-up of description, tension and atmosphere have been clearly understood. The comments on the effects of 'infusing', the imagery of Victor's dead mother, and the effects even of simple words like 'ugly' are perceptive. The consideration of the effects of features such as syntax and punctuation further enhance this response.

The response to *Dracula* is less detailed, although some interesting points are made. These could have been developed further, and this would have made the response more effective. Also, this response lacks a real sense of *comparing* the two extracts and the approaches that the two writers take.

Summary of examiner's advice

❏ Focus closely on the effects of individual words.
❏ Focus on the effects of imagery, etc.
❏ Be sensitive to atmosphere and tone.
❏ Be sensitive to the connotations of words, phrases, etc.
❏ Deal with the two texts fairly evenly – don't spend all the time writing about one and then just a couple of lines on the other – go for **balance.**
❏ **Compare** the texts. Don't just write about them in isolation – draw comparisons.

The next two extracts are from Eric Lomax's *The Railway Man* and Pat Barker's *The Ghost Road*. The extracts are the opening sections of the books. Read them carefully.

Extract A is the opening of *The Railway Man* by Eric Lomax. This book is non-fiction and in it Lomax describes his experiences as a prisoner of war held by the Japanese during the Second World War when he worked on the Burma–Siam Railway – 'The Railway of Death'.

Extract A

I have a painting in the hallway of my house in Berwick-upon-Tweed, by the Scottish artist Duncan Mackellar. It is a large work set in St Enoch Station in Glasgow on a dusty summer evening in the 1880s. A woman in late middle age, dressed in dark and modest clothes and carrying a parasol, is standing tense and distraught, looking out beyond us, oblivious of any other presence. Behind her the high smoke-grimed glass and wrought-iron walls of the station rise up. She is gazing off the edge of the platform at a vanishing train, so that we see her through the eyes of a receding traveller, and she has the flat restrained face of a person who has learned to swallow grief. Her sudden loneliness is captured as she strains to keep an image of her child, or so we assume, who is on the train heading for the emigrant ship or a colonial war – India, Afghanistan, the Gold Coast.

Although it is a conventional image, it is genuinely moving. I have always loved it. Railway stations have always attracted me, not just because trains are there, but because they are also ambivalent places, echoing with completed journeys and shrill with the melancholy noises of departure. Mackellar's painting is about the inevitability of separation, the cost of journeying. And we have never created any sound so evocative of separation as the whistle of a steam locomotive, that high note of inhuman relief as vaporized water is blown off and meets the cold air.

Once in the 1970s I went to St Enoch and stood on the platform at the spot that Mackellar's painting creates for the viewer, and the back of the great shed, like an enormous Victorian conservatory, seemed hardly to have changed. The station was not yet quite disused and silent, though a few years later it was destroyed, like so many of the other steam cathedrals. That age is gone now, finally, but the reality of grief, and the consequences of grief, of which Mackellar caught something in his painting, are not so easily banished.

The passion for trains and railways is, I have been told, incurable. I have also learned that there is no cure for torture. These two afflictions have been intimately linked in the course of my life, and yet through some chance combination of luck and grace I have survived them both. But it took me nearly fifty years to surmount the consequences of torture.

(Eric Lomax, *The Railway Man*)

Extract B is the opening of *The Ghost Road* by Pat Barker. This is a novel set during the First World War in which Barker explores the psychological effects of warfare on the minds of young soldiers. The book, although basically a work of fiction, does contain real figures from history. Much of the action of the novel is seen through the eyes of an army officer, Billy Prior.

Extract B

In deck-chairs all along the front the bald pink knees of Bradford businessmen nuzzled the sun.

Billy Prior leant on the sea-wall. Ten or twelve feet below him a family was gathering its things together for the trek back to boarding-house or railway station. A fat, middle-aged woman, swollen feet bulging over lace-up shoes, a man with a lobster-coloured tonsure – my God, he'd be regretting it tomorrow – and a small child, a boy, being towelled dry by a young woman. His little tassel wobbled as he stood, square-mouthed with pain, howling, 'Ma-a-am.' Wet sand was the problem. It always was, Prior remembered. However carefully you tiptoed back from that final paddle, your legs got coated all over again, and the towel always hurt.

The child wriggled and his mother slapped him hard, leaving red prints on his chubby buttocks. He stopped screaming, gulped with shock, then settled down to a persistent grizzle. The older woman protested, 'Hey, our Louie, there's no need for that.' She grabbed the towel. 'C'mon, give it here, you've no bloody patience, you.'

The girl – but she was not a girl, she was a woman of twenty-five or twenty-six, perhaps – retreated, resentful but also relieved. You could see her problem. Married, but the war, whether by widowing her or simply by taking her husband away, had reduced her to a position of tutelage in her mother's house, and then what was the point? Hot spunk trickling down the thigh, the months of heaviness, the child born on a gush of blood – if all that didn't entitle you to the status and independence of a woman, what did? Oh, and she'd be frustrated too. Her old single bed back, or perhaps a double bed with the child, listening to snores and creaks and farts from her parents' bed on the other side of the wall.

She was scrabbling in her handbag, dislodging bus tickets, comb, purse, producing, finally, a packet of Woodbines. She let the cigarette dangle wetly from her lower lip while she groped for the matches. Her lips were plump, a pale salmon pink at the centre, darkening to brownish red at the edges. She glanced up, caught him looking at her, and flushed, not with pleasure – his lust was too blatant to be flattering – but drawn by it, nevertheless, into the memory of her unencumbered girlhood.

Her mother was helping the little boy step into his drawers, his hand a dimpled starfish on her broad shoulder. The flare of the match caught her attention.

'For God's sake, Louie,' she snapped. 'If you could only see how common you look . . . '

Louie's gaze hadn't moved. Her mother turned and squinted up into the sun, seeing the characteristic silhouette that said 'officer'. 'Look for the thin knees,' German snipers were told, but where they saw prey this woman saw a predator. If he'd been a private she'd have asked him what the bloody hell he thought he was gawping at. As it was, she said, 'Nice weather we're having, sir.'

Prior smiled, amused, recognizing his mother's speech, the accent of working-class gentility. 'Let's hope it lasts.'

He touched his cap and withdrew, thinking, as he strolled off, that the girl was neither a widow nor married. The way the mother's voice had cracked with panic over that word 'common' said it all. Louie's knees were by no means glued together, even after the child. And her mother was absolutely right, with that fag stuck in her mouth she did look common. Gloriously, devastatingly, *fuckably* common.

(Pat Barker, *The Ghost Road*)

ACTIVITY   Evaluate the effectiveness of each of these extracts as an opening to the respective books. You should examine the ways in which the writers use language in each to create their effects, and think about the kind of impact that each opening has on you, the reader. Refer to specific details of language in your response.

The following two extracts are the opening sections of *Snow Falling on Cedars* by David Guterson and *The Shipping News* by E. Annie Proulx. Read each of them through carefully.

Extract A

The accused man, Kabuo Miyamoto, sat proudly upright with rigid grace, his palms placed softly on the defendant's table – the posture of a man who has detached himself insofar as this is possible at his own trial. Some in the gallery would later say that his stillness suggested a disdain for the proceedings; others felt certain it veiled a fear of the verdict that was to come. Whichever it was, Kabuo showed nothing – not even a flicker of the eyes. He was dressed in a white shirt worn buttoned to the throat and gray, neatly pressed trousers. His figure, especially the neck and shoulders, communicated the impression of irrefutable physical strength and of precise, even imperial bearing. Kabuo's features were smooth and angular; his hair had been cropped close to his skull in a manner that made its musculature prominent. In the face of the charge that had been leveled against him he sat with his dark eyes trained straight ahead and did not appear moved at all.

In the public gallery every seat had been taken, yet the court-room suggested nothing of the carnival atmosphere sometimes found at country murder trials. In fact, the eighty-five citizens gathered there seemed strangely subdued and contemplative. Most of them had known Carl Heine, a salmon gill-netter with a wife and three children, who was buried now in the Lutheran cemetery up on Indian Knob Hill. Most had dressed with the same communal propriety they felt on Sundays before attending church services, and since the courtroom, however stark, mirrored in their hearts the dignity of their prayer houses, they conducted themselves with churchgoing solemnity. This courtroom, Judge Llewellyn Fielding's, down at the end of a damp, drafty hallway on the third floor of the Island County Courthouse, was run-down and small as courtrooms go. It was a place of gray-hued and bleak simplicity –   ➡

a cramped gallery, a bench for the judge, a witness stand, a plywood platform for the jurors, and scuffed tables for the defendant and his prosecutor. The jurors sat with studiously impassive faces as they strained to make sense of matters. The men – two truck farmers, a retired crabber, a bookkeeper, a carpenter, a boat builder, a grocer, and a halibut schooner deckhand – were all dressed in coats and neckties. The women all wore Sunday dresses – a retired waitress, a sawmill secretary, two nervous fisher wives. A hairdresser accompanied them as alternate.

The bailiff, Ed Soames, at the request of Judge Fielding, had given a good head of steam to the sluggish radiators, which now and again sighed in the four corners of the room. In the heat they produced – a humid, overbearing swelter – the smell of sour mildew seemed to rise from everything.

Snow fell that morning outside the courthouse windows, four tall, narrow arches of leaded glass that yielded a great quantity of weak December light. A wind from the sea lofted snowflakes against the windowpanes, where they melted and ran toward the casements. Beyond the courthouse the town of Amity Harbor spread along the island shoreline. A few wind-whipped and decrepit Victorian mansions, remnants of a lost era of seagoing optimism, loomed out of the snowfall on the town's sporadic hills. Beyond them, cedars wove a steep mat of still green. The snow blurred from vision the clean contours of these cedar hills. The sea wind drove snowflakes steadily inland, hurling them against the fragrant trees, and the snow began to settle on the highest branches with a gentle implacability.

The accused man, with one segment of his consciousness, watched the falling snow outside the windows. He had been exiled in the county jail for seventy-seven days – the last part of September, all of October and all of November, the first week of December in jail. There was no window anywhere in his basement cell, no portal through which the autumn light could come to him. He had missed autumn, he realized now – it had passed already, evaporated. The snowfall, which he had witnessed out of the corners of his eyes – furious, wind-whipped flakes against the windows – struck him as infinitely beautiful.

(David Guterson, *Snow Falling on Cedars*)

Extract B

Here is an account of a few years in the life of Quoyle, born in Brooklyn and raised in a shuffle of dreary upstate towns.

Hive-spangled, gut roaring with gas and cramp, he survived childhood; at the state university, hand clapped over his chin, he camouflaged torment with smiles and silence. Stumbled through his twenties and into his thirties learning to separate his feelings from his life, counting on nothing. He ate prodigiously, liked a ham knuckle, buttered spuds.

His jobs: distributor of vending machine candy, all-night clerk in a convenience store, a third-rate newspaperman. At thirty-six, bereft, brimming with grief and thwarted love, Quoyle steered away to Newfoundland, the ➡

rock that had generated his ancestors, a place he had never been nor thought to go.

A watery place. And Quoyle feared water, could not swim. Again and again the father had broken his clenched grip and thrown him into pools, brooks, lakes and surf. Quoyle knew the flavor of brack and waterweed.

From this youngest son's failure to dog-paddle the father saw other failures multiply like an explosion of virulent cells – failure to speak clearly, failure to sit up straight; failure to get up in the morning; failure in attitude, failure in ambition and ability; indeed, in everything. His own failure.

Quoyle shambled, a head taller than any child around him, was soft. He knew it. 'Ah, you lout,' said the father. But no pygmy himself. And brother Dick, the father's favorite, pretended to throw up when Quoyle came into a room, hissed 'Lardass, Snotface, Ugly Pig, Warthog, Stupid, Stinkbomb, Fart-tub, Greasebag,' pummeled and kicked until Quoyle curled, hands over head, sniveling, on the linoleum. All stemmed from Quoyle's chief failure, a failure of normal appearance.

A great damp loaf of a body. At six he weighed eighty pounds. At sixteen he was buried under a casement of flesh. Head shaped like a crenshaw, no neck, reddish hair ruched back. Features as bunched as kissed fingertips. Eyes the color of plastic. The monstrous chin, a freakish shelf jutting from the lower face.

Some anomalous gene had fired up at the moment of his begetting as a single spark sometimes leaps from banked coals, had given him a giant's chin. As a child he invented stratagems to deflect stares; a smile, downcast gaze, the right hand darting up to cover the chin.

His earliest sense of self was as a distant figure: there in the foreground was his family, here, at the limit of the far view, was he. Until he was fourteen he cherished the idea that he had been given to the wrong family, that somewhere his real people, saddled with the changeling of the Quoyles, longed for him. Then, foraging in a box of excursion mementoes, he found photographs of his father beside brothers and sisters at a ship's rail. A girl, somewhat apart from the others, looked toward the sea, eyes squinted, as though she could see the port of destination a thousand miles south. Quoyle recognized himself in their hair, their legs and arms. That sly-looking lump in the shrunken sweater, hand at his crotch, his father. On the back, scribbled in blue pencil, 'Leaving Home, 1946.'

At the university he took courses he couldn't understand, humped back and forth without speaking to anyone, went home for weekends of excoriation. At last he dropped out of school and looked for a job, kept his hand over his chin.

Nothing was clear to lonesome Quoyle. His thoughts churned like the amorphous thing that ancient sailors, drifting into arctic half-light, called the Sea Lung, a heaving sludge of ice under fog where air blurred into water, where liquid was solid, where solids dissolved, where the sky froze and light and dark muddled.

(E. Annie Proulx, *The Shipping News*)

ACTIVITY Compare these two passages as openings to narratives. Examine the ways in which the writers use language to create their effects and describe the impact that each has on you, the reader. You should refer closely to the language style and structure of each piece in your response.

We will now look at some of the types of questions that you might encounter in the examination. Of course, you may not have studied the texts used in these examples, but the format of the question will be similar no matter which texts you have studied. Look carefully at the question before reading the student response which follows. Each response has accompanying 'Examiner's comments', which you should consider after you have read each response.

The first question focuses on a comparative study of *Measure for Measure* by William Shakespeare and *Murmuring Judges* by David Hare.

Example 1

Compare the ways in which Shakespeare and Hare present the theme of justice through the language of the play. In your answer you should refer to

❏ lexical choice
❏ metaphorical features
❏ form and structure

Student response

Shakespeare and Hare seem to show the same feelings towards justice and the justice system. This illustrates that the justice system has hardly changed in 400 years. They both believe that justice can be corrupted by people of high status because of power and greed, but in the end justice will prevail; although Hare does leave this last point to the imagination of the audience.

In *Measure for Measure*, Angelo is the one who corrupts the system and the ideals of justice, while in *Murmuring Judges* by David Hare, justice is corrupted by Barry Hopper who is a Detective Constable and mainly by Sir Peter Edgecombe QC who sees the law as a lucrative game. Both Angelo and Sir Peter have very high status within their respective societies.

In *Measure for Measure* Shakespeare uses metaphors when he refers to justice, as when Angelo gives his view on the law:

> . . . We must not make a scarecrow of the law,
> Setting it up to fear the birds of prey,
> And let it keep one shape, till custom underlie it
> Their perch and not their terror . . .

Angelo is claiming that law now fears the criminals and for justice to prevail the law has to become strong again.

Shakespeare also uses imagery when Isabella is trying to show Angelo that he is letting the power that he possesses take over his mind and blur his judgement:

> . . . O, tis excellent
> To have a giant's strength, but it is tyrannous
> To use it like a giant . . .

Isabella is showing Angelo that it is right to enforce the law but he is being too strict in his punishment.

Despite the imagery and metaphors used by Shakespeare in *Measure for Measure*, the vocabulary and syntax that Shakespeare uses when referring to justice are actually quite simple, which is usual for him:

> . . . Condemn the fault, and not the actor of it?
> Why, every fault's condemned ere it be done . . .

Angelo is saying that there is no point in condemning the act but not the criminal, and goes on to say that that would not bring justice:

> . . . Mine were the very cipher of a function,
> To fine the faults whose fine stands on record,
> And let go by the actor . . .

Shakespeare has Angelo make a mockery of justice by making him go against all the things that he has said when he attempts to bribe Isabella, and what makes it worse is that he also lies to her about saving Claudio's life:

> . . . Redeem thy brother
> By yielding up thy body to my will . . .

Here he is going to commit the same crime as Claudio. However, everything in the end is resolved and justice is done by the Duke when he reveals Claudio is still alive. Angelo has to marry Mariana, the fiancée he left when she lost her dowry, and Lucio has to marry the prostitute he has given a child to. Here justice has prevailed and it seems that Shakespeare believes that it always will.

Although Hare does not use metaphors or write in verse, he often uses images when explaining why people are corrupt in the justice system. Barry uses the image that everything is always done by the book in films and the hero is always perfect, but in real life this is not the case. To get justice you have to bend the rules:

> . . . I used to go to the pictures . . . and this bloke'd get up
> and he'd say, 'I don't care what any of you think of me . . . I
> think this is wrong . . .'

Sir Peter's reason for not really caring for his clients is that they are lower than him, they are scum:

> . . . There is a glass screen. And our clients, I'm afraid, live on the one side of it. We on the other . . .

The use of imagery shows that Hare does use some methods like Shakespeare's, but Shakespeare's are usually a little more poetic as Hare's are straight to the point.

The vocabulary that Hare uses is simple like Shakespeare's when he is talking about the theme of justice:

> . . . What you've got is an unsafe prosecution . . .

One thing that Hare uses that Shakespeare does not is questions to introduce a conversation about justice and fairness:

> . . . You mean you're bent?
> You mean those men are innocent? . . .

At the end of Hare's play it seems that justice may run its course, as it did in *Measure for Measure*. However, the audience never actually finds out because the play ends:

> . . . I want the Chief Superintendent. I wonder. Could I have a word? . . .

It seems that Shakespeare and Hare share the same ideal that justice will prevail, but Hare does leave the audience guessing a little.

One ideal that both Shakespeare and Hare have is that it is the women in society who fight for justice. In *Measure for Measure* the Duke is the man who puts everything right, but it is Isabella who pleads with Angelo to spare the life of her brother and tells the Duke about Angelo's proposition:

> . . . I have a brother is condemned to die.
> I do beseech you, let it be his fault
> And not my brother . . .

These were her first words for Angelo and in their second meeting she finds out what Angelo is really like and she says:

> . . . I'll tell the world
> What man thou art . . .

It is easy to see that she is fighting for her brother.

In *Murmuring Judges* it is Irina and Sandra who believe in the true value of justice and who put up a fight against the corruptness in the system. Irina confronts Sir Peter when she finds out about the dodgy arrest involving Gerard:

... The police were on the fiddle ...
... You don't believe him ...
... You don't believe what Gerard says ...

It is Sandra who confronts Barry about his methods of arrest.

... You mean you're bent ...
... Barry you're out of your mind ...
... That doesn't make it right ...

It is also Sandra who goes to see the Chief Superintendent at the end of the play.

Although Shakespeare and Hare have different styles of writing, with Shakespeare writing mainly in verse and having a very poetic style compared to Hare's everyday language written in prose, they do share some same features and ideals when presenting the theme of justice. They both keep their language simple, they both use imagery, and both believe that it is the people of higher status who corrupt justice. There are differences between the two writers but there are also a lot of similarities considering that they wrote their plays in different centuries.

Examiner's comments

- ❏ The student begins the essay in an interesting way, bringing together both texts.
- ❏ The discussion of justice is introduced – again with comments relating to both texts.
- ❏ The student then goes on to discuss *Measure for Measure* in more detail, maintaining focus on the idea of justice.
- ❏ The language of *Murmuring Judges* is compared to that of *Measure for Measure*, again keeping focus on the idea of justice.
- ❏ Links are made between the theme of justice and the role of women in society.
- ❏ This leads to a consideration of the characters of Irina and Sandra.
- ❏ The texts are brought together again in the conclusion of the essay.

Overall this essay packs in a good many relevant points and supports the ideas well. Although there are one or two weaknesses of phrasing or expression, it is a sound essay that addresses the question and keeps focus throughout.

Example 2

Compare and contrast the methods Simon Armitage and Carol Ann Duffy use to write about life experiences in their poetry. Your answer should include a comparative analysis of register, lexis, poetic form and structure, metaphorical and phonological techniques.

Student response

Carol Ann Duffy often uses her own life experiences as subject matter for her poetry. In the poem 'Confession', which is based on her own past experience and takes a sinister look at the interaction that takes place in a confessional box, there are many linguistic features which complement the sentiments expressed by the poet. In this poem, there are no full stops to indicate sentence endings. This gives the accusatory tone of the main speaker's voice a sense of urgency and continuity as he tries, forcefully, to persuade the confessor to 'Come away into this dark cell and tell your sins to a hidden man . . . '. The sinister tone of the poem is further enhanced by the poet's choice of vocabulary. Words such as 'evil', 'damnation', and 'hell' add to the threatening tone of the poem as do the images of 'musty gloom' and 'hidden man'. Duffy often uses similes to express her ideas and these work well in this poem, both to convey the vulnerability of the confessor, 'your white hands clasping each other like Hansel and Gretel in the big black wood', and the disturbing nature of the surroundings, 'It smells in here doesn't it smell like a coffin'. In addition, Duffy's metaphorical depiction of sins being 'little maggoty things that wriggle in the soul . . . ' works as a powerful negative image of the soul being rotten and consumed with guilt and shame, and the adjective 'wee' used to describe the confessor's voice adds to the sense of vulnerability. It is interesting to see how the insignificance and powerlessness felt by the confessor is expressed by Duffy's use of language. The words of the confessor are few and in the form of a prayer, thus enhancing the feeling of powerlessness and, as the words on the page are written in italics, a sense that they are spoken in a quiet voice is achieved. The main speaker's comment that ' . . . you do well to stammer' also adds to the image of the confessor being weak, afraid and submissive.

Like Carol Ann Duffy, Simon Armitage also uses personal life experiences within his poetry. Likewise, he too incorporates the theme of religion in his poems to explore ideas of punishment and guilt. However, in the poem 'Chapter and Verse', as the title suggests, Armitage presents his ideas almost as a factual, historical event. Based on the biblical account of the way soldiers were chosen to fight in battle, this poem is structured as a biblical extract and tells of the punishment received by those who fail to meet expectations or, more importantly, sin because of vanity: ' . . . but moreover for kissing themselves on the lips in the lake. They were all of them guilty and gathered together and thumped'. It is interesting to see how Armitage, through writing in the third person, creates a sense of cold detachment from these apparent injustices. This stands in stark contrast to Duffy's 'Confession' where, as the poem is written as dialogue, a sense of the poet's emotional interaction is conveyed. However, Armitage's cold detachment in this poem also creates a disturbing feel to it and, like 'Confession', a sinister tone is evident. Armitage's use of irony also adds to the sinister, disturbing tone of the poem. Although it is those who bent 'kneeling and lapping the water like dogs' who were punished for admiring their reflections, it is those who were 'taking the water like gods' who made 'such a lasting impression'. It is also interesting to see how Armitage plays with the word 'gods', which he uses to describe those who were 'saved', as he uses the anagram 'dogs' as a derogatory term to describe the 'guilty'. Just as the men were treated according to their physical position by the lake, the physical positioning of the letters determined their status.

Both Duffy and Armitage use past experiences as subject matter for their poetry and both of them express their memories in a similar 'snapshot' fashion. For instance, in Duffy's 'Brothers' we see glimpses of her past being expressed in short phrases: ' . . . a boy playing tennis with a wall', 'a baby crying in the night'. Indeed, the word 'photographs' is mentioned in the poem itself, thus enhancing this idea. Likewise, Armitage in his poem 'White Christmas' includes snippets of memory expressed in a similar way: ' . . . my mother is Marie Curie, in the kitchen discovering radium', 'my two-year-old niece is baby Jesus, passing between us . . . '. Both poets appeared to have captured through language the way in which memories are recalled as short, incomplete images – just as they would have been captured on camera. Coupled with the theme of 'memory' is the theme of 'time' which is included in both 'Brothers' and 'White Christmas', albeit to create differing effects. In 'White Christmas' time appears to pass slowly. The subject of the poem, who ironically has been given a watch as a present, appears to be merely 'filling in' time whilst his wife is away: ' . . . so I walk through the snow . . . at a steady pace'. Indeed, the idea that he has too much time is confirmed in the last few lines: 'I'm the man in the joke, the man in a world of friends where all the clocks are stopped – synchronizing his own watch'. However, in the poem 'Brothers', time, in the form of age, appears to pass quickly. Duffy starts the poem with her brothers being 'men who share an older face' and who, by the second verse, 'shrink to an altar boy, a boy practising scales, a boy playing tennis with a wall, a baby . . . '. In this poem time seems mercilessly rapid in its passing as, at the end of the fourth and final verse, Duffy talks of death: 'One day I shall pay for a box and watch them shoulder it'. Indeed, the sense that we are at the mercy of time is expressed in the line 'but time owns us'.

Examiner's comments

❏ The essay addresses the question directly without any unnecessary and time-wasting preamble.

❏ The response is sensitive to tone.
❏ There is close focus on choice of vocabulary and its effect.
❏ There is clear awareness of the use of metaphorical features and the effects they create in the poems.
❏ Good links are made between the poetry of Duffy and Armitage.
❏ The comparison is integrated – there is a sophisticated structure to the essay.
❏ The response maintains focus throughout.

Overall this is a good response to the question. The student maintains a clear view of the question from beginning to end, and a good many relevant and perceptive points are made. There is also a good deal of analytical comment here.

ACTIVITY Having studied the examples of questions given here, think about the texts you are studying for the comparative Unit. Devise **two** questions, each focusing on different aspects of the texts. When you are satisfied with your questions write an essay in answer to each of them.

How this Unit links to other sections of the course

The table below shows the major links between this Unit and others on the course.

Question	Skills learned	Links to other parts of the Specification

Comparative Literary Studies	Knowledge, understanding and insight gained from combined literary and linguistic study
	
	Using literary and linguistic frameworks to explain features of texts
	
	Making valid and informed comparisons and connections between texts
	
	Becoming aware of the ways contextual variation shapes meaning of texts
		• Poetic Study
		  Unit 2
		• The Language of Prose
		  Unit 3 Section A
		• Dramatic Study
		  Unit 5 Section A

6 Texts and Audience: Dramatic Study

In this chapter you will focus on the ways in which language is used in drama texts and the interrelationship between that language and the effects created on the audience. In looking at the language of drama, both linguistic and literary issues will be examined, and the aim of your studies will be to develop a full understanding of the ways in which dramatists use language in their plays to create a whole range of effects, which in turn provoke responses in the audience.

In the examination for AQA Specification A, the section on Dramatic Study will offer you a choice of six drama texts for study, all published before 1770. The unit is a Closed Book unit, so you will not be allowed to take your texts with you into the examination. You will study one text and in the examination two questions will be set on each text. You will select one question to answer on the text that you have studied.

Whatever text you study and whichever question you choose to answer, the question will require you to use analytical techniques in your answer. You will be tested on your ability to:

❏ identify and assess the ways in which values are communicated to the audience
❏ show understanding of the contexts of the writing of the text and how choices of form, style and vocabulary shape the meaning of texts.

As well as identifying these key objectives, the examination board's specification offers the following advice on the possible form of questions:

❏ candidates will be required to answer on the whole text, analysing theatricality through characters' use of language, presentation of character and development and context of plot
❏ candidates may be required to outline the ways in which issues are raised by dramatists and the attitudes they seek to promote as well as the reactions of the audience.

The nature of drama

Drama is different from other forms of literature that you have studied in a number of respects. One key difference is that by its very nature drama focuses on the spoken word rather than the written word. Sometimes we lose sight of this, because very often in studying drama for examination purposes the focus is on the written text of a play rather than the spoken performance of it. It is important, even when sitting at a desk with only the written text in front of you, that you consider the 'performance' aspect of drama. In many respects a play can be fully appreciated only when seen in performance, and this is why it is so important to try to see a live performance of the play or plays you are studying. If you cannot see the play on the stage, try to get hold of a video or film performance of it. Sometimes it is impossible to see any kind of performance of a play, in which case you will need to rely on your own imagination to re-create a performance of the play inside your head.

Another difference between drama and other literary forms is the fact that drama relies upon certain conventions – it has distinct rules of structure, format and presentation. We will look at these conventions in more detail a little later.

As a drama text presents the core for a 'performance', it is often a more 'public' form of literary communication than other forms. As such, its audience is a particularly important element. When seen live on stage, the experience of a performance is a shared activity and there is a direct relationship between the way the dramatist writes, the way that this is put into performance, and the response of the audience.

If a dramatist's work is to survive, his or her works must be performed, and therefore the expectations of the audience need to be taken into account. Sometimes, when presented with something that doesn't meet their expectations, audiences can make their feelings felt and this can lead the dramatist to make alterations to the text. For example, when *The Rivals* was first performed the audience response to it was so hostile that Sheridan withdrew it after the first night and substantially re-wrote a large proportion of it. Shakespeare often deliberately includes things in his plays that he knows will appeal to and gain the approval of his audience. Although a dramatist does write about and explore themes and ideas that he or she is interested in and wants to present to the audience, no dramatist can afford to lose sight of the audience being written for and the fact that plays must contain some appeal for that audience.

ACTIVITY

Think about a dramatization (stage play, video, film or television) of a novel you have read. Write about the strengths and weaknesses of the dramatization. If you had been the producer, how would you have made your dramatization different?

Now think about plays that you have read and those that you have seen. What do you feel are the main advantages to be gained from:

a seeing a play in performance

b reading a play on your own or as part of a group?

Features of drama

Conflict

At the centre of all drama is a sense of conflict, in one form or another. This could consist of conflict in the conventional sense such as in *Henry IV Part 1* where Henry faces rebellion and battles ensue. Equally, conflict could be between individual characters and their ideals or values. The conflict could stem from within a character, perhaps torn between certain courses of action, or it could be spiritual or moral in nature. Whatever form it takes, this conflict will be ever present throughout the play and form the basis for sustaining the dramatic tension and the interest of the audience.

Of course this is explored and exploited in different ways by different dramatists. In *Othello*, for example, we see the emotional conflicts set up within Othello himself by Iago sowing the seeds of jealousy in his mind. A more subtle use of conflict can be found in the comedy *Much Ado About Nothing*, in the opposition between Beatrice and Benedick. In a more modern drama such as *Murmuring Judges*, conflicts operate in different ways. We have the conflict of views of the role of the barrister as represented by the attitudes of Irina and Sir Peter, or the conflict of views on the right way of policing as seen through the characters of Sandra and Barry, for example.

ACTIVITY Think about any plays that you have studied in the past or are currently studying. Draw up a table for each of them showing what conflicts occur within each drama and how important each is to the overall effects of the play.

Realism

The question of realism is one that is often raised in relation to drama, and it has provoked much debate. One view of realism in drama is that put forward by the poet and philosopher Samuel Taylor Coleridge, who felt that in watching a play the audience are prepared to 'willingly suspend disbelief' and believe in the reality of the characters and the action they see before them on the stage. Some drama does work like this, and in the 1950s a whole style of drama, including plays such as *Look Back in Anger* by John Osborne, became known as 'Kitchen Sink Dramas' because of their portrayals of 'real life' in the colloquial language of everyday speech.

It's quite clear, though, that not all drama sets out to be 'realistic' in that sense and some dramatists deliberately set out to present a different picture from the world we know. In Shakespeare's *The Winter's Tale*, for example, there are features such as a statue apparently coming to life, and in *The Tempest* Prospero deals in magic, and spirits of the air do his bidding. In the plays of Beckett all kinds of strange things happen, such as in *Endgame* where the characters live in dustbins.

In reconciling these apparent opposites we come to the understanding that there are two kinds of realism – one is the surface or physical realism where the characters, the things they say and do, the language they use and so on are immediately recognizable as representing 'real life'. The other kind of realism is psychological realism, in which the dramatist focuses on the feelings, thoughts, emotions, fears, inner desires and life of the characters. Both kinds of drama, or varying degrees of each, are open to the dramatist depending on the effect and appeal to the audience he or she wishes to create.

The theatre

One final consideration when studying a play, as opposed to other kinds of literature, is the fact that, as we have said, a play is meant to be seen on the stage. The dramatist will have given thought to the mechanics of performing the play in the theatre. Some dramatists give little guidance in this respect, while others give detailed stage directions to do with things like the set and lighting. These features are integral to the play and are generally designed to enhance the performance, the visual effect or the impact of the spoken language of the play. The spoken language of the play is still the heart of the drama but you need to be aware of how it interrelates with the other elements of drama that bring language to life.

Plot and structure

The plot is obviously of central importance to most plays, although there are certain kinds of plays (those of Samuel Beckett for example) where the lack of a conventional plot is essential for the overall effect of the drama. However, in the drama written before 1770 that you will study, you will find plot is a key element. The plot, however, is much more than simply the 'story' of the play. The way plot develops is an essential part of the way a play is put together – in other words, with its structure. From a dramatist's point of view this structure is something that needs careful thought and planning, because ultimately it can have a bearing on whether the play is a successful one or not.

ACTIVITY From an audience's point of view, what features do you think a successful play should have in terms of plot?

Here are some points you might have thought about. An effective plot should:

❏ maintain the interest of the audience from beginning to end
❏ move the action on from one episode to the next
❏ arouse the interest of the audience in character and situation
❏ create high points or moments of crisis at intervals
❏ create expectation and surprise.

Generally speaking, if a play contains most or all of these features then it is likely to be well received by an audience.

In studying plays you will see that most of them follow a particular pattern in the way that they are structured, and it is possible to identify the following key elements.

1 **Exposition:** this opens the play, often introduces the main characters and provides background information.

2 **Dramatic incitement:** this is an incident that provides the starting point for the main action of the play.

3 **Complication:** this usually forms the main action of the play – the characters respond to the dramatic incitement and other developments that stem from it.

4 **Crisis:** this constitutes the climax of the play.

5 **Resolution:** this is the final section of the play, where things are worked out and some kind of conclusion is arrived at.

ACTIVITY | Examine the structure of the play that you are studying. Draw a diagram to represent the way the action of the play develops and the way it fits into this pattern. Make a note of the 'key moments' of the development of the plot.

This is how the above pattern applies to Shakespeare's *As You Like It*.

1 **Exposition:** The play begins with the audience being given the information that a good duke has been usurped by his ruthless brother, Frederick, and has taken to the forest with a few faithful courtiers. There they live simply but happily. Rosalind, the good duke's daughter, has stayed behind at court to be with her friend and cousin, Celia, who is Frederick's daughter.

2 **Dramatic incitement:** Rosalind displeases Frederick, who banishes her from court.

3 **Complication:** Rosalind disguises herself as a boy and leaves to search for her father, taking with her Celia and the Court jester, Touchstone. Another character, Orlando, leaves to seek his brother, Oliver, who has

withheld his inheritance and treats him cruelly. Various complications ensue.

4 **Crisis:** Rosalind realizes she must find a way to reveal her true self to Orlando.

5 **Resolution:** All the exiles meet together and the love affairs are happily resolved. Duke Frederick resigns his usurped kingdom and everyone gets what is rightfully theirs.

The language of drama

The type of language used in a play – formal, serious, colloquial, slang, and so on – will depend on the kind of effects that the dramatist wants to achieve, and the functions language is to perform. For example, we can learn about characters through their language, or language can add colour to a scene, create atmosphere, and alter the tone and mood of a play.

Dialogue

The most obvious way in which dramatists use language in their plays is in dialogue, through which the characters convey information and interact with each other. There are dialogues of all kinds in plays and the language the dramatist uses will be chosen carefully to reflect the tone, atmosphere and content of the particular scene. Dialogue is a verbal exchange between two or more characters but it can take many forms – for example, it could present the tender exchange of love between two characters, it could involve characters plotting an evil deed together or it could be an argument.

Read the following extracts carefully. Extract 1 is from *The Recruiting Officer* by George Farquhar. Captain Plume talks to Sergeant Kite about the recruitment of men for the army.

Extract 1

Plume	By the Grenadier March that should be my drum, and by that shout it should beat with success – let me see – (*looks on his watch*) – four o'clock – at ten yesterday morning I left London – a hundred and twenty miles in thirty hours is Pretty smart riding, but nothing to the fatigue of recruiting.
	Enter **Kite**
Kite	Welcome to Shrewsbury, noble Captain: from the banks of the Danube to the Severn side, noble Captain, you're welcome.
Plume	A very elegant reception indeed, Mr Kite. I find you are fairly entered into your recruiting strain – pray, what success?

➡

Kite	I have been here but a week and I have recruited five.
Plume	Five! Pray, what are they?
Kite	I have listed the strong man of Kent, the king of the gypsies, a Scotch pedlar, a scoundrel attorney, and a Welsh parson.
Plume	An attorney! Wert thou mad? List a lawyer! Discharge him, discharge him this minute.
Kite	Why, sir?
Plume	Because I will have nobody in my company that can write; a fellow that can write, can draw petitions – I say, this minute discharge him.
Kite	And what shall I do with the parson?
Plume	Can he write?
Kite	Umh – he plays rarely upon the fiddle.
Plume	Keep him by all means. But how stands the country affected? Were the people pleased with the news of my coming to town?
Kite	Sir, the mob are so pleased with your honour, and the justices and better sort of people are so delighted with me, that we shall soon do our business. But, sir, you have got a recruit here that you little think of.
Plume	Who?
Kite	One that you beat up for last time you were in the country: You remember your old friend Molly at the Castle?
Plume	She's not with child, I hope.
Kite	No, no, sir: she was brought to bed yesterday.
Plume	Kite, you must father the child.
Kite	Humph – and so her friends will oblige me to marry the mother.

Extract 2 is from *King Lear*. Lear has given everything to his daughters and in return wants to retain a hundred knights for himself. However, his daughters Goneril and Regan are not satisfied with this arrangement.

Extract 2

Lear	I can be patient. I can stay with Regan. I and my hundred knights.
Regan	Not altogether so. I looked not for you yet, nor am provided For your fit welcome. Give ear, sir, to my sister, For those that mingle reason with your passion Must be content to think you old, and so But she knows what she does.
Lear	Is this well spoken?
Regan	I dare avouch it, sir. What, fifty followers? Is it not well? What should you need of more? Yea, or so many, sith that both charge and danger Speak 'gainst so great a number? How in one house

➡

	Should many people under two commands
	Hold amity? 'Tis hard, almost impossible.
Goneril	Why might not you, my lord, receive attendance
	From those that she calls servants, or from mine?
Regan	Why not, my lord? If then they chanced to slack ye,
	We could control them. If you will come to me
	(For now I spy a danger) I entreat you
	To bring but five and twenty, to no more
	Will I give place or notice.
Lear	I gave you all.
Regan	And in good time you gave it.
Lear	Made you my guardians, my depositaries.
	But kept a reservation to be followed
	With such a number. What, must I come to you
	With five and twenty? Regan, said you so?
Regan	And speak 't again, my lord. No more with me.
Lear	Those wicked creatures yet do look well-favoured
	When others are more wicked. Not being the worst
	Stands in some rank of praise. [*To Goneril*] I'll go with
	thee;
	Thy fifty yet doth double five and twenty,
	And thou art twice her love.
Goneril	Hear me, my lord:
	What need you five and twenty? Ten? Or five?
	To follow in a house where twice so many
	Have a command to tend you?
Regan	What need one?

Extract 3 is taken from *A Midsummer Night's Dream*, and in it Hermia and Lysander regret the difficulties and brevity of love.

Extract 3

Lysander	How now, my love? Why is your cheek so pale?
	How chance the roses there do fade so fast?
Hermia	Belike for want of rain, which I could well
	Between them from the tempest of my eyes.
Lysander	Ay me! For aught that I could ever read,
	Could ever hear by tale or history,
	The course of true love never did run smooth;
	But either it was different in blood
Hermia	O cross! Too high to be enthralled to low.
Lysander	Or else misgraffed in respect of years
Hermia	O spite! Too old to be engaged to young.
Lysander	Or else it stood upon the choice of friends
Hermia	O hell, to choose love by another's eyes!

➡

Lysander   Or, if there were a sympathy in choice,
War, death, or sickness did lay siege to it,
Making it momentany as a sound,
Swift as a shadow, short as any dream,
Brief as the lightning in the collied night,
That in a spleen unfolds both heaven and earth,
And, ere a man hath power to say 'Behold',
The jaws of darkness do devour it up.
So quick bright things come to confusion.

ACTIVITY   Examine each of these examples of dialogue and compare the ways in which language is used in each one, bearing in mind the following features:

- ❏ the lexis
- ❏ the tone created
- ❏ metaphorical and rhetorical features
- ❏ the overall effects created.

Here are some features you might have noted:

Extract 1   This exchange between the Sergeant and his officer is direct and the short-question-and-response format appears naturalistic, but it is carefully contrived to provide the audience with information. The language contains the mannered formality typical of Restoration drama.

Extract 2   Notice how this is a three-way dialogue and Goneril and Regan work together against their father. Their language is very supportive of each other, and although they are superficially respectful to their father, using terms like 'My Lord' and 'Sir', these words are full of insincerity. Lear's language contains an element of hopelessness as he looks from one to the other of his daughters for support, but does not find it.

Extract 3   This piece of dialogue has often been likened to a duet, where each speaker's words pick up on and complement the other's. Notice the formality of the phrasing, the rhythmical nature of the verse, and the rhetorical effect of the language.

ACTIVITY   From the play you are studying, pick three examples where the dramatist uses dialogue in different ways to create different effects. Analyse closely the language use in each example.

Presenting character

A key element in the overall effectiveness of a play is the extent to which the dramatist is successful in creating interesting and convincing characters.

Although characters on the stage can be revealed through what they do, language has a key role to play in developing our perceptions of them. Sometimes dramatists make use of stage directions to tell us how they intend a character to appear to the audience. Of course, when watching a play on stage you will be seeing these directions translated into actions, rather than reading them.

Some dramatists, Shakespeare included, tend to provide little information of this type, however. They rely on other methods of revealing characters to the audience. These methods include:

- ❏ what characters say
- ❏ how characters speak
- ❏ how characters are described by others and what is said about them.

Characters in plays usually have distinctive voices, which the dramatist creates in order to shape the kind of response he or she wants from the audience. In simple terms this can present a single dimension of a character. For example, read the following extract from *Romeo and Juliet*, which shows the character of Tybalt:

Extract 4

Romeo	O she doth teach the torches to burn bright.
	It seems she hangs upon the cheek of night
	Like a rich jewel in an Ethiop's ear;
	Beauty too rich for use, for earth too dear.
	So shows a snowy dove trooping with crows,
	As yonder lady o'er her fellows shows.
	The measure done, I'll watch her place of stand,
	And touching hers make blessed my rude hand.
	Did my heart love till now? Forswear it sight,
	For I ne'er saw true beauty till this night.
Tybalt	This by his voice should be a Montague.
	Fetch me my rapier, boy. What dares the slave
	Come hither, covered with an antic face,
	To fleer and scorn at our solemnity?
	Now by the stock and honour of my kin,
	To strike him dead I hold it not a sin.
Capulet	Why how now kinsman, wherefore storm you so?
Tybalt	Uncle, this is a Montague, our foe;
	A villain that is hither come in spite,
	To scorn at our solemnity this night.
Capulet	Young Romeo is it?
Tybalt	'Tis he, that villain Romeo.
Capulet	Content thee gentle coz, let him alone.
	'A bears him like a portly gentleman;

➡

And to say truth, Verona brags of him
To be a virtuous and well-governed youth.
I would not for the wealth of all this town
Here in my house do him disparagement.
Therefore be patient, take no note of him;
It is my will, the which if thou respect,
Show a fair presence, and put off these frowns,
An ill-beseeming semblance for a feast.

Tybalt   It fits when such a villain is a guest.
I'll not endure him.

Capulet   He shall be endured.

ACTIVITY Examine how Shakespeare uses language here to give an impression of the character of Tybalt. What kind of impression of him do you get?

Tybalt's distinctive voice is belligerent and aggressive, and it is the only aspect of his character that is revealed in the play. Most major characters in drama, however, have different sides to their personalities and behave in different ways in different situations. In *King Lear*, for example, the changes that come about in Lear's personality are reflected in his language as he changes from commanding king to bitter father, to helpless old man, to one who has found salvation. Look carefully at these four extracts:

Extract 5

Gloucester   My Lord of Kent: remember him hereafter as my honourable friend.

Edmund   My services to your Lordship.

Kent   I must love you, and sue to know you better.

Edmund   Sir, I shall study deserving.

Gloucester   He hath been out nine years, and away he shall again. The King is coming.

Sennet. Enter one bearing a coronet, **King Lear,**
Cornwall, Albany, Goneril, Regan, Cordelia,
and Attendants

Lear   Attend the Lords of France and Burgundy,
Gloucester.

Gloucester   I shall, my Liege.

Lear   Meantime, we shall express our darker purpose.
Give me the map there. Know that we have divided
In three our kingdom; and 'tis our fast intent
To shake all cares and business from our age,
Conferring them on younger strengths, while we

➡

Unburthened crawl toward death. Our son of
  Cornwall,
And you, our no less loving son of Albany,
We have this hour a constant will to publish
Our daughters' several dowers, that future strife
May be prevented now. The Princes, France and
  Burgundy,
Great rivals in our youngest daughter's love,
Long in our court have made their amorous
  sojourn,
And here are to be answered.

Extract 6

Albany	What's the matter, Sir?
Lear	I'll tell thee. [*To* **Goneril**] Life and death! I am ashamed

That thou hast power to shake my manhood thus,
That these hot tears, which break from me
  perforce,
Should make thee worth them. Blasts and fogs
  upon thee!
Th'untented woundings of a father's curse
Pierce every sense about thee! Old fond eyes,
Beweep this cause again, I'll pluck ye out,
And cast you, with the waters that you loose,
To temper clay. Yea, is't come to this?
Ha! Let it be so: I have another daughter,
Who, I am sure, is kind and comfortable:
When she shall hear this of thee, with her nails
She'll flay thy wolvish visage. Thou shalt find
That I'll resume the shape which thou dost think
I have cast off for ever.   [*Exit*

Extract 7

Goneril	Hear me, my Lord.

What need you five-and-twenty, ten, or five,
To follow in a house where twice so many
Have a command to tend you?

Regan	What need one?
Lear	O! reason not the need; our basest beggars

Are in the poorest thing superfluous:
Allow not nature more than nature needs,
Man's life is cheap as beast's. Thou art a lady;
If only to go warm were gorgeous,
Why, nature needs not what thou gorgeous wear'st,

➡

Which scarcely keeps thee warm. But, for true
   need, –
You heavens, give me that patience, patience
   I need! –
You see me here, you Gods, a poor old man,
As full of grief as age; wretched in both!
If it be you that stirs these daughters' hearts
Against their father, fool me not so much
To bear it tamely; touch me with noble anger,
And let not women's weapons, water-drops,
Stain my man's cheeks! No, you unnatural hags,
I will have such revenges on you both
That all the world shall – I will do such things,
What they are, yet I know not, but they shall be
The terrors of the earth. You think I'll weep;
No, I'll not weep:
I have full cause of weeping, [*Storm heard at a
   distance*] but this heart
Shall break into a hundred thousand flaws
Or ere I'll weep. O Fool! I shall go mad.

Extract 8

Lear   Come, let's away to prison;
We two alone will sing like birds i'th'cage:
When thou dost ask me blessing, I'll kneel
   down,
And ask of thee forgiveness: so we'll live,
And pray, and sing, and tell old tales, and laugh
At gilded butterflies, and hear poor rogues
Talk of court news; and we'll talk with them too,
Who loses and who wins; who's in, who's out;
And take upon's the mystery of things,
As if we were God's spies: and we'll wear out,
In a walled prison, packs and sects of great ones
That ebb and flow by th'moon.

ACTIVITY

Examine Lear's language in each of the four extracts focusing on the
following aspects of each:

❏ the lexis
❏ the way the language reflects Lear's mood and state of mind
❏ what impression you get of Lear.

As you think about these points, look out for particular features of language
– are there any key words or phrases? Is imagery used? If so, what is its
effect? What about the rhythm and syntax of the speech – does it flow
smoothly, or is it disjointed?

Here is how one student responded to these four extracts.

In this first speech Shakespeare has created Lear to act with total responsibility and freedom. He speaks with utter confidence that evokes admiration of his character. Lear acts imperiously and savours the patriarchal performance. He enters in full panoply of power which seems to be an abdication ritual. Lear is boasting to the court his daughters' loyalty, it is an attempt to show off and Goneril and Regan play along with his plans.

In this speech Lear uses the royal plural as is appropriate. Lear is the medieval sovereign with two bodies, one personal and one belonging to the role and he proposes to divide them. In lines 39–44 Lear introduces the motives behind the formal court meeting, but his words have an ironic twist as his actions are more likely to create strife rather than stop it. Also Lear claims there is also a 'darker purpose', another plan other than the division of the kingdom. This is of course to arrange a marriage for Cordelia. This speech marks the beginning of Lear's identity being stripped away especially with the use of phrases like 'divest us'.

In Act I Scene 4, Lear's parting words to Goneril highlight the situation he has found himself in and reveal more of his character. This marks the point where Lear realizes he is losing control. Although Goneril does not, Lear still sees himself as being the king: 'I'll resume the shape . . . '

Again there is irony in this speech because Lear is made to describe Regan attacking Goneril in the manner of one wolf attacking another: 'with her nails she'll flay thy wolvish visage'.

Goneril's actions cause Lear to cry and it shames him to do so, and he sees himself as being foolish. To Lear crying is seen as a female weapon and it contradicts his masculinity. As the play progresses it becomes clear that Lear's masculinity is important to him. Hunting and being with his knights are all values associated with manliness and so in Act II rather than cry at his daughters' mistreatment he goes off into a rage. Lear claims to rather break into thousands of pieces than cry. It is here that Lear for the first time describes age as being wretched.

In this speech Lear makes reference to need and nature and the idea of identity, these all being key ideas in sanity. Lear asks for patience but immediately he moves to anger and revenge, the opposite of patience. This marks the onset of Lear's madness and he makes reference to nature and beasts. He compares man's life to that of a beast without luxuries.

Throughout the play Lear makes reference to nature and animals but more so when in a rage. Lear's identity has been stripped away which leads to his madness but when at the end of the play Lear is reunited with Cordelia his redemption is complete. He recognizes the important things in life. His mind has been healed through Cordelia's love. Lear also comes to terms with his own femininity, which he has been at odds with throughout the play. In Lear's final speech to Cordelia he hastens to reassure her and his tone is that of a father comforting a distraught and frightened child. Lear insulates himself from reality. His vision is self-centred and pathetic but also shows a renunciation of power. This final speech is ironic because Cordelia alone exists for Lear and yet at the beginning he banished her from his sight.

Throughout all the speeches Lear makes there are ironies, references to nature and animals and continuous switches between verse and prose. Verse is usually used for the important speeches as in the beginning, but the use of prose seems to show the onset of madness that is sinking in.

Amrit

Examiner's comments

The student begins by going straight to the point, focusing on the regal nature of Lear. True, the opening sentence is not phrased as effectively as it might be, but the student makes some perceptive points to do with Lear's confidence and the admiration that he inspires in others, and she sums up his attitude very well in writing that he ' . . . acts imperiously and savours the patriarchal performance.'

The 'Royal We' is picked up on, and the issue of the public versus private man is perceived. The student also detects the motives behind the formality of the court meeting – the formal swearing of allegiance and the arranged marriage of Cordelia. Notice the very perceptive point made that the speech marks the beginning of the process of Lear's identity being stripped away, through the use of phrases like 'divest us'.

The student continues to explore ways in which the language reveals to us Lear's character and traces his loss of control, and comments on the irony of Lear's words. More perceptive points are made relating to Lear and his preoccupation with his masculinity. There is an interesting pick-up on the references to 'age' and being 'wretched' too. Reference is also made here to key images relating to nature and identity, and the significance of these images in terms of the changes taking place in Lear's character.

The effects on Lear of his experiences are well observed in the final stages of the essay. The way the language reflects the healing that has taken place is observed, and the essay finishes with a brief summary drawing its ideas together.

ACTIVITY   Now think about the play you are studying. Choose one of the main characters and find three speeches he or she makes in the play where language is used differently in each one. Analyse the ways in which language is used in each speech, and describe the effects created.

Soliloquies

The soliloquy is another way that the dramatist can develop character through the language of the play. The soliloquy is a speech that a character delivers when alone on the stage. Through this device the dramatist has much scope for allowing characters to express their thoughts and feelings aloud, and therefore to let the audience know what is going on in their minds. It is often used to allow characters to reveal their true feelings, plans or motives.

The Revenger's Tragedy by Cyril Tourneur opens with the protagonist, Vindice, revealing his thoughts on some of the other characters and on his own circumstances.

Extract 9

Vindice   Duke: royal lecher: go, grey haired Adultery,
And thou his son, as impious steeped as he:
And thou his bastard true-begot in evil:
And thou his duchess that will do with devil:
Four ex'lent characters! – Oh that marrowless age
Would stuff the hollow bones with damned desires,
And 'stead of heat kindle infernal fires
Within the spendthrift veins of a dry duke,
A parched and juiceless luxur. Oh God! One
That has scarce blood enough to live upon,
And he to riot it like a son and heir?
Oh the thought of that
Turns my abusèd heart-strings into fret.
Though sallow picture of my poisoned love,
My study's ornament, thou shell of Death,
Once the bright face of my betrothed lady,
When life and beauty naturally filed out
These ragged imperfections;
When two heaven-pointed diamonds were set
In those unsightly rings – then 'twas a face
So far beyond the artificial shine
Of any woman's bought complexion
That the uprightest man – if such there be,
That sin but seven times a day – broke custom
And made up eight with looking after her.

Oh she was able to ha' made a usurer's son
Melt all his patrimony in a kiss,
And what his father fifty years told
To have consumed, and yet his suit been cold:
But oh accursed palace!
Thee when thou wert apparelled in thy flesh,
The old duke poisoned,
Because thy purer part would not consent
Unto his palsey-lust; for old men lustful
Do show like young men angry-eager, violent,
Out-bid like their limited performances –
Oh 'ware an old man hot and vicious:
'Age as in gold, in lust is covetous'.

ACTIVITY

Look carefully at this soliloquy.
What do you learn from it about:

a the character of Vindice

b his view of other characters?

Think about the tone of the soliloquy. Do you detect any shifts of tone here?

Now think about the play that you are studying. Make a list of each soliloquy in the play and for each one note down the following details:

a who is speaking

b the context of the soliloquy

c what is being said

d why the dramatist uses a soliloquy at that point in the drama.

Asides

Asides are also used to reveal character and motivation. The 'aside' is a kind of 'stage whisper', or behind-the-hand comment. Sometimes it is directed to another character but often it is aimed at the audience or the character is apparently speaking to himself or herself. For example, in *The Revenger's Tragedy* it leaves us with an uneasy feeling when Vindice uses the aside when speaking to his mother.

Extract 10

Vindice   Mother I must take leave of you.
Gratiana   Leave for what?
Vindice   I intend speedy travel.   ➡

Hippolito   That he does madam.

Gratiana   Speedy indeed!

Vindice   For since my worthy father's funeral,
My life's unnatural to me, e'en compelled,
As if I lived now when I should be dead.

Gratiana   Indeed he was a worthy gentleman
Had his estate been fellow to his mind.

Vindice   The duke did much deject him.

Gratiana   Much?

Vindice   Too much.
And through disgrace oft smothered in his spirit
When it would mount. Surely I think he died
Of discontent, the nobleman's consumption.

Gratiana   Most sure he did.

Vindice   Did he? 'Lack, – you know all,
You were his midnight secretary.

Gratiana   No,
He was too wise to trust me with his thoughts.

Vindice   [*Aside*] I' faith then father thou wast wise indeed,
'Wives are but made to go to bed and feed'. –
Come mother, sister; you'll bring me onward, brother?

Hippolito   I will.

Vindice   [*Aside*] I'll quickly turn into another.   *Exeunt*

ACTIVITY   In the drama text you are studying, find three or four examples of the use of the aside.

In each case:

a Who is speaking?

b What is being said?

c What is the purpose of the aside?

Creating atmosphere

The theatres in which pre-1770 plays were first performed obviously did not have the sophisticated technology and elaborate sets that are available to the modern dramatist. Much of the creation of scene, atmosphere and mood was done through the language of the play. In Elizabethan times, for example, the plays were performed in daylight with no sets and so all effects were created in the imagination of the audience, through the words of the play.

Shakespeare's plays were originally performed in daylight, as they are today in the recreated Globe Theatre in London's Bankside

Look at the following example from *King Lear*, where Lear is without shelter on the heath at the height of a terrible storm. Read it carefully.

Extract 11

Another part of the heath. Storm still

Enter **Lear** *and* **Fool**

Lear   Blow, winds, and crack your cheeks! Rage! Blow!
You cataracts and hurricanoes, spout
Till you have drenched our steeples, drowned the
  cocks!
You sulph'rous and thought-executing fires,
Vaunt-couriers of oak-cleaving thunderbolts,
Singe my white head! And thou, all-shaking
  thunder,
Strike flat the thick rotundity o'th'world!
Crack Nature's moulds, all germens spill at once
That makes ingrateful man!

Fool   O Nuncle, court holy-water in a dry house is
better than this rain-water out o'door. Good
Nuncle, in, ask thy daughters' blessing; here's a
night pities neither wise men nor Fools.

Lear   Rumble thy bellyful! Spit, fire! Spout, rain!
Nor rain, wind, thunder, fire, are my daughters:
I tax you not, you elements, with unkindness;
I never gave you kingdom, called you children,
You owe me no subscription: then let fall
Your horrible pleasure; here I stand, your slave,
A poor, infirm, weak, and despised old man.
But yet I call you servile ministers,
That will with two pernicious daughters join
Your high-engendered battles 'gainst a head
So old and white as this. O, ho! 'tis foul.

ACTIVITY Analyse the ways in which Shakespeare's language here creates an impression of a storm. How does the atmosphere created relate to Lear's state of mind?

Here are some things you might have thought about:

❑ The lexis creates a vivid impression of the violence of the storm – 'Blow', 'crack', 'range', 'cataracts', 'hurricanoes', 'oak-cleaving thunderbolts' all build to create a sense of the violence of the storm.

❑ The sentences are structured using lists of nouns or verbs, 'spit, fire; spout, rain', 'rain, wind, thunder, fire'. This builds up a strong physical image of the violence of the storm.

❑ Lear places himself at the forefront of the storm, and its rage is reflected in that rage Lear feels within himself.

❑ Lear's commands help to create the atmosphere of the scene.

ACTIVITY Select two contrasting passages from the play you are studying and examine the ways in which language is used to create a sense of atmosphere and mood.

Remember to use specific examples from each passage to illustrate your comments.

Opening scenes

We have already seen that plays usually begin with some kind of exposition, which sets the scene and gives the audience information. This can be important in order for them to understand what is going on, or to inform them of events that happened before the play starts. As we have also seen, one way of doing this is to start the play with a soliloquy in which a character gives the audience information indirectly, and another way is for information to be disclosed through conversation between two or more characters. Very often the seeds of the later action are sown in the opening scene.

However dramatists choose to begin their plays, it is vital that the drama captures the interest and imagination of the audience from the start. The central conflict must be introduced quickly, and the audience must become eager to know what happens next. In creating this atmosphere of expectancy and anticipation, the dramatist's use of language is central.

Look at the following opening scenes.

Extract 12   *Hamlet*

> *Elsinore*
>
> *Enter* **Barnardo** *and* **Francisco**, *two sentinels*

Barnardo Who's there?   ➡

Francisco	Nay, answer me. Stand and unfold yourself.
Barnardo	Long live the King!
Francisco	Barnardo?
Barnardo	He.
Francisco	You come most carefully upon your hour.
Barnardo	'Tis now struck twelve, get thee to bed Francisco.
Francisco	For this relief much thanks, 'tis bitter cold,
	And I am sick at heart.
Barnardo	Have you had quiet guard?
Francisco	Not a mouse stirring.
Barnardo	Well, good night.
	If you do meet Horatio and Marcellus,
	The rivals of my watch, bid them make haste.

Enter **Horatio** *and* **Marcellus**

Francisco	I think I hear them. Stand ho, who is there?
Horatio	Friends to this ground.
Marcellus	And liegemen to the Dane.
Francisco	Give you good night.
Marcellus	O, farewell honest soldier.
	Who hath relieved you?
Francisco	Barnardo has my place.
	Give you good night. [*Exit*
Marcellus	Holla, Barnardo!
Barnardo	Say,
	What, is Horatio there?
Horatio	A piece of him.
Barnardo	Welcome Horatio, welcome good Marcellus.
Horatio	What, has this thing appeared again tonight?
Barnardo	I have seen nothing.
Marcellus	Horatio says 'tis but our fantasy,
	And will not let belief take hold of him
	Touching this dreaded sight twice seen of us.
	Therefore I have entreated him along,
	With us to watch the minutes of this night,
	That if again this apparition come,
	He may approve our eyes and speak to it.
Horatio	Tush, tush, 'twill not appear.
Barnardo	Sit down awhile,
	And let us once again assail your ears,
	That are so fortified against our story,
	What we have two nights seen.
Horatio	Well, sit we down,
	And let us hear Barnardo speak of this.
Barnardo	Last night of all,
	When yond same star that's westward from the
	pole

➡

Had made his course t'illume that part of
  heaven
Where now it burns, Marcellus and myself,
The bell then beating one –

Enter **Ghost**

Marcellus   Peace, break thee off. Look where it comes
  again!
Barnardo   In the same figure like the King that's dead.
Marcellus   Thou art a scholar, speak to it Horatio.

Extract 13   *The Way of the World*

A Chocolate-house.

Mirabell *and* **Fainall**, *rising from cards;* Betty *waiting.*

Mirabell   You are a fortunate man, Mr Fainall.
Fainall   Have we done?
Mirabell   What you please. I'll play on to entertain you.
Fainall   No, I'll give you your revenge another time, when you are
  not so indifferent; you are thinking of something else now,
  and play too negligently. The coldness of a losing gamester
  lessens the pleasure of the winner. I'd no more play with a
  man that slighted his ill fortune than I'd make love to a
  woman who undervalued the loss of her reputation.
Mirabell   You have a taste extremely delicate and are for refining on
  your pleasures.
Fainall   Prithee, why so reserved? Something has put you out of
  humour.
Mirabell   Not at all; I happen to be grave today, and you are gay;
  that's all.
Fainall   Confess, Millamant and you quarrelled last night, after I
  left you; my fair cousin has some humours that would tempt
  the patience of a stoic. What, some coxcomb came in, and
  was well received by her, while you were by.
Mirabell   Witwoud and Petulant, and what was worse, her aunt, your
  wife's mother, my evil genius; or to sum up all in her own
  name, my old Lady Wishfort came in.
Fainall   Oh, there it is then! She has a lasting passion for you, and
  with reason. What, then my wife was there?
Mirabell   Yes, and Mrs Marwood and three or four more, whom I
  never saw before. Seeing me, they all put on their grave
  faces, whispered one another; then complained aloud of the
  vapours, and after fell into a profound silence.
Fainall   They had a mind to be rid of you.
Mirabell   For which reason I resolved not to stir. At last the good old
  lady broke through her painful taciturnity, with an invective   ➡

against long visits. I would not have understood her, but Millamant joining in the argument, I rose and with a constrained smile told her, I thought nothing was so easy as to know when a visit began to be troublesome. She reddened and I withdrew, without expecting her reply.

Fainall   You were to blame to resent what she spoke only in compliance with her aunt.

Mirabell   She is more mistress of herself than to be under the necessity of such a resignation.

Fainall   What? though half her fortune depends upon her marrying with my lady's approbation?

Mirabell   I was then in such a humour, that I should have been better pleased if she had been less discreet.

Fainall   Now I remember, I wonder not they were weary of you. Last night was one of their cabal-nights; they have 'em three times a week, and meet by turns, at one another's apartments, where they come together like the coroner's inquest, to sit upon the murdered reputations of the week. You and I are excluded; and it was once proposed that all the male sex should be excepted; but somebody moved that, to avoid scandal, there might be one man of the community; upon which motion Witwould and Petulant were enrolled members.

Mirabell   And who may have been the foundress of this sect? My Lady Wishfort, I warrant, who publishes her detestation of mankind, and full of the vigor of fifty-five, declares for a friend and ratafia; and let posterity shift for itself, she'll breed no more.

Fainall   The discovery of your sham address to her, to conceal your love to her niece, has provoked this separation. Had you dissembled better, things might have continued in the state of nature.

ACTIVITY   Compare the ways in which the dramatists open their plays in these extracts. What information do you learn from each, and what effect do you think each would have on the audience?

Here are some ideas about these opening scenes.

One of the important elements in the opening of *Hamlet* is the atmosphere that is created. It is midnight, bitterly cold and we are on the battlements of a castle. The guards are clearly on edge, expecting something to happen. Horatio and Marcellus arrive and we learn that for the past two nights a ghost has appeared. Horatio has dismissed this as imagination, but he has come to see for himself. Tension mounts as the ghost appears – it looks just like the king who recently died.

If you can imagine being in a theatre, you will see that this is an effective opening. The atmosphere of fear and tension would immediately capture the interest of the audience, and when the ghost appears the audience learns about the dead king.

The seeds of the whole drama are sown here, as the appearance of Hamlet's father's ghost begins the train of events that eventually lead to the tragic conclusion of the play.

In *The Way of the World*, Congreve begins with a conversation between two of the central characters in the play, the hero Mirabell and the scheming Fainall. Those two are therefore set up in opposition right from the start.

We also gain a good deal of information as to what is going on from the dialogue. A number of other key characters are mentioned and we learn about Mirabell's relations with them. We also learn something about how these people spend their time – Mirabell and Fainall have been playing cards in a chocolate house, and there are frequent social gatherings in the evenings where gossip is bandied about and scandals are discussed.

ACTIVITY

Look at the opening of the play you are studying. What kind of opening does the dramatist create? How does the dramatist:

❑ hold the attention of the audience?
❑ create atmosphere?
❑ convey important information?
❑ create a sense of character?

Themes

Plays address particular themes that the dramatist is interested in exploring and presenting to an audience. Although playwrights may make use of visual effects to examine these themes, the language of the play is the key element through which they are drawn to the attention of the audience. As plays usually contain more than one theme, the language can become a complex structure in which various thematic strands are woven together to present a unified whole.

In *Measure for Measure*, for example, one of the key themes that Shakespeare explores is that of 'appearance versus reality'. The fact that this is going to be an important issue in the play is signalled early on. Having appointed Angelo to act as his deputy in his absence, the Duke confides to Friar Thomas:

> . . . Lord Angelo is precise;
> Stands at a guard with Envy; scarce confesses
> That his blood flows; or that his appetite
> Is more to bread than stone. Hence shall we see
> If power change purpose, what our seemers be.

(Act I Scene 3)

In giving the Duke this comment, Shakespeare reveals to the audience one of the reasons for the Duke's strange and hasty departure and at the same time signals a central theme of the play. The word 'seemers' here sounds a keynote and if you examine the play you will find the word 'seem' or 'seeming' used over and over again throughout the drama.

For example, in Act III Scene 1 the Duke refers to Angelo as 'this well-seeming Angelo' and Angelo recognizes the deceit in his own character:

> O place, O form,
> How often dost thou with thy case, thy habit,
> Wrench awe from fools, and tie the wiser souls
> To thy false seeming!

> *(Act II Scene 4)*

When Isabella finally realizes that Angelo is blackmailing her, she responds:

> Ha? Little honour, to be much believ'd
> And most pernicious purpose! Seeming, seeming!
> I will proclaim thee, Angelo, look for't.

> *(Act II Scene 4)*

There are many more such references in the play, as well as other words that signal a mismatch between appearance and reality. Together they create a structure within the language that keeps this theme in the forefront of the audience's minds and explores different aspects of the issue.

ACTIVITY Look at the play you are studying. What themes does your play explore? For each theme you have identified find four or five examples to show how the dramatist uses the language of the play to draw attention to and explore these themes.

Metaphorical techniques

Like other writers, dramatists make use of imagery, metaphor, simile and symbolism to create effects through the language of their plays. Sometimes dramatists use the technique of repeating similar images in order to build up a certain sense or a particular effect. For example, read the following two extracts from *Othello*. In the first, Othello has been led to believe from Iago's insinuation that his wife, Desdemona, has been unfaithful to him. He is struggling not to believe it but nevertheless the thought has brought unpleasant images to mind. In the second extract, Othello's jealousy has taken over completely and he charges his innocent wife with adultery.

Extract 14

Othello   This fellow's of exceeding honesty,
And knows all qualities with a learnèd spirit
Of human dealings. If I do prove her haggard,
Though that her jesses were my dear heart-strings,
I'd whistle her off, and let her down the wind
To prey at fortune. Haply, for I am black
And have not those soft parts of conversation
That chamberers have; or for I am declined
Into the vale of years – yet that's not much –
She's gone: I am abused, and my relief
Must be to loathe her. O, curse of marriage!
That we can call these delicate creatures ours
And not their appetites! I had rather be a toad
And live upon the vapour of a dungeon
Than keep a corner in the thing I love
For others' uses. Yet 'tis the plague of great ones;
Prerogatived are they less than the base.
'Tis destiny unshunnable, like death:
Even then this forkèd plague is fated to us
When we do quicken. Desdemona comes:

Enter **Desdemona** *and* **Emilia**

If she be false, O, then heaven mocks itself!
I'll not believe't.

Extract 15

Desdemona   Upon my knees, what doth your speech import?
I understand a fury in your words,
But not the words.
Othello   Why, what art thou?
Desdemona   Your wife, my lord; your true and loyal wife.
Othello   Come, swear it; damn thyself;
Lest being like one of heaven, the devils themselves
Should fear to seize thee. Therefore be double-damned:
Swear thou art honest.
Desdemona   Heaven doth truly know it.
Othello   Heaven truly knows that thou art false as hell.
Desdemona   To whom, my lord? With whom? How am I false?
Othello   Ah, Desdemona! Away, away, away!
Desdemona   Alas, the heavy day! Why do you weep?
Am I the motive of these tears my lord?
If haply you my father do suspect
An instrument of this your calling back,
Lay not your blame on me. If you have lost him,
I have lost him too.

Othello   Had it pleased heaven
To try me with affliction, had they rained
All kind of sores and shames on my bare head,
Steeped me in poverty to the very lips,
Given to captivity me and my utmost hopes,
I should have found in some place of my soul
A drop of patience. But alas, to make me
A fixèd figure for the time of scorn
To point his slow unmoving finger at!
Yet could I bear that too, well, very well:
But there where I have garnered up my heart,
Where either I must live, or bear no life,
The fountain from the which my current runs,
Or else dries up – to be discarded thence
Or keep it as a cistern for foul toads
To knot and gender in! Turn thy complexion there,
Patience, thou young and rose-lipped cherubin,
Ay, there look grim as hell!

ACTIVITY Examine the ways in which Shakespeare uses imagery to create a sense of
Othello's state of mind and mood in each extract. You should pay particular
attention to the use of:

❏ metaphor
❏ simile
❏ symbolism
❏ repeated images.

Here is how one student responded to these extracts.

Othello's state of mind in the extracts is one of anger and depression
focused on his wife, Desdemona. In the first extract there is a mood of
uncertainty and confusion over whether or not he believes she has
betrayed him. Further in the extract, however, violent imagery is
applied through Othello's soliloquy that emphasizes his feelings clearly.
By the time Desdemona arrives and converses with him on the matter,
in the second extract, Othello's mood and state of mind is distinct. He is
extremely angry, and fails to recognize her truths by not permitting her
to explain herself. Shakespeare mixes the strong imagery in Othello's
speeches and a sense of anguish towards his wife is created.

At the beginning of the first extract, Othello is not entirely sure as to
whether these 'crimes' allegedly committed by Desdemona are true, as
he has 'still to prove her hagggard'. Yet, as he continues to contemplate
the possibility Shakespeare uses extraordinary and very strong, harsh
images that seem to push Othello into the belief that Desdemona has
been unfaithful to him:

> 'I am abused, and my relief
> Must be to loathe her.'

By the use of the words 'abused' and 'loathed' Shakespeare has created an image of a torn, decayed figure in the form of Othello who must turn to abhor the woman he loved. The word 'abused' signifies Othello's distress and indicates that his mind must have been in a distraught and delicate state. Additionally Shakespeare uses a paradox in the form of 'O curse of marriage!' Whilst metaphorically this suggests that his marriage has been cursed, the statement is also a paradox because 'curse' symbolizes woe and tribulations, while 'marriage' signifies hope and expectation. This image, therefore, further enhances the idea of Othello's instability. Further on in the first extract, Othello's anger seems accentuated through the use of intense imagery. For example he claims:

> 'Yet 'tis the plague of great ones.'

The use of 'plague' suggests terror, pain and death, thus showing the way that Othello's mind is suffering torment.

Towards the end of the first extract the idea of 'death' is introduced, showing again the feelings of anguish that Othello is suffering and the power of his rage against Desdemona:

> ' 'Tis destiny unshunnable, like death.'

This simile shows that Othello is placing his wife's betrayal (as he perceives it) on a parallel with death itself. There is also a sense here in which he seems to accept all this as a kind of destiny.

In the second extract there is a repetition of many of the images of the first. For example, Shakespeare again introduces the image of the plague and affliction is used again:

> 'Had it pleased heaven
> To try me with affliction, had they rained
> All kinds of sores and shames on my bare head.'

Similarly he feels that he could have coped with 'poverty to the very lips' or being put into captivity and it would have hurt less than Desdemona's infidelity to him. Through this imagery Shakespeare seems to portray Othello as almost suicidal. This combination of Othello's thoughts implies that he is now certain that his wife has betrayed him.

Perhaps the most powerful image that reflects Othello's state of mind occurs in both extracts. In the first extract he says:

> 'I would rather be a toad
> And live upon the vapour of a dungeon
> Than keep a corner in the thing I love
> For others' uses.'

The image of the toad here creates a sense of baseness and bleakness through the imagery of the dungeon and this emphasizes the strength of Othello's feeling in that he would rather be this than allow another man to sleep with his wife. In the second extract the image of the toad is used again, but rather differently this time. Othello says:

> '. . . where I have garnered up my heart,
> Where either I must live, or bear no life,
> The fountain from which my current runs,
> Or else dries up – to be discarded thence
> Or keep it as a cistern for foul toads
> To knot and gender in!'

The image has become more intense here. The 'toad' has now become 'foul toads' and an unpleasant sexual element has been introduced with 'knot and gender' – as the thought of Desdemona with another man eats away at Othello's mind.

Examiner's comments

Overall the student has handled the task quite well. She is clearly aware of Othello's state of mind and mood in each extract, and she is also aware of some of the ways in which Shakespeare creates a sense of this mood. The response begins with a clear statement of Othello's state of mind and, although there are one or two minor technical infelicities, the sense of understanding is here.

From stating the more general points the student then begins to look at specific examples of the lexis of the two extracts and comments on the connotations and effects of individual words. The response develops with an analysis of the effects of the repeated use of the 'toad' as an image. Although the essay does lack analysis at a deeper level and the idea of the symbolic use of language is not really taken up, the response does cover a range of relevant points.

ACTIVITY

Now think about the play you are studying.

1 Make a list of any groups of images the dramatist uses, and within each group find examples of specific images used in the play. Remember to make a note of where these come from (Act, Scene and line number).

2 Choose two passages from the play where the dramatist uses imagery, and write an analysis of each showing how language is used in each in order to create the effects desired.

Rhetorical techniques

Dramatists also make use of rhetorical techniques in their writing, to give to their characters the kind of language use that can be used to persuade the audience or shape their responses in a particular way. Here are some of the features that you will find in the language of plays:

❏ repetition of sounds, words, sentence structures, etc.
❏ listing
❏ alliteration
❏ onomatopoeia
❏ assonance
❏ hyperbole
❏ puns
❏ antithesis.

For example, in *Measure for Measure*, Shakespeare uses **repetition** as Isabella calls for justice against the corrupt Angelo, who has just used his powers and position to try to blackmail her into sleeping with him.

Extract 16

Isabella	Justice, justice, justice, justice!
Duke	Relate your wrongs: in what? By whom? Be brief.
	Here is Lord Angelo shall give you justice;
	Reveal yourself to him.
Isabella	Oh worthy Duke,
	You bid me seek redemption of the devil.
	Hear me yourself: for that which I must speak
	Must either punish me, not being believed,
	Or wring redress from you. Hear me, oh hear me, here!
Angelo	My Lord, her wits I fear me are not firm;
	She hath been a suitor to me for her brother
	Cut off by course of justice.
Isabella	By course of justice!
Angelo	And she will speak most bitterly and strange.
Isabella	Most strange, but yet most truly will I speak.
	That Angelo's forsworn, is it not strange?
	That Angelo's a murderer, is't not strange?
	That Angelo is an adulterous thief,
	An hypocrite, a virgin-violator,
	Is it not strange, and strange?
Duke	Nay, it is ten times strange.
Isabella	It is not truer he is Angelo
	Than this is all as true as it is strange;
	Nay, it is ten times true, for truth is truth
	To th'end of reck'ning.

Note here how the almost ritualistic, incantatory effect of the repetition adds power to Isabella's words.

Listing can also be used to accumulate words or phrases like a list, to add impact as in this example from *The Merchant of Venice*:

> Hath not a Jew eyes? Hath not a Jew hands, organs,
> dimensions, senses, affections, passions,
> fed with the same food, hurt with the same weapons,
> subject to the same diseases, healed by the same
> means, warmed and cooled by the same winter
> and summer as a Christian is?

ACTIVITY Remind yourself of alliteration, assonance and onomatopoeia (see pages 53–56), which you worked on in the Poetry Unit. Now look at the play you are studying and find five or six examples of each. In each case, describe what effect the particular feature adds to the overall impact of the language.

We looked at the idea of **antithesis** in relation to poetry, but this technique is very commonly used in drama too. Some of Shakespeare's most famous lines are examples of antithesis:

> To be, or not to be
> *(Hamlet)*
> Fair is foul, and foul is fair
> *(Macbeth)*
> My only love sprung from my only hate
> *(Romeo and Juliet)*

We mentioned earlier that conflict is at the heart of drama and that language expresses the conflict, of whatever kind it might be. The opposition of words in antithesis often reflects the oppositions or conflicts at the centre of the drama. The fact that Othello's jealousy has taken him to the extremes of love and hate is summed up in the antithesis in his final lines of the play, which are addressed to the dead Desdemona:

> **Othello**   I kissed thee, ere I killed thee: no way but this,
>   Killing myself, to die upon a kiss.

ACTIVITY Look at the play you are studying and see if you can find some examples of antithesis. Describe the effects created.

Another rhetorical technique you are likely to find used in the play you study is that of **hyperbole**. Hyperbole means an exaggerated and extravagant use of language in order to create a particular effect or impact. Christopher

Marlowe often makes use of hyperbole in his plays, as in this speech from *Doctor Faustus* where Faustus becomes carried away with visions of what will be possible if he sells his soul to the devil.

Extract 17

Faustus   How am I glutted with conceit of this!
Shall I make spirits fetch me what I please,
Resolve me of all ambiguities,
Perform what desperate enterprise I will?
I'll have them fly to India for gold.
Ransack the ocean for orient pearl,
And search all corners of the new-found world
For pleasant fruits and princely delicates;
I'll have them read me strange philosophy
And tell the secrets of all foreign kings;
I'll have them wall all Germany with brass
And make swift Rhine circle fair Wittenberg;
I'll have them fill the public schools with silk
Wherewith the students shall be bravely clad;
I'll levy soldiers with the coin they bring
And chase the Prince of Parma from our land
And reign sole king of all our provinces;
Yea, stranger engines for the brunt of war
Than was the fiery keel at Antwerp's bridge
I'll make my servile spirits to invent.

Puns were particularly popular with Elizabethan audiences, but it is likely that you will find some in any pre-1770 text that you study. A pun is a play on words – when a word has two or more different meanings, the ambiguity can be used for a witty or amusing effect.

For example, Mercutio in *Romeo and Juliet*, although mortally wounded by Tybalt, keeps up his reputation for wordplay to the end by telling his friends:

Ask for me tomorrow, and you will find me a grave man.

ACTIVITY   Look through the play you are studying and make notes on the use of hyperbole and punning. Identify what these elements add to the drama.

Irony in drama

A dramatist might use two types of irony. In both types, the irony lies in the fact that the audience knows something that a character or characters on stage do not know.

Dramatic irony occurs when what is said by a character contrasts with what happens elsewhere in the action. Look at this example from Hamlet:

Extract 18

King	O my offence is rank, it smells to heaven;
	It hath the primal eldest curse upon't,
	A brother's murder. Pray can I not,
	Though inclination be as sharp as will.
	My stronger guilt defeats my strong intent,
	And like a man to double business bound,
	I stand in pause when I shall first begin,
	And both neglect. What if this cursed hand
	Were thicker than itself with brother's blood,
	Is there not rain enough in the sweet heavens
	To wash it white as snow? Whereto serves mercy
	But to confront the visage of offence?
	And what's in prayer but this two-fold force,
	To be forestalled ere we come to fall,
	Or pardoned being down? Then I'll look up;
	My fault is past. But O what form of prayer
	Can serve my turn? 'Forgive me my foul murder'?
	That cannot be since I am still possessed
	Of those effects for which I did the murder,
	My crown, mine own ambition, and my Queen.
	May one be pardoned and retain th' offence?
	In the corrupted currents of this world
	Offence's gilded hand may shove by justice,
	And oft 'tis seen the wicked prize itself
	Buys out the law. But 'tis not so above;
	There is no shuffling, there the action lies
	In his true nature, and we ourselves compelled,
	Even to the teeth and forehead of our faults
	To give in evidence. What then? What rests?
	Try what repentance can – what can it not?
	Yet what can it, when one can not repent?
	O wretched state, O bosom black as death,
	O limed soul, that struggling to be free,
	Art more engaged! Help, angels, make assay.
	Bow stubborn knees, and heart with strings of steel,
	Be soft as sinews of the new-born babe.
	All may be well. [*Kneels*

Enter **Hamlet**   ➡

Hamlet	Now might I do it pat, now he is praying;
	And now I'll do't – and so he goes to heaven;
	And so am I revenged. That would be scanned:
	A villain kills my father, and for that,
	I his sole son do this same villain send
	To heaven.
	Why, this is hire and salary, not revenge.
	'A took my father grossly full of bread,
	With all his crimes broad blown, as flush as May,
	And how his audit stands who knows save heaven?
	But in our circumstance and course of thought,
	'Tis heavy with him; and am I then revenged,
	To take him in the purging of his soul,
	When he is fit and seasoned for his passage?
	No.
	Up sword, and know thou a more horrid hent,
	When he is drunk asleep, or in his rage,
	Or in th' incestuous pleasure of his bed,
	At game, a-swearing, or about some act
	That has no relish of salvation in 't –
	Then trip him that his heels may kick at heaven,
	And that his soul may be as damned and black
	As hell whereto it goes. My mother stays.
	This physic but prolongs thy sickly days. [*Exit*
King	[*Rising*] My words fly up, my thoughts remain
	below.
	Words without thoughts never to heaven go. [*Exit*

ACTIVITY This is an example of dramatic irony. Explain why this situation is ironical.

Verbal irony occurs when a character says one thing but means another. For example, again in *Hamlet*, Claudius says that he is sending Hamlet to England for safety's sake when in fact the audience knows (and Hamlet guesses) that he is really planning to have him killed.

ACTIVITY Look at the play you are studying and find three or four examples of the use of irony. Explain what the irony consists of, and its significance in the play.

Drama and contextual variation

In terms of studying a drama text for A-level, **contextual variation** can refer to two quite separate elements of the play.

First, the language of the play can vary depending on the context of the particular scene, groupings of character, and so on. For example, in *Othello*, Iago uses language in different ways according to the context in which he is speaking – whom he is speaking to, for what purpose and so on.

The **context** of the play is also the larger cultural frame of reference within which the play came about – for example, the kind of society and the historical period within which the work was produced. In studying a Shakespeare play it can be useful to have an understanding of the kind of theatres they were originally performed in or the kind of beliefs the people of that time held. A knowledge of the Elizabethans' belief in the divine right of kings can do much to help you understand why people act as they do in *Richard II*.

ACTIVITY
> Think about the pre-1770 drama text you are studying. What can you learn about the context in which the play was written from studying the play? How far does a knowledge of the period in which it was written inform your understanding of the play itself?

Now let us think about the ways in which language can be used differently in a play according to the context in which the speaker is operating. The Duke in *Measure for Measure* has many 'languages' according to whom he is speaking to, at what point in the play he is speaking, and what his purpose is. In other words, his language varies according to context.

ACTIVITY
> Look at the following extracts from the play which show the Duke using language in different ways.
>
> The first comes right at the beginning of the play. What first impression do you form from the way he speaks? How does his language change after he has sent for Angelo?

Extract 19

Within Vienna

Enter **Duke**, **Escalus**, **Lords** *and* **Attendants**

Duke	Escalus.
Escalus	My lord.
Duke	Of Government the properties to unfold
	Would seem in me t'affect speech and discourse,
	Since I am put to know that your own science
	Exceeds, in that, the lists of all advice
	My strength can give you. Then no more remains
	But that, to your sufficiency, as your worth is able,

➡

And let them work. The nature of our people,
Our city's institutions, and the terms
For common justice, y'are as pregnant in
As art and practice hath enriched any
That we remember. There is our commission,
From which we would not have you warp. Call
  hither,
I say, bid come before us Angelo.

[*Exit an* **Attendant**]

What figure of us, think you, he will bear?
For you must know, we have with special soul
Elected him our absence to supply;
Lent him our terror, drest him with our love,
And given his deputation all the organs
Of our own power. What think you of it?

Here the Duke, disguised as a friar, visits the condemned Claudio in prison.

Extract 20

Duke   Be absolute for death: either death or life
Shall thereby be the sweeter. Reason thus with life:
If I do lose thee, I do lose a thing
That none but fools would keep. A breath thou art,
Servile to all the skyey influences
That dost this habitation where thou keep'st
Hourly afflict. Merely, thou art Death's fool;
For him thou labour'st by the flight to shun,
And yet run'st toward him still. Thou art not noble;
For all th'accommodations that thou bear'st
Are nursed by baseness. Thou'rt by no means
  valiant;
For thou dost fear the soft and tender fork
Of a poor worm. Thy best of rest is sleep;
And that thou oft provok'st, yet grossly fear'st
Thy death, which is no more. Thou art not thyself;
For thou exists on many a thousand grains
That issue out of dust. Happy thou art not;
For what thou hast not, still thou striv'st to get,
For what thou hast, forget'st. Thou art not certain;
For thy complexion shifts to strange effects
After the moon. If thou art rich, thou'rt poor;
For, like an ass whose back with ingots bows,
Thou bear'st thy heavy riches but a journey,
And Death unloads thee. Friends hast thou none;

➡

For thine own bowels which do call thee sire,
The mere effusion of thy proper loins,
Do curse the gout, serpigo, and the rheum
For ending thee no sooner. Thou hast nor youth,
    nor age,
But as it were an after-dinner's sleep
Dreaming on both; for all thy blessed youth
Becomes as aged, and doth beg the alms
Of palsied eld: and when thou art old and rich,
Thou hast neither heat, affection, limb, nor beauty
To make thy riches pleasant. What's yet in this
That bears the name of life? Yet in this life
Lie hid moe thousand deaths; yet death we fear
That makes these odds all even.

ACTIVITY   Look at his word choice here and the pattern of his speech. What do you notice about them? What gives the speech a 'sermon-like' quality?

Here the Duke, still disguised as a friar, speaks to Lucio, who has been slandering the Duke. Lucio does not know he is talking to the Duke and the Duke cannot reveal himself.

Extract 21

Duke   Either this is envy in you, folly, or mistaking. The very
stream of his life, and the business he hath helmed,
must upon a warranted need give him a better
proclamation. Let him be but testimonied in
his own bringings-forth, and he shall appear to the
envious a scholar, a statesman, and a soldier.
Therefore you speak unskilfully: or, if your knowledge
be more, it is much darkened in your malice.

Lucio   Sir, I know him and I love him.

Duke   Love talks with better knowledge, and knowledge
With dearer love.

Lucio   Come, sir, I know what I know.

Duke   I can hardly believe that, since you know not
what you speak. But if ever the Duke return –
as our prayers are he may – let me desire you to make
your answer before him. If it be honest you have
spoke, you have courage to maintain it; I am bound
to call upon you, and I pray you your name.

Lucio   Sir, my name is Lucio, well known to the Duke.

Duke   He shall know you better, sir, if I may live to
report you.

ACTIVITY   What clues can you find in the language to tell you how the Duke is feeling here? Is he speaking as the Duke or as a friar? Why do you think that the Duke speaks in prose here rather than verse?

APPROACHES TO EXAMINATION QUESTIONS

Now let us look at the kinds of questions that you will need to deal with in the examination, and apply some of the points we have discussed in order to answer them.

A reminder that the following questions test your ability to:

❏ communicate clearly the knowledge, understanding and insights gained from combined literary and linguistic study, using appropriate terminology and accurate written expression

❏ show understanding of the ways contextual variation and choices of form, style and vocabulary shape the meaning of texts.

❏ identify and consider the ways attitudes and values are conveyed in speech and writing.

Don't forget – you will not have the text with you in the examination.

Note   These questions have deliberately been made generic so that you can apply them to whatever text you are studying. In the examination, the questions will focus specifically on named texts. These generic questions, however, have been designed to show you the kinds of issues that questions in the examination are likely to raise.

1 Discuss the ways in which the dramatic use of form, style and vocabulary creates attitudes and values for one or two main characters throughout the play. In your answer you should also consider the ways contextual variation and choices of language shape the meaning of the text.

2 Examine the ways in which the dramatist creates a sense of dramatic tension through the interaction of characters in the play you have studied. You should consider the following in your answer: choices of form, style and vocabulary.

3 Examine the ways in which the dramatist develops the themes of the play through his or her use of language. You should refer to metaphorical, rhetorical and representational features in your answer.

7 Adaptation of Texts for an Audience

As you have already seen, both when you analysed texts and when you constructed texts of your own, audience is a key factor for any text. In Unit 5, the role of the audience is the cohesive element that draws the two parts of the paper together. Let us re-examine the definition of audience that we worked with when looking at constructing our own texts in Chapter 1.

Audience	Who the text is written for or aimed at; the audience can vary from the very general to the very specific

We can broaden this for the purposes of this Unit, since we also look at the likely **reaction** of the people for whom a text or piece of drama is written, and how the writer conveys attitudes, values and concerns in his or her piece of text.

In Section A of Unit 5 (see Chapter 6) you examined the way the writer of a text takes into account the audience of the theatre, and considered the theatricality of the text you are studying. In Section B, the emphasis switches somewhat as you will need to consider which adaptations and changes you need to bring to bear on specific texts when you construct your new text, arising from original texts, for a new audience.

For both sections you need to be confident about using frameworks for analysis and production. As this particular Unit also requires you to evaluate the success of your own text in comparison to one (or possibly both) of the others, you are working to a very tight schedule.

The final skill you need to develop is the ability to plan, write and revise each of your answers in 45 minutes. This is a tall order but, given that you will have prepared your dramatic text and that you are given stringent word limits for your textual adaptation and comparative analysis, you should be able to learn to do this, with frequent practice.

The audience

As you have seen in the previous chapter, any dramatic text places great value on its audience and the reaction that can be attained; theatrical productions of dramatic texts are given individuality and angled towards particular audience reactions by means of the interpretation that the director imposes on the production. This notion of a play being given an interpretation by an individual director can be applied to the tasks that appear in the next section of the specification.

In Section B of Unit 5, the specification gives guidance on the nature of the tasks that students will be expected to do. It states that candidates will be asked to adapt and recast two or more printed passages for a new audience and purpose; in addition, candidates will need to comment on some of the ways the process has taken place by focusing on certain areas in a comparative commentary.

The first of these tasks, adapting writing to a particular requirement, could be compared with the job of a theatrical director. You are asked to take material you are unfamiliar with and place your stamp of individuality on it by 'interpreting' it, through textual adaptation and recasting, so that a new audience can view it. As we have already noted, the main focus of this Unit is the way texts are targeted at their audience, and the importance of textual construction. This is reflected in the assessment objectives, which target your ability to synthesize the knowledge and understanding gained from combined literary and linguistic study in constructing a new text (in other words your appreciation of audience, purpose and form), as well as writing accurately to a specific brief using unfamiliar material. The second task is another opportunity for you to demonstrate one of the most important aspects of study at A2-level, that is comparing and contrasting two texts and evaluating their relative effectiveness through comparative analysis.

Textual adaptation

As in all cases where you are expected to produce answers that require a systematic approach, it is a good idea to adopt a framework to help you construct your text and then use an analytical framework to deconstruct parts of it.

It is vital therefore to remind yourself of two parts of the specification that directly feed into this section. You should re-read Chapter 1 on Language Production to help you focus on how to construct texts. Secondly, it is important for you remind yourself of the process you have adopted for textual analysis, as you will need to be aware of the stylistic features you are going to target in your comparative analysis. It is best to make these decisions before you recast your text, as it will help you to focus on the relevant features and issues – in other words, you are killing two birds with one stone.

Having reminded yourself of the relevant processes, you can now look at one particular way of approaching this section.

Approaching and analysing the task

The first words you will be confronted with on the examination paper are those of the task. The material for adaptation is printed after this, for the sound reason that candidates need to focus on the *whole* of the task (remembering there are two parts to the question). It also allows you to focus on the particulars of the text adaptation: what you have to do, who you have to do it for and (perhaps) how you have to do it. (The 'how' part of the task may not be delineated, depending upon the nature of the material you are given.) Your first job, therefore, is to look carefully at the task and pick out the key words; this will enable you to focus on the main issues. You should then be able to target the necessary parts of the texts you are given to adapt, and leave out redundant material.

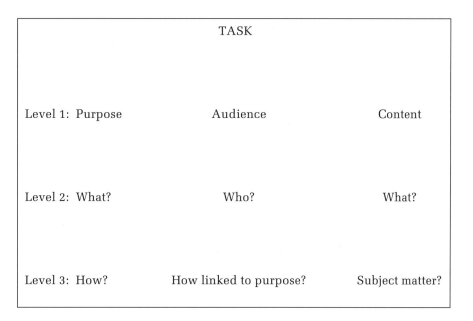

The framework in the diagram above shows that there are three levels to task analysis; if you follow this methodology, you should have the main points of the task firmly in your mind *before* you read the materials for adaptation. The framework functions as follows:

1 Level 1 questions help you to establish the main criteria and parameters of your adapted piece of writing. You need to identify if there is an intended:

   ❏ purpose – are you asked to write for a particular reason?
   ❏ audience – are you asked to write for a particular group of people?
   ❏ content base – are you given a subject to write about?

2   Level 2 questions go beyond this by identifying the nature of the task.

- ❏ What is the purpose? What is it that you are actually required to do?
- ❏ Who is the audience? Who do you have to write for?
- ❏ What is the content? What material are you likely to need?

3   Level 3 questions are not always needed but it is safer to ask them since it helps you to focus even more closely on the task.

- ❏ Purpose: How are you meant to convey your information? Do you need to adopt a particular viewpoint or a particular style?
- ❏ Audience: Are there issues of audience that link to the purpose of the task? Is the audience limited in any way that affects what you do and how you do it?
- ❏ Subject matter: What limitations are put on your subject matter? Is there a word limit?

ACTIVITY

Use the following specimen question (it appears in full at the end of this chapter with a student response) to work through the task-related questions at the three levels you have just learned.

Read the following two texts. Text A is an extract from a history book on the First World War. Text B is a review of the film 'The Trench' which was published in *The Independent* newspaper.

Using information from Texts A and B, write a first-person account that records the experiences and feelings of a soldier during the First World War. Your writing should take the form of **one** of the following:

- ❏ a letter home
- ❏ part of an autobiography
- ❏ a section from a diary.

You must state which form you have chosen and aim to write between 300 and 400 words. You should seek to include as much relevant information as possible from the texts, while seeking to create an appropriate style for your first-person account.

Reflecting on your knowledge of the type of text you are to produce

It is likely that the new text you are asked to produce will be of a type that you have seen or read. You will have read all kinds of texts to help you prepare for this section, and you will have some notion of their forms and styles as well as some of the communicative methods used by their writers. The task above requires one of three types of text – a letter, an extract from an autobiography, or a diary section – and you will have acquired an awareness of these three forms from your own reading.

ACTIVITY Look at the following list of forms of writing. Think about what you know about each from your own reading. Note down next to each one some of your ideas on form and possible styles of writing.

Writing form	Ideas on form and style
An entry for a children's encyclopaedia	
An editorial for a tabloid newspaper	
A letter to a Member of Parliament	
A leaflet on the dangers of smoking for teenagers	
A consumer report on a particular product, e.g. mini-disc players	
A quick-start instruction sheet for computers	
An advertisement for high-class wines in a magazine	
A travel piece for a broadsheet newspaper	
A review of a one-off rock concert or festival	

It is always useful to reflect on the knowledge you have about particular texts before you start reading the source material or writing your own text. Note down any ideas you have, as this may help you take a particular stance later in the recasting process.

Reading through the source materials

It is likely that you will be faced with at least two pieces of source material, one of which will probably be non-fiction. You may find that the materials are linked in one of the following ways:

- ❑ theme or subject matter
- ❑ historical period
- ❑ genre
- ❑ audience
- ❑ context.

It is useful to have a pencil or highlighter in your hand so you can identify and mark the relevant information as you read through the source. Since you have already analysed the task in detail, you should be focused on the material you will need. Remember that your word limit is likely to be around 400 words, which means you have hardly any latitude with the material. Make sure that you select only the necessary content and do not get sidetracked. You might like to consider the following list of techniques that writers often use to help them get their points across. Examine such techniques carefully, since they may be there only to improve the effectiveness of the writer's message:

- ❏ imagery or use of other literary conventions
- ❏ analogy or parallel situations
- ❏ use of rhetorical features for effect
- ❏ use of exemplar material to illustrate the point
- ❏ use of humour.

However, these methods may give you ideas on how to deal with the content in your own piece of writing, so do not ignore the writer's methodologies altogether!

ACTIVITY

Using the following extract, imagine you have to write a piece for a history textbook for teenagers, on the effects of the atomic bomb dropped on Hiroshima. Select the relevant material and facts from this passage, as you would in your first read-through in an exam situation. Remember, all you are doing here is identifying the material you will use.

Text *Visiting Hiroshima, 9 September, 1945* by Marcel Junod

The bare cone of Fujiyama was just visible on the horizon as we flew over the 'inland sea' which lay beneath us like a lavender-blue carpet picked out in green and yellow with its numerous promontories and wooded islands.

Towards midday a huge white patch appeared on the ground below us. This chalky desert, looking almost like ivory in the sun, surrounded by a crumble of twisted ironwork and ash heaps, was all that remained of Hiroshima.

The journalist described the main official buildings of the town, which were built of reinforced concrete and dominated a sea of low-roofed Japanese houses extending over six miles to the wooded hills I could see in the distance.

'The town was not much damaged,' he explained. 'It had suffered very little from the bombing. There were only two minor raids, one on March 19th last by a squadron of American naval planes, and one on April 30th by a Flying Fortress. On August 6th there wasn't a cloud in the sky above Hiroshima, and a mild, hardly perceptible wind blew from the south. Visibility was almost perfect for ten or twelve miles.

'At nine minutes past seven in the morning an air-raid warning sounded and four American B-29 planes appeared. To the north of the town two of them turned and made off to the south and disappeared in the direction of the Shoho Sea. The other two, after having circled the neighbourhood of Shukai, flew off at high speed southwards in the direction of the Bingo Sea. At 7.31 the all-clear was given. Feeling themselves in safety people came out of their shelters and went about their affairs and the work of the day began.

'Suddenly a glaring whitish pinkish light appeared in the sky accompanied by an unnatural tremor which was followed almost immediately by a wave of suffocating heat and a wind which swept away everything in its path.

'Within a few seconds the thousands of people in the streets and the gardens in the centre of the town were scorched by a wave of searing heat. Many were killed instantly, others lay writhing on the ground screaming in agony from the intolerable pain of their burns. Everything standing upright in the way of the blast, walls, houses, factories and other buildings, was annihilated and the debris spun round in a whirlwind and was carried up into the air. Trams were picked up and tossed aside as though they had neither weight nor solidity. Trains were flung off the rails as though they were toys. Horses, dogs and cattle suffered the same fate as human beings. Every living thing was petrified in an attitude of indescribable suffering. Even the vegetation did not escape. Trees went up in flames, the rice plants lost their greenness, the grass burned on the ground like dry straw.

'Beyond the zone of utter death in which nothing remained alive houses collapsed in a whirl of beams, bricks and girders. Up to about three miles from the centre of the explosion lightly built houses were flattened as though they had been built of cardboard. Those who were inside were either killed or wounded. Those who managed to extricate themselves by some miracle found themselves surrounded by a ring of fire. And the few who succeeded in making their way to safety generally died twenty or thirty days later from the delayed effects of the deadly gamma rays. Some of the reinforced concrete or stone buildings remained standing but their interiors were completely gutted by the blast. About half an hour after the explosion whilst the sky all around Hiroshima was still cloudless a fine rain began to fall on the town and went on for about five minutes. It was caused by the sudden rise of over-heated air to a great height, where it condensed and fell back as rain. Then a violent wind rose and the fires extended with terrible rapidity, because most Japanese houses are built only of timber and straw.

'By the evening the fire began to die down and then it went out. There was nothing left to burn. Hiroshima had ceased to exist.'

The Japanese broke off and then pronounced one word with indescribable but restrained emotion: 'Look.'

We were then rather less than four miles away from the Aioi Bridge, which was immediately beneath the explosion, but already the roofs of the houses around us had lost their tiles and the grass was yellow along the roadside. At three miles from the centre of the devastation the houses were already

➡

destroyed, their roofs had fallen in and the beams jutted out from the wreckage of their walls. But so far it was only the usual spectacle presented by towns damaged by ordinary high explosives.

About two and a half miles from the centre of the town all the buildings had been burnt out and destroyed. Only traces of the foundations and piles of debris and rusty charred ironwork were left. This zone was like the devastated areas of Tokyo, Osaka and Kobe after the mass fall of incendiaries.

At three-quarters of a mile from the centre of the explosion nothing at all was left. Everything had disappeared. It was a stony waste littered with debris and twisted girders. The incandescent breath of the fire had swept away every obstacle and all that remained upright were one or two fragments of stone walls and a few stoves which had remained incongruously on their base. We got out of the car and made our way slowly through the ruins into the centre of the dead city. Absolute silence reigned in the whole necropolis.

Evaluating the source materials

Having identified the main content to be used in your new text, the final job you need to do prior to writing is to evaluate the material in terms of its linguistic content so that you can ensure that the changes you make are appropriate for the new target audience and purpose. This allows you to focus on the kinds of changes you will make, and thus reflect on them in your comparative commentary.

Use the following checklist to make a linguistic evaluation of your source material, ensuring that this includes consideration of the particular features you need to focus on in your adaptation.

Evaluate: SOURCE TEXTS		Consideration of changes for: ADAPTED TEXT
Audience: – who? – how linked to style?	⇨	Identify: – new audience – new style
Mode: – speech – writing – mixed modes	⇨	Identify: – new mode? – same mode? – mixed modes?
Genre: – what?	⇨	Identify – new genre? – same genre? – mixed genres?

Written style:		Identify:
– use of lexis		– lexical changes
– use of syntax	⟹	– syntactical changes
– use of grammar		– grammatical changes
– phonological features		– phonological changes
– rhetorical features		– rhetorical changes

Structure and cohesion:		Identify:
– order	⟹	– new order
– chronology		– new chronology

Graphological features:		Identify:
– any presentational devices	⟹	– new presentational devices (if needed)

Obviously, since there are only 45 minutes at your disposal for the whole of this exercise, it is essential that this part of the process is undertaken quickly and efficiently; however, by focusing on the way you are to adapt your text at this stage and engaging in a hypothetical comparison, you will save yourself time when planning the comparative commentary, since you will already have identified the major areas for analysis.

The second part of the question we looked at earlier in this section is as follows:

> Compare Text A, Text B and your new text in order to highlight the choices you have made in your own writing. In your comparison you should show:
>
> ❑ how language has been used to suit the purposes and audience for the writing and the forms taken
> ❑ how vocabulary and other stylistic features have been used to shape meaning and for particular effects.
>
> You should aim to write about 400–500 words.

Here you are asked to reflect on the stylistic choices you have made and how they helped you to meet the demands of the new purpose and audience, through comparison with the source texts. You should have taken these key areas into account prior to the writing of your new text.

Adopting an approach to or perspective on the source material

It may be that the task you are set does not specify the nature of the writing you have to do beyond its subject matter. In the question we have been examining, three alternative writing styles are given, all of which have an impact on the style and communicative strategies that could be used. All three require a first-person pronominative form, but there are subtle differences between writing for yourself (a diary), writing for a known family audience (a letter) or writing for an unknown formal audience (an autobiography).

If you are not given a particular angle from which to write, there are many methods you could consider. Examine some of the following ideas.

Use of narrators, characters or figures

❑ first-person pronominative form, adopting a persona through which you can deliver your material
❑ third-person narrative: construction of a particular character through which the source information can be channelled
❑ creation of a situation where characters interact, using the source material as a narrative base

Use of particular forms

❑ a personal diary or reflective journal
❑ the epistolary form
❑ a short story or narrative

Use of the spoken mode

❑ dialogue between a number of characters
❑ a range of different narrators, each with his or her own distinctive speech style, accent, dialect forms, etc.

Use of presentational features

❑ time-lines or chronological representations
❑ summaries, précis, abstracts and synopses
❑ glossaries, word boxes and definitions
❑ bullet points and subheadings

Use of graphological devices

❑ illustrations, images and pictures (where appropriate)
❑ headlines, titles and captions

Remember that your choice of strategy for delivering your new text, should you have the opportunity to choose it, is very important and will help to ensure the overall success of your piece.

Structuring selected material to use in your new text

As with any piece of written work you undertake, planning is vital. Because you have been given word limits and parameters within which to write, it is best if you first prepare an outline of your text.

A paragraph plan is usually the best way of doing this. Simply note down the order of the details you wish to use, remembering the overall angle or approach you have chosen. You should consider cohesive details such as plot, story line, sequencing and chronology here, too.

Marrying the outline with the style

Having established the approach you are to take with your material, you can now decide upon the ways in which you are going to write your new text. At this point you need to reflect on the stylistic details that will enhance your new text, giving it the elements that will help it to succeed. Use the following framework to help you.

Lexical and semantic choices

❏ semantic field
❏ connotations and denotations of words
❏ formality
❏ jargon or specialist terms
❏ abstract ideas or concrete facts

Grammatical choices

❏ pronouns and pronominative form
❏ noun types: abstract or concrete
❏ use of modifiers: adjectives (factual, emotive, descriptive, evaluative); adverbials (time, place, direction, situation, quality)

Sentence types

❏ statements, questions, commands, etc.
❏ simple, compound or complex
❏ co-ordination and subordination
❏ pre-modification and post-modification

Verb usage

❏ tense
❏ voice

Use of rhetorical and phonological devices

❏ repetition and patterning
❏ imagery and other literary devices

Writing your new text

It is now time to write. You will have practised the work outlined in the previous sections until you can do it effortlessly, so it should have taken you about 15–20 minutes to do, leaving you about 25 minutes to write your new text. When you write, take the following points into consideration:

❑ double space your text in case you want to amend or add to it when you re-read your piece
❑ stick to the word limit – quantity does not necessarily equal quality in this section
❑ check back to your plan at every opportunity to ensure consistency of style and delivery
❑ focus on those aspects of the adaptation that will be part of your comparative analysis; underline them in another colour (*not* red or green) if necessary to remind you to refer to them in the next question
❑ re-read your text once you have finished; it is surprising how many mistakes you can make when writing under such intense pressure.

Recasting

Here is the recasting methodology in outline.

1 Analyse the task and adopt an approach.
2 Reflect on your own knowledge of the type of text you will produce.
3 Read through the source materials.
4 Evaluate the source materials for content and appropriate stylistic changes.
5 Adopt an approach to or perspective on the source material.
6 Structure the material you have selected to use in your new text.
7 Marry your text outline with your chosen style.
8 Write your new text.
9 Revise text as necessary

ACTIVITY

Here is a sample recasting question for you to attempt.

Read the following first-person accounts of the *Titanic* disaster.

Your task is to write a journalistic report for *The Times* of the details of the disaster, a day after your newspaper has already reported that the ship has sunk. This first story had few factual details. With more details to hand, you can now write your piece.

Your word limit is 350–400 words. You should include a headline to your piece.

Text A

A Fireman's Story

I was in my bunk when I felt a bump. One man said, 'Hello. She has been struck.' I went on deck and saw a great pile of ice on the well deck before the forecastle, but we all thought the ship would last some time, and we went back to our bunks. Then one of the firemen came running down and yelled, 'All muster for the lifeboats.' I ran on deck, and the Captain said, 'All firemen keep down on the well deck. If a man comes up I'll shoot him.'

Then I saw the first lifeboat lowered. Thirteen people were on board, eleven men and two women. Three were millionaires, and one was Ismay [J. Bruce Ismay, Managing Director of the White Star Line; a survivor].

Then I ran up on to the hurricane deck and helped to throw one of the collapsible boats on to the lower deck. I saw an Italian woman holding two babies. I took one of them, and made the woman jump overboard with the baby, while I did the same with the other. When I came to the surface the baby in my arms was dead. I saw the woman strike out in good style, but a boiler burst on the *Titanic* and started a big wave. When the woman saw that wave, she gave up. Then, as the child was dead, I let it sink too. I swam around for about half an hour, and was swimming on my back when the *Titanic* went down. I tried to get aboard a boat, but some chap hit me over the head with an oar. There were too many in her. I got around to the other side of the boat and climbed in.

Text B

The Wireless Operator's Story

From aft came the tunes of the band. It was a ragtime tune. I don't know what. I went to the place I had seen the collapsible boat on the boat deck, and to my surprise I saw the boat, and the men still trying to push it off. I guess there wasn't a sailor in the crowd. They couldn't do it. I went up to them and was just lending a hand when a large wave came awash of the deck. The big wave carried the boat off. I had hold of an oarlock and I went with it. The next I knew I was in the boat. But that was not all. I was in the boat, and the boat was upside-down, and I was under it. And I remember realizing I was wet through and that whatever happened I must not breathe, for I was under water. I knew I had to fight for it, and I did. How I got out from under the boat I do not know but I felt a breath of air at last. There were men all around me – hundreds of them. The sea was dotted with them, all depending on their lifebelts. I felt I simply had to get away from the ship. She was a beautiful sight then. Smoke and sparks were rushing out of her funnel. There must have been an explosion, but we heard none. We only saw the big stream of sparks. The ship was turning gradually on her nose – just like a duck that goes for a dive. I had only one thing on my mind – to get away from the suction. The band was still playing. I guess all of them went down. I swam with all my might. I suppose I was 150 feet away when the *Titanic,* on her

➡

nose, with her after-quarter sticking straight up in the air, began to settle – slowly.

When at last the waves washed over her rudder there wasn't the least bit of suction I could feel. She must have kept going just so slowly as she had been . . . I felt after a little while like sinking. I was very cold. I saw a boat of some kind near me, and put all my strength into an effort to swim to it. It was hard work. I was all done when a hand reached out from the boat and pulled me aboard. It was our same collapsible. The same crowd was on it. There was just room for me to roll on the edge. I lay there not caring what happened. Somebody sat on my legs. They were wedged in between slats and were being wrenched. I had not the heart left to ask the man to move. It was a terrible sight all around – men swimming and sinking.

I lay where I was, letting the man wrench my feet out of shape. Others came near. Nobody gave them a hand. The bottom-up boat already had more men than it would hold, and it was sinking. At first the larger waves splashed over my clothing. Then they began to splash over my head, and I had to breathe when I could. As we floated around on our capsized boat and I kept straining my eyes for a ship's lights, somebody said, 'Don't the rest of you think we ought to pray?' The man who made the suggestion asked what the religion of the others was. Each man called out his religion. One was a Catholic, one a Methodist, one a Presbyterian. It was decided the most appropriate prayer for all was the Lord's Prayer. We spoke it over in chorus with the man who first suggested that we pray as the leader. Some splendid people saved us. They had a right-side-up boat and it was full to capacity. Yet they came to us and loaded us all into it. I saw some lights off in the distance and knew a steamship was coming to our aid.

Text C

From a Lifeboat

We did not begin to understand the situation till we were perhaps a mile or more away from the *Titanic*. Then we could see the rows of lights along the decks begin to slant gradually upward from the bow. Very slowly the lines of light began to point downward at a greater and greater angle. The sinking was so slow that you could not perceive the lights of the deck changing their position. The slant seemed to be greater about every quarter of an hour. That was the only difference.

In a couple of hours, though, she began to go down more rapidly. Then the fearful sight began. The people in the ship were just beginning to realize how great their danger was. When the forward part of the ship dropped suddenly at a faster rate, so that the upward slope became marked, there was a sudden rush of passengers on all the decks towards the stern. It was like a wave. We could see the great black mass of people in the steerage sweeping to the rear part of the boat and breaking through into the upper decks. At the distance of about a mile we could distinguish everything through the night, which was

➡

perfectly clear. We could make out the increasing excitement on board the boat as the people, rushing to and fro, caused the deck lights to disappear and reappear as they passed in front of them.

This panic went on, it seemed, for an hour. Then suddenly the ship seemed to shoot up out of the water and stand there perpendicularly. It seemed to us that it stood upright in the water for four full minutes.

Then it began to slide gently downwards. Its speed increased as it went down head first, so that the stern shot down with a rush.

The lights continued to burn till it sank. We could see the people packed densely in the stern till it was gone.

As the ship sank we could hear the screaming a mile away. Gradually it became fainter and fainter and died away.

Evaluating your writing

Once you have written your own text, the final part of the Unit requires you to reflect on the ways in which you have constructed it by comparing it to the original source texts in some way. This could include any of the following areas:

❏ specific comparative issues, such as the use of lexis and grammatical constructions
❏ a comparison of the audiences of the texts
❏ a comparative examination of the purposes of the pieces
❏ an evaluation of the effectiveness of each piece of writing
❏ a simple comparison of the original text(s) with the new text.

Naturally, since this is the second and more demanding part of the course, the comparative angle is very important; you will have noted already that it is an integral part of each Unit at A2 level. It is therefore imperative that you leave yourself enough time to do justice to this section of the paper.

Analysing the demands of the task

Your first step is to analyse the task so that you can build your own analytical framework through which to highlight the differences between the source text(s) and your new text.

If you have done your planning and writing in a systematic way in the previous section, you should be able to tackle this as an extension of the recasting process. Remind yourself of the section where you evaluated the source material and decided on the nature of the changes that were necessary.

At the beginning of the recasting process, you will have examined the nature of the task and you should have noted:

❏ the purpose of the task – what it is you are required to do
❏ the intended audience of the piece – who you are addressing
❏ the content from the source texts that you can usefully adapt.

Your next step was to identify the **methods** you needed to consider for effective textual transmission. You should have noted:

❏ how you are meant to convey your information – careful consideration of viewpoint and style
❏ how issues of audience link to the purpose of the task – a reflection on any audience limitation
❏ how to use your subject matter – judgement of limitations and word limit, which texts have the relevant material, and textual length.

If these parts of the process have been addressed, the final question will be less daunting since your framework for analysis will already be established in your mind.

Firming up your analytical framework

When you evaluated the source material in the previous section you used a particular process; this process allowed you to be systematic in your textual construction. For your evaluation of your own writing through comparison to the source texts, simply follow the same process, reflecting on whether any consideration of each particular point was needed before progressing on to the next. This will allow you construct your comparative framework:

❏ audience
❏ mode
❏ genre
❏ written style:
  – use of lexis
  – use of syntax
  – use of grammar
  – phonological features
  – rhetorical features
❏ structure and cohesion of the material
❏ graphological features.

Once you have reminded yourself of the outline of how you constructed your text in the light of the source texts, you can start to consider some of the details which highlight the differences between the original texts and your own text.

Fleshing out your analytical comparison

One way of putting flesh on the bones of your analytical comparison is to consider the outline above in terms of a table, as below. This is an easy way of selecting the material you are to discuss.

Source texts		Adapted text	
Issues	*Intended effect and illustrative example*	*Issues*	*Intended effect and illustrative example*
Audience: – who?		**Audience:** – new	
– how it is linked to style		– new style	
Mode		**Mode**	
Genre		**New genre**	
Written style		**New style**	
– use of lexis		– lexical changes	
– use of syntax		– syntactical changes	
– use of grammar		– grammatical changes	
– phono-logical features		– phono-logical changes	
– rhetorical features		– rhetorical changes	
Structure and cohesion		**New order or chronology**	
Presentational devices		**New presentational devices**	

You may find the above table useful in the practice stages of writing your evaluative commentary, and you may be able to come up with a shorthand version for use in the timed situation of the examination. The advantage of using a table such as this is that it allows you to reflect on your processes of initial textual consideration and appraisal of the source texts, and follow them up by selecting and emphasizing the changes you made in your adaptation. Obviously some of these areas will require little or no attention in your comparative commentary; others may need only one comparative example, while there will be some you want to emphasize by giving a couple of examples. Remember your time limitations and that your word limit is around 500 words.

Writing your analytical comparison

When you begin your comparative analysis, remember the analytical model you were given at the start of this book, which will help to keep your comparison focused on explanation and interpretation. You can chain your comparative points together by using the three-point critical sentence:

1 Identify the point you want to discuss from both texts in order to show the nature of your adaptation

2 Give working examples from both texts

3 Explain and interpret how they work within the text in terms of purpose, audience, subject matter, etc.

This will help you build up an effective comparative commentary that will be systematic, since it uses the outline above and also an analytical model that covers identification, description and explanation of linguistic issues.

It is vital that you cover the range of methods you have drawn on to help you make your adaptation. This is where your knowledge of other, similar texts you have read might help you. You should draw on your knowledge of the variety of literary and non-literary texts you have read and make reference to them wherever necessary. Try to relate this to your understanding of audience and purpose also, by showing how language is used in targeting audience and helping to underpin the purpose of the text.

Be brief and focused in your comparative analysis so that you are not spending unnecessary time on one area when you could be discussing other issues. Remember, if your adaptation has been successful, there will be a range of areas to choose from and discuss.

If the question asks you to focus on specific areas – lexical and grammatical issues, for instance – there is no need to mention the other areas that have been outlined above. The nature of the comparative commentary will often be dictated by the demands of the initial adaptation task.

The following activity is the follow-up task to the adaptation question given earlier in this chapter.

ACTIVITY

Compare the ways that you have used language in writing your new text, with **one** of the source texts. In your comparison you should show:

❏ how you have targeted your particular audience
❏ how you have used vocabulary and other stylistic features to help shape the meaning of your text.

You should aim to write no more than 400–500 words in your comparative commentary.

APPROACHES TO EXAMINATION QUESTIONS

1 Textual adaptation

Read the following two texts. Text A is an extract from a history book on the First World War. Text B is a review of the film 'The Trench' which was published in *The Independent* newspaper.

Using information from Texts A and B, write a first-person account that records the experiences and feelings of a soldier during the First World War. Your writing should take the form of **one** of the following:

- ❏ a letter home
- ❏ part of an autobiography
- ❏ a section from a diary

You must state which form you have chosen and aim to write between 300 and 400 words. You should seek to include as much relevant information as possible from the texts, while seeking to create an appropriate style for your first-person account.

2 Comparative commentary

Compare Text A, Text B and your new text in order to highlight the choices you have made in your own writing. In your comparison you should show:

- ❏ how language has been used to suit the purposes and audience for the writing and the forms taken
- ❏ how vocabulary and other stylistic features have been used to shape meaning and for particular effects

You should aim to write about 400–500 words.

Text A

The volunteers flocked to the recruiting offices at Kitchener's call: 'Your country needs you.' Kitchener had expected to assemble an army of 500,000 volunteers; by the end of 1914 he had nearly 1,000,000, and the machinery for training and equipping them creaked badly.

At the front, the British regulars were sceptical. Kitchener's 'ridiculous and preposterous army of twenty-five corps is the laughing stock of every soldier in Europe', declared one senior general, and ' . . . under no circumstances could these mobs take the field for two years'. The generals expected, anyway, to have broken through the German lines long before then.

The winter of 1914-15 in fact gave the Allied commanders no grounds for this optimism. The invincible sweep of machine-gun fire across No Man's Land was already demonstrating its defensive power, and the enemy's barbed wire entanglements, covered too by machine-guns, were proving a murderous barrier in front of his better-sited trenches.

➡

The wire became the new horror. It 'terrified and obsessed the infantryman. All his daring and courage came to naught when he ran against an incompletely destroyed network. He knew that he would get caught and lacerated in its entangled mass of snares and meshes. His would be a slow and agonising death.' The German wire had to be destroyed if any attack was to succeed, and high explosive shells were the weapon. But these were in desperately short supply. Starting with more in the first place, the Germans had been quicker than the Allies to expand their own supplies of artillery and ammunition. The French, having concentrated on their light 75s designed for offensive action in open country, were seriously short of heavy guns capable of oblique fire; but the British lack of guns and shells was far more critical. The fire-power of the British artillery was quite inadequate even for the defence of its own trenches, let alone for the pulverisation of the enemy's wire. In the factories in Britain, Kitchener's recruiting for the army had resulted in a grave shortage of skilled munition workers, which in turn led to a disastrous shell shortage.

Lacking artillery support, lacking the weapons of trench warfare, the mortar and the hand-grenades, dependent on their own rifle fire to contend with patrols and local attacks, short of trained junior officers and NCOs, the British infantry had to man their trenches in strength, unable to rely on their guns to ease the burden of defence.

The pattern of trench warfare, which was to eat up the years, was now emerging. The German defence, with strong, permanent trenches guarded by the almost unbreakable partnership of barbed wire and machine guns, was building itself a fortified barrier of enormous strength. The Allied generals, with an optimism which was to prove quite unfounded, believed that they could break through with well-prepared offensive actions, supported by a concentration of artillery fire-power which they did not yet possess. Joffre, and his subordinate General Ferdinand Foch, now in command of the French armies in the north of France, though temperamentally different, were united in their amazing optimism, and in their plans for early offensive action and for tying in the British with their schemes.

Haig saw the immediate obstacle clearly, the lack of guns and shells, but thought too readily that artillery would utterly destroy the German defences: his dream of the final cavalry manoeuvre – his own arm – blinded him perhaps to the infantryman's tactical problems. Although some of Haig's instructions in 1914 and early 1915 show that he was aware of the problem of the machine-gun, he was also capable of pronouncing at this time that it was 'a much overrated weapon'. Like most other commanders, French and British, he underestimated the strength of the German positions, summing the matter up for *The Times* correspondent in January 1915: ' . . . as soon as we were supplied with ample artillery ammunition of high explosive, I thought we could walk through the German lines at several places.'

So the stage was set for the five offensives the British and French were to make against the German lines in 1915 – each of them planned to be the great breakthrough. The men themselves – as well as the generals – were keen; the French to redeem their sacred soil, the British to have another go at the Hun as a change from the wretched winter, crowded in their inadequate, half-flooded trenches.

Source: Alistair Horne, *Death of a Generation* (Macdonald)

Text B

Oh what a lonely war! – Anthony Quinn

On the morning of 1 July 1916, a continuous line of British soldiers climbed out of their trenches along the Somme and began to walk slowly towards the German lines. There was a general belief that the furious bombardment of the enemy during the previous week had destroyed their positions. That belief proved unfounded, and by the end of the day the British Army had suffered the bloodiest slaughter in its history, with 60,000 casualties, killed or wounded.

The novelist William Boyd has taken on this momentous subject for his directorial debut – momentous in that it marks the point when the Twentieth Century really began – yet 'The Trench' is no more a 'war movie' than was Terrence Malick's 'The Thin Red Line' earlier this year. While both films concentrate on the psychological torment of men preparing to face their death, Malick treated this in a dreamy, expansive, near-philosophical way. Boyd, in contrast, pulls the focus tight into a tense, airless space.

Set over the 48 hours leading up to the Battle of the Somme, 'The Trench' acquaints us with a squad of young soldiers, the volunteers of Kitchener's Army who joined up in the first flush of patriotic ardour, little suspecting what was awaiting them at the front.

As in R. C. Sherriff's play *Journey's End,* the intention is to undermine the romantic conception of the Great War. But where Sherriff's men were of the educated, well-spoken officer class, 'The Trench' mostly explores the earthier comradeship of soldiers such as 17-year-old Billy Macfarlane (Paul Nicholls), the platoon's tough-nut Sergeant Winter (Daniel Craig) and the nerve-jangled Second Lieutenant Hart (Julian Rhind-Tutt), who keeps himself going on crafty nips of scotch. Navigating the claustrophobic spaces, the camera absorbs not just the dread but the boredom, discomfort, squalor, sleeplessness and dislocation of trench life, these miseries counterpointed by the mirth and energetic profanity of what were essentially young lads together. When a toe-rag corporal named Dell (Danny Dyer) charges his fellows a penny each for a look at his porn photos, you're tempted to snort at such juvenile behaviour – until you remember that most of these soldiers are juveniles.

Boyd has previously covered the horrors of the Western Front in his capacious and brilliant novel *The New Confessions* (1987), from which he ➡

occasionally borrows details. When Billy's brother Eddie is shot in the mouth by a sniper, a soldier standing nearby catches one of his teeth in the face, a direct quotation from the moment in the novel when Todd, on his first unprotected view of no-man's land, is hit just above the eye from a flying tooth fragment.

Later on, Billy comes across a ration party that has been blasted by a direct hit, all that remains of them a hideous confusion of flesh and bone. The camera glimpses this briefly before turning back to Billy, yet its impact cannot match Todd's description of a similarly unspeakable sight: 'I saw what looked like a horrifically mangled side of beef, flayed by a maniac butcher with an axe. At the top there was an ear, some hair and part of a cheek.' It seems to me that the novel's description is more unsettling than what we witness in the film, because the suggestiveness of the words 'flayed' and 'maniac butcher' force us towards the perilous uncertainties of our own imagination – far scarier than what we see in plain view.

This is not the place to discuss the superiority of the novel over film, though it must be said that in terms of richness of characterisation, Boyd's soldiers on film pale beside Todd's platoon in the book, whose names I can still recall from the last time I read it.

The young cast of 'The Trench' certainly look the part, from their close-cropped beads to their eager, open faces, yet in general we accumulate little sense of them as individuals. A notable exception is the uneasy relationship between the hard-bitten Sergeant Winter played by Daniel Craig and Julian Rhind-Tutt's ineffectual junior officer; both actors have a presence which they use to tremendous effect in a sequence near the end of the film. The platoon's rum ration – vital Dutch courage for those about to go over the top – has been stolen, and in desperation Winter asks the Second Lieutenant to donate his personal supply of whisky for the sake of his men. The latter refuses, and for the first and last time we feel the repressed hostility crackle between the two; only afterwards did I remember that Winter himself was teetotal, his persistence an act of true selflessness. It's one of the film's great moments. The film's other problems are mainly to do with budget. The interior recreation of the trench never quite allows you to ignore the studio lighting or the slightly artificial atmosphere: there seems a peculiar absence of flies and mosquitoes for a reeking, mud-bound trench in high summer. I also didn't much care for the cymbal crashes on the score whenever a dramatic title – 'The Trench, 1st July 1916' – flashed up on screen. These are minor shortcomings. What Boyd and his team have done, given their means, is remarkable. One emerges from it with a sense of tragic limitation, of young men who barely accustomed themselves to life before they were suddenly forced to confront death. It addresses with profound seriousness and humanity an experience of war that still holds and horrifies, even as it fades from the edges of living memory.

Source: The Independent 17 September 1999

World War I soldiers had to live and fight in horrific conditions

Student answer

> **Textual adaptation: Life during World War I: a letter home**
>
> *18th November 1915*
>
> Dearest Family,
>
> I am scrawling this note from our trench – we have not moved now for four weeks. Winter is beginning to set in and I am sure there will be casualties from the perishing weather that will follow. The cold! The boredom! The smell! These remain our worst enemies along with the dreaded Hun.
>
> I am afraid that I must be the bearer of terrible news. Lieutenant Hart died yesterday morning. He was on routine patrol duty when an enemy sniper shot him dead. He took one shot in the head – he did not suffer. I am not sure how I will manage now that he is gone. His jokes and his constant offerings of warming whiskey kept me going. I trust you will break it to Jeanie gently.
>
> I, myself, am as well as can be expected, in body at least. I am not sure that my mind is in quite such good health. I feel, after all the death, all the loss, that my mind, my humanity, my soul, died a good few months ago now.
>
> I have been out here just short of a year, but I feel sure the war will be over quite soon. We are desperately short of ammunition and weaponry. We have no shells for our artillery, which means we cannot bombard the enemy lines, we cannot attack, move forward. We have to sit here and defend what we have got – which is not much and is beginning to decrease.
>
> I am told that Kitchener has thousands of volunteers, millions maybe, all ready to come out here and fight for their country. What a waste!

They will only make things worse, because there will be more men for fewer arms. The generals think that they can smash through the German lines with sheer weight of numbers. They are wrong. The Huns' trenches are strong, well built, deep. I came across one on recon patrol once that was over 30 feet deep. Ours are usually around 20. They also have machine gun turrets. These guns can cut down swathes of men without reloading.

The lads are not so scared of the guns, though. It is over so swiftly that you have no time to think about dying. It is an honourable way to go. What everyone fears more than anything is the wire. If it is not completely destroyed by the shells, the wire can kill all by itself. It catches and slashes, often fatally. A slow death. These are becoming more and more frequent because of the shell shortage – shorter bombardments, more dangerous wire. The fear is spreading.

However, I will fight on. The thought of you all keeps me going. You are in my prayers and dreams every night, every day. I will see you all very soon, though not soon enough.

With warmest love,
Billy.

Comparative commentary

I chose to write in the form of a letter home, because I felt that this would be the most flexible style and allow me to be more familiar with my audience. It allowed me to write in a personal, emotive manner, whilst at the same time, giving me licence to explain things which needed explaining. Emotion is probably the biggest difference between my piece and the two sources. Text B does contain some voiced opinions, but these are concerning the quality of the film, not the quality of life of the soldiers, so it is entirely different. I wanted the voice of the soldier to surface and so I allowed him certain comments on his situation, such as the simple use of a pattern of three noun phrases at the start of the letter: 'The cold! The boredom! The smell!' This contrasts with the long and frequently complex sentences of both pieces.

I tried to create in my piece an undercurrent of dying hope, as though the soldier is beginning to accept that he will probably die but never articulates this overtly:

> *'The lads are not so scared of the guns, though. It is over so swiftly that you have no time to think about dying. It is an honourable way to go.'*

The use of the negated and modified verb 'not so scared' after the informal and chatty use of the noun 'lads' alleviates the gravity of the situation. The adverb 'swiftly' and the adjective 'honourable' convey his grip on reality as well as his principles. Billy also uses many abstract terms, which all serve to distance the horror of the Front from his family: 'health . . . death . . . loss . . . humanity . . . soul.' I attempted to highlight how the soldiers became 'terrified and obsessed' by the wire (Text A). I used this and introduced some phonological effects through the assonance of: 'It catches and slashes, often fatally.'

There is also the hint of the hatred and fear that it represents in the use of the verb 'slashes' which is also alluded to in the first text:

> *' . . . caught and lacerated in its entangled mass of snares and meshes.'*

I cut the more formal 'His would be a slow and agonising death' to a simple noun phrase that I believe is both stark and a real fact: 'A slow death.'

'Billy' and 'Lieutenant Hart' are both characters mentioned in the review of the film (Text B), and it would be a perfectly valid decision for me to translate these into my piece. The other name I use, 'Jeanie', is purely my creation and I consider it to be of sufficient informality and appropriateness to mesh in seamlessly.

The recounting of Lieutenant Hart's death in my piece also adds a personal touch and voice. By mentioning the death of one man in particular, it includes a sense of first-hand experience. Text A mentions individual men such as General Haig, but these are men who were leaders. But by inserting this death and loss into my piece, it adds an emotional edge to the letter. I supplement this by use of emotive adjectives: 'afraid . . . terrible . . . ' conveying the personal grief of Billy. This, coupled with the fact that he mentions someone called 'Jeanie', someone we presume to be his wife, serves to emphasize the personal involvement one would expect to find in a letter of this kind.

Another choice relates to the amount of detail I included in my piece. In Text B we are given descriptions of flying tooth fragments and the sight of mutilated bodies after a shell explosion. I felt such details had no place in my letter because the soldier is writing home to his family, and so would wish to spare them such gruesome description. Instead, I included a bulk of information on the soldier's opinions about the shell shortage and the number of volunteers going to the front line. This was, I felt, a subject the soldier could go into in some detail. It is shocking, the fact that they were low on ammunition, but it is not shocking in the way that a description of a man missing half of his head would be to his family.

I also aimed at a certain formality of style which I feel would be apparent in letters of almost 100 years ago. I use no contractions or abbreviated forms:

> *'I, myself, am as well as can be expected, in body at least. I am not sure that my mind is in quite such good health.'*
>
> *I believe this adds to the authenticity of the piece of writing and ensures its cohesion.*

Examiner's comments

This answer serves to highlight what you can do with material and the many ideas that can be gleaned from the source texts. This student concentrates on the material that is appropriate to his audience and their sensibilities. He chooses his lexis carefully, and where it is value-laden and emotional, it is for a particular effect, which he remarks upon in his comparative commentary. His own new text is of the right word length, although his commentary strays over the guidelines by some 200 words. That said, he crams a great deal of information into his analysis and covers all the areas he is asked to cover, and more!

How this Unit links to other sections of the course

Unit 5 has its genesis in Units 1 and 3 of the specification. It is designed to continue on from these two Units, but it also feeds into the next and final module, the Synoptic Unit. This Unit is also designed to help you cope with the rigours of increased examination demands: additional tasks, more examination time and unseen comparative analysis.

The table below shows the major links between this Unit and others on the course.

Question	Skills learned	Links to other parts of the Specification
Dramatic Study Question	Identifying how values are communicated to an audience	• Language of Prose and Speech Unit 3 Sections A and B • Synoptic question Unit 6 Question 1
	Showing understanding of contexts	• Language of Prose and Speech Unit 3 Sections A and B • Comparative Literary Studies Unit 4
	Dealing with the closed book examination	• Language of Prose Unit 3 Section A
Adaptation Question	Writing for different purposes	• Production question Unit 1 Question 1 • Synoptic question Unit 6 Question 2
	Identification of audience and writing for a specific audience	• Production question Unit 1 Question 1 • Synoptic question Unit 6 Questions 1 and 2
	Learning to use, select and adapt source material	• Production question Unit 1 Question 1
	How to use a framework for production	• Synoptic question Unit 6 Question 2
Comparative Commentary	Reflecting on choices made in own writing	• Production question Unit 1 Question 2
	Use of quotation to evidence stylistic points in own writing	• Production question Unit 1 Question 2
	Assimilation of subject matter and content of texts	• Production question Unit 1 Question 2
	Reflecting on how language is used to help target an audience	• Language of Speech Unit 3 Section B • Synoptic question Unit 6 Question 1

8 Language in Context

The final section of AQA Specification A is the synoptic Unit, which is weighted as 20 per cent of the course. It deals with unseen material in an examination of 2½ hours. There are two questions in a format that will always remain the same; first, there will be an analytical comparison of at least three unseen texts (there may be more than three texts if they are brief) followed by an evaluation of the analytical methods you used in your comparative analysis.

The synoptic Unit

As you have seen in the previous two Units, the comparative angle to text analysis is a key element of study at A2-level. The comparative part of this final paper is very important and needs to be considered in both questions. In the subject specification, you are told that you will be tested on the following areas in the first comparative question. These bullet points will also appear on the examination paper itself – they are printed there to emphasize their importance and to remind you to cover these particular areas in your answer.

Question 1 **tests** your ability to:

❑ respond with knowledge and understanding to texts of different types and from different periods, exploring and commenting on relationships and comparisons between them
❑ use different literary and linguistic approaches to the study of written and spoken language
❑ identify and consider the ways attitudes and values are created and conveyed in speech and writing.

Question 1 also **draws on** your ability to:

❑ use appropriate terminology and accurate written expression
❑ show understanding of the ways contextual variation and choices of form, style and vocabulary shape the meanings of texts.

In other words, this Unit is testing your overall ability by drawing on the parts of the course that are the most important for an integrated study of language and literature. You should be using the terminology in a natural and unforced way by this point in the course, so that it facilitates your textual interpretation rather than being some kind of bolt-on exercise.

Similarly, the practice you have had during the course should enable you to fuse technical vocabulary with an analytical framework that helps you deal with the texts in a logical fashion.

However, there is also an evaluative part to this Unit. Along with the comparative element in all Units at A2, evaluation is a key issue. Previously you have evaluated the effectiveness of your textual comparison in Unit 4 and of your textual adaptation in Unit 5. The synoptic Unit, however, moves you into a new area of evaluation: that of the analytical method you used to help you compare and analyse the unseen texts, and how the use of your particular approach has helped your appreciation of the texts. The specification and the examination paper both point out how you will be assessed in this evaluative question.

Question 2 **tests** your ability to:

❏ evaluate different literary and linguistic approaches to the study of written and spoken language, showing how these approaches inform your readings.

Question 2 also **draws on** your ability to:

❏ communicate clearly the knowledge and insights gained from combined literary and linguistic study, using appropriate terminology and accurate written expression
❏ demonstrate expertise and accuracy in writing for a variety of specific purposes and audiences.

This is a new departure for English students, since you are being asked to reflect not only on your interpretation and analysis but also on how effective your analysis is. There will be more on this later in the chapter.

The analytical comparison

The three texts which will appear in this synoptic Unit and form the basis of your answers to both questions are all unseen and are drawn from a range of sources. The groups of texts will always have representations of the following among them:

❏ a piece of literary writing
❏ a piece of non-literary writing
❏ a spontaneous unscripted extract of speech
❏ texts drawn from a range of historical periods.

Obviously, it is important that you are familiar with the form and nature of these types of texts before you begin the comparative analysis.

There will always be some unifying link between the three texts; this link will be important, as it will provide the first clue you need, to be able to put together your comparative framework for analysis. These links could include:

- ❏ theme
- ❏ audience or intended audience
- ❏ historical period
- ❏ representation or treatment of a particular issue
- ❏ mode issues
- ❏ purpose
- ❏ context.

It is likely that your analysis will always have to take mode issues into consideration whether it is a link or not, since there will always be both writing and speech as part of the unseen material. Similarly, you will probably take into account both audience and purpose, which are two of the key textual determinants we have emphasized during the course. However, the link that connects the three texts should be your first consideration in constructing your analytical framework. Once you have established this, you can start to flesh out the structure of your analysis.

Deciding upon an analytical framework

This isn't as daunting as it first sounds. Throughout the book, we have emphasized the need to answer any question in a structured, logical fashion. It is imperative that you do so throughout the course so that when you reach this point, the construction of your analytical framework is second nature to you as well as an integral part of your planning procedure.

You have to deal with at least three texts here, so it is crucial that you use an analytical framework to help you engage in unseen analysis to this extent. A framework will give you the opportunity to cover the necessary ground in a logical way, while also drawing on the expertise you have developed in each of the other five modules by employing such analytical frameworks.

Your first job when tackling the analytical comparison in the synoptic Unit, therefore, is to decide upon the nature of your framework by examining the texts closely. You need to view this Unit as the culmination of your studies, where you can bring all your critical experience to bear on the texts; it is your final opportunity to ensure that the examiner hears your personal, informed voice as you respond to the material in front of you. The most effective way to do this is to decide on the parameters of your analysis by constructing an effective framework before you begin.

Areas to consider for your analytical framework

You should consider all the areas you have learned about in your studies and select the appropriate ones to aid your comparison. At the end of this book there is a Literary and Linguistic Toolkit (see page 280). To continue the analogy of the toolkit, when a mechanic examines an engine he or she does not use every tool, but selects only the appropriate tools that will help to do the job effectively and efficiently. The same applies here: select only the relevant terminology and analytical tools and apply them to the appropriate parts of the texts that will help inform the textual comparison.

Having used the information in the question to establish the unifying link between the texts, you need to consider certain levels of textual discrimination, as outlined in the diagram below. By working your way through these levels in a systematic way, you will ensure full coverage of the key areas.

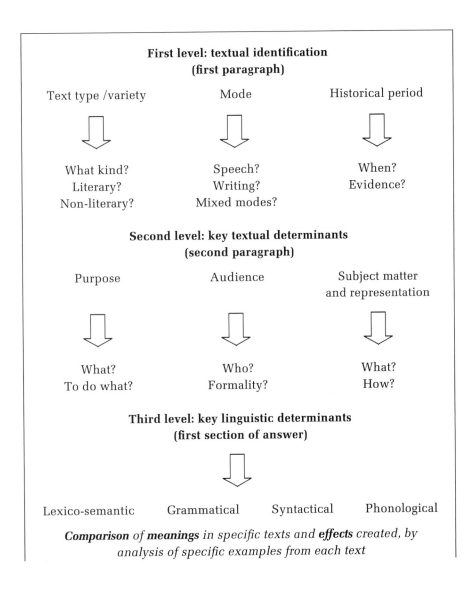

First level: textual identification
(first paragraph)

Text type /variety   Mode   Historical period

What kind?   Speech?   When?
Literary?   Writing?   Evidence?
Non-literary?   Mixed modes?

Second level: key textual determinants
(second paragraph)

Purpose   Audience   Subject matter
          and representation

What?   Who?   What?
To do what?   Formality?   How?

Third level: key linguistic determinants
(first section of answer)

Lexico-semantic   Grammatical   Syntactical   Phonological

Comparison of *meanings* in specific texts and **effects** created, by
analysis of specific examples from each text

Fourth level: mode determinants
(second section of answer)

Identification *of specific mode features and* **differences** *created by*
them, by **analysis** *of specific examples from each text*

Fifth level: transmission of values
(third section of answer)

How *each writer/speaker* **conveys** *his or her values through use of*
language, by **analysis** *of specific examples from each text*

Sixth level: evaluation
(final paragraph)

Cohesion　Authorial detachment　Emotional reaction　Reaction of others
Evaluation *of textual* **success** *through comparative methods you have*
employed

The main areas you need to work on have all been covered elsewhere in
the book. The diagram above gives an outline from which to design your
own analytical framework: it is simply to remind you of the areas that need
to be covered in a comparative analysis of this type.

Your major task is to identify the way in which you will construct your
analysis. It may be that you focus on one of the key areas from the first two
levels, such as intended audience, and compare the ways that the writers or
speakers in the texts use language in targeting their audiences. You need to
remember that it would be virtually impossible to cover all the areas that are
listed above in detail; you should concentrate on selecting an appropriate
focus for your comparative analysis and ensuring that you cover the
necessary linguistic and literary points. It would be perfectly possible to
amalgamate coverage of the third, fourth and fifth levels if you have mastered
the art of integrated analysis. This is perhaps something to work towards,
since it will enable you to make a comparative analysis in a vibrant and
meaningful way.

In whatever way you decide to construct your analytical framework, you
need to keep its form and purpose in mind so that when you come to the
second question you can reflect upon the key areas that have shaped your
analysis. Rather like the second section of Unit 5, where there is a natural
relationship between the changes you made in your new text and the

wording of the original source texts, the two tasks in Unit 6 are integrated, with the success of each being dependent on the other.

Some issues of mode comparison

When we looked at the differences between modes in Chapter 4, The Study of Speech, we limited our analysis to the features of each mode. In this section of the paper, as we have already mentioned, there will be a need to compare the nature of the different modes, and in particular the lexical, syntactic and grammatical features of the two modes. Naturally, we do not have the space to cover all possible issues in this book, but if we look at the major comparative areas this will help you practise making meaningful comparisons.

Lexical issues

You will have found that there are very obvious differences between the types of linguistic units used in written and spoken texts. This is mainly due to the fact that when we speak we tend to use many more grammatical (or function) words than lexical (or content) words. This means that speech has **low lexical density**; that is, when we calculate the proportion of grammatical words in relation to lexical words, we see that the latter are not as heavily represented as the function words. Writing, especially literary writing, has **high lexical density**.

The following example is taken from *English in Speech and Writing* by Rebecca Hughes. It shows these differences quite succinctly.

Written text (function words in italics)
The essence *of* television is *this*: *it* is *about* entertainment, *not* government. *It* is *about* ratings *and about* competition *between* channels.

Spoken text (function words in italics)
And that really is *the* essential *about* television *it's about* entertainment *and not* government *that it's about the* ratings *that it's about the* competition *between each* channel.

When we speak we tend to use lexical words that are from a simple stock of core content words which we use day in, day out. Often these words are fairly concrete and simplistic in nature. The use of abstract terms can be fairly limited in speech, simply because the mode is more suited to concrete terminology. When abstracts are used, they are often formulated into verbs. For example, we could convert the abstract noun *hatred* into the form of a pronoun and verb such as *I hate* . . . These words are in contrast to the more literary lexis used in written prose. We can see this very clearly when we re-examine the introductory lines from two texts (first quoted in Chapter 4) which provide an interesting comparison between speech and writing.

ACTIVITY

> Re-read the openings of the two texts printed below.
>
> **A** Highlight the grammatical (function) words in each text and calculate which is the more lexically dense from your results.
> **B** Identify the content words in each text and compare the use of those content words in Extract 1 with Extract 2. What word classes do they fall into? What conclusions can you reach, even from this small sample?

Extract 1

I have very pale skin, very red lips. The lips are a fleshy cushion of pink, but I colour them dark scarlet. The skin is naturally pale, that prized magnolia of lovers, the skin of fairy tales and calves, and it is dusted with Shiseido, a white powder. The journalists have always talked about my skin.

Extract 2

My name's Joanne (0.5) I'm eighteen years old (1.0) an' I live in a small village (0.5) called Castleton (0.5) near Whitby (.) on in the middle o' the North Yorkshire Moors (0.5) with m' mum 'n dad (1.0) an' ma brother Simon (0.5) who's twenty-three a:::nd (0.5) erm (0.5) ma sister Emma.

Grammatical issues

One of the key issues that you will be able to discuss when comparing the use of different modes is that a wide range of grammatical features are unique to speech, and can thus form an interesting and rich comparison to the grammatical complexities of writing.

We have already mentioned the fact that **elliptical forms** are very common in speech, such as *don't care* for *I don't care*. In a construction such as this, the subject, in the form of the first-person pronoun, is missed out because the context would probably indicate that it is the speaker who is reflecting this attitude. Similarly, we have already mentioned the high occurrence of **contracted forms** such as *he's* for *he is* and *it's* for *it is*.

We can go on to examine the clause structure of spontaneous speech. Often, there is a high incidence of subject-verb construction, followed by a post modifying object, complement or adverbial. These **simple clauses** are often connected by a variety of co-ordinating features such as fillers, relative pronouns, adverbs, determiners and elliptical forms.

Look at the following utterance, taken from near the opening of a conversation where two people are trading their experiences from their summer holidays. Typically, the first topic of conversation is the weather!

R: I had a smashing holiday
J: Yeah
R: went to Scotland (.) an' we had great weather (0.5) it was sunny nearly all the time

If we break down the component parts of just this small part of the conversation, we can see that there is a high incidence of the simple clause structure described above:

	S(ubject)	V(erb)	O(bject)
	I	**had**	**a smashing holiday**
	S	V	A(dverbial)
	[Elliptical subject]	**went**	**to Scotland**
contracted co-ordinator	S	V	C(omplement)
an'	**we**	**had**	**great weather**

Here it is easy to see where each clause starts and the next begins, but as a speaker becomes more animated or excited you will find that clauses become more complex in their construction, or there is a high incidence of co-ordination between the clauses, or the clauses become pared-down phrases – quite often noun phrases – which take the place of a full clause. It is fairly common in unscripted speech for the co-ordinating conjunction *and* to be used as an **indication of continuation** by the speaker. (This is also why so many children repeatedly use the word in stories when they first learn to write; they are simply replicating a pattern they have heard and use in speech.)

Another grammatical issue we have made passing reference to is **deixis,** which is a kind of linguistic pointing, in that it is word usage that relies totally on context. **Deictic expression** falls into two broad categories. **Proximal** terms are those expressions that refer to things near to the speaker, such as *this, here* or *now.* **Distal** terms relate to things that are away from the speaker, such as *that* or *then.*

Another key grammatical area used in speech is **reference.** This allows us to identify things, people, places and so on. The three major areas are **anaphoric, exophoric** and **cataphoric** reference.

❑ **Anaphoric reference** is by far the most common. It allows us to refer back to something that was mentioned earlier in the conversation.

Example
Look at that **bloke** (.) **he**'s got orange hair

The third-person singular pronoun *he* is an example of anaphoric reference. Since the last noun mentioned was *bloke,* it obviously refers back to that word. We use anaphora all the time in speech, since it allows us to be speedier in communicating what we want to say, as well as making speech less repetitive.

❏ **Exophoric reference** means referring to something that only the context or situation can identify.

Example
Let's go over **there**

The deictic term *there* is obviously context dependent, and only the shared understanding of the two or more people who are party to this utterance would identify what it means. It is therefore an example of exophoric reference.

❏ **Cataphoric reference** is much less frequent in speech; it is a device often used by writers to withhold information, since it refers forward to something mentioned later.

Example
He's over there. **George Smith**!

The third-person singular pronoun *he* is mentioned prior to the name of the person referred to, in this case *George Smith*.

Issues of transmission of values

In speech, attitudes are often indicated by use of:

❏ prosody (the way we utter words, including pitch, pace, rhythm and volume)
❏ standard and non-standard forms (whether we take care with our speech and conform to the accepted norms, or deviate and use non-standard words and constructions)
❏ lexical choice and use of modifiers (certain words are chosen for emphasis or contrast)
❏ grammatical construction (where the manner in which you construct your utterances reflects a certain attitude).

In writing, authors use a wide range of devices all the time to add emphasis and lend weight to their words, as discussed in Chapter 3, The Language of Prose.

Evaluating your analytical methodology

As mentioned earlier, this evaluation is a new requirement for English students, but is included in every specification. The main assessment objective that will be tested is your ability to:

❏ evaluate different literary and linguistic approaches to the study of written and spoken language, showing how these approaches inform your readings.

Since you will have constructed your own framework for analysing the unseen texts in the first question of this paper, it should be a relatively simple task to discuss each main analytical focus in your answer.

It is essential that you plan out this answer; there will be an enormous temptation to rush this, but you should note that it accounts for a quarter of the marks on this Unit, which could make the difference between one grade and another in your final result.

However, there is no need to write a great deal here; as long as you pick out each major focus of your integrated, analytical comparison, describe how this approach helped your understanding of the texts, and reinforce your points with some well-chosen examples, you should succeed in this section.

Remember that the main focus of this course has been the integrated study of language and literature; this should remain in the forefront of your mind when you tackle this question. Your analytical framework will have taken account of both literary and linguistic matters, so you should always comment on both of these in your answer. Obviously, the approach you adopted in analysing the texts will dictate the extent to which you comment on literary and linguistic issues, as well as the interrelation between the two as seen through your analysis.

As always, it is necessary to use an outline for answering the question. You will probably want to comment on the core aspects of any text, that is audience, purpose, context and mode. These areas will essentially form the backdrop to what you write in your answer, since the textual interpretation you have adopted will be driven by a focus on these areas. The nature of your comparative study will dictate which of them is given prevalence.

About half of your answer should be devoted to delineating your approach. You then need to turn your attention to looking at other possible ways you might have approached your textual analysis – if you used a variety of approaches in your answer, you can discuss these alternative approaches. If you want to achieve higher marks for this question, you must show that you recognize there are different ways to approach any textual analysis.

You must be able to show that you have learned to select and use different analytical frameworks to help you understand different texts, and be aware that alternative approaches can yield slightly different readings of a text. A writer producing a text can be likened to a brewer using a range of ingredients to make beer; the proportion of the ingredients is vital, and results in different tastes depending on the mixture used. The taste of the beer will also be differently perceived by different drinkers, and they will personally assess whether it is, for instance, too strong or weak, rather as you assess texts you are studying.

Some of the issues you might like to consider when you tackle this part of the question are detailed below.

1 **Authorial intention** One very productive way of reflecting upon your analysis is to consider what the writer set out to do in the first place – the purpose of the text. You can evaluate to what extent the writer has succeeded by reflecting on your analytical results. This is a useful way of seeing whether a text works or not, since you will be examining the linguistic and literary choices and effects very closely.

2 **Critical approaches** Some critical theories yield startling results. For instance, a feminist approach to textual analysis specifically examines the portrayal of women and women's issues in writing and speech. In a male-oriented world it can produce very interesting readings. Similarly, a deconstructive approach to textual analysis and interpretation could bring many alternative readings to the surface, since this approach aims to see the text as open and possessing a variety of meanings.

3 **Critical frameworks** You may become so confident and articulate in your application of self-constructed critical frameworks that you may be able to offer two or more approaches of your own. This is perfectly valid and, in many ways, a laudable means of answering the question.

4 **Exploration of issues, themes or ideas** As indicated earlier, this may be a popular approach to framing your answer since there will be obvious links of this kind between the texts. You may decide to focus on the text by concentrating on one issue rather than another; you can follow this up by describing what the reading would have yielded had you taken a slightly different perspective.

5 **Mode use** In the first, comparative question, you will need to comment on the differing ways modes are used and represented. You may wish to take a more linguistic approach and examine some of the formalized mode theories that have been propounded in recent years, such as those put forward by Michael Stubbs or Leech, Deuchar and Hogenraad.

6 **Representation** Another method of weighing up different approaches to textual interpretation is to consider the ways writers and speakers represent the ideas and biases that they manifest in their texts. This could be seen as an extension of the critical approach, but some universal issues such as age, politics, and morality can all be given an interesting 'spin' by the writer and then interpreted in an individual fashion by the reader.

No single approach to this question should be regarded as an ideal; you can decide on your own critical route through the texts and describe the discoveries you make during your journey. The individual student's reflections on that journey are of most interest to the examiner, not the reflections of a teacher or lecturer!

APPROACHES TO EXAMINATION QUESTIONS

Practice Synoptic Paper 1

Question 1 (1 hour 45 minutes)
Analytical comparison

Read the three texts printed on the following pages. These texts all contain speech representations of some kind. **Text A** is an article from a football fanzine. **Text B** is from a contemporary thriller. **Text C** is a transcript of two old ladies being interviewed on the BBC.

Compare all **three** texts, commenting in detail on the ways language is used to target purpose, audience and context. Your analysis should include consideration of:

❏ the writer's/speaker's choice of vocabulary and grammar
❏ the use of particular mode features
❏ the ways in which the writers/speakers convey their attitudes and values to their intended audience
❏ any other areas which you consider are important in your reading, analysis and comparison of these texts.

Question 2 (45 minutes)
Evaluation of analytical methods

Using the three texts you have analysed in Question 1, highlight the ways in which you have interpreted these three texts and evaluate the approach to analysis you have used, saying which you have found the most useful in shaping your responses to the three texts.

Text A: The Lowdown . . . Paul 'Ga-Ga' Gascoigne from *The Onion Bag* (Issue 12)
(This text appeared in a football fanzine when Paul Gascoigne, affectionately known as Gazza, was playing for Glasgow Rangers. The text appeared shortly after England had beaten Scotland in the European Championships, where Gascoigne had scored a wonder goal.)

Full name: Paul Gascoigne the Amazing Giant Baby.
Mental age: 3¼
Team: I'm one of the Powah-Rangers, me. Vroom-vroom! Thakka-thakka-thakka! Ker-POWWWWW!
Previous clubs: Chad Valley, Fisher Price.
International honours: Throwing temper-tantrums, crying, blowing raspberries, being naughty, saying poo an' wee-wee to referees for ma country, Thelma pet.
Biggest influence on career: Having to play in Pampers.
With which historical figure do you most associate yourself? People say I look like Baby-Face Finlayson out of the Beano, and he's a canny lad, like. But ➡

one blurk I really look up to is Michael Jackson – he's mad, bad and reet dangerous on the swings.

What did you think when you first saw Sheryl's new breasts? Lunch.

Favourite cartoon: Scrappy-Doo. Or 'Paul Ince' as we call him oot in the playgroond, like.

Food/drink: Gerber doner kekab an' chilli sauce is me favourite flavah jar; and as for a bevvie I like Newcastle Broon mixed with rurse-hip syrup in me bottle.

Hobby: Inapprurpriate surcial behaviah. Ye can call us a sentimental simpleton, but givin' them 'You Bet!' contestants fifty quid for the bairns was straight from the bottom of me gret big Geordie heart. And as for me heartbreakin' revelations on the Danny Baker show . . .

PG Skill-Tip: Divven't sell a defendah a dummy 'til you're burped an' settled in yer cot, like.

PG Training Tip: Fifteen bottles o' Broon doon me neck followed up with half an hoor o' keep-fit in the doorframe, workin' off the calories in me Giant Baby-Booncer, like.

Most likely to say: 'Haway, Five-Bellies, man! Bleeeeeeurch! Fooled the jocko bastards! Broon and birianis aal roond – an' divven't forget the comedy breasts!'

Least likely to say: Nothing.

If you weren't a footballer, what do you think you'd be? A village idiot.

Text B: From *Quite Ugly One Morning* by Christopher Brookmyre
(*At this point in this thriller, Jack Parlabane, a journalist nicknamed 'Scotland' by his American friend Larry Freeman, seeks help in researching a particularly interesting but potentially dangerous story.*)

A strange scent in the nostrils, stronger all the time. The feeling of being on to something big but not knowing what it was. A lot of corpses and the broken traces of a connection; like discovering short stretches of an overgrown path through a dense forest, but not yet able to see where those stretches came from or were leading to.

Lieutenant Larry Freeman had been nervous. Larry was about seven feet tall with shoulders 'the size of a Kansas prairie', as his wife put it, a frightening sight in black shades and a black, bald head. And Larry was never nervous.

'Something in the air then, big man?'

'Uh-huh,' he had said slowly in that rumbling burr you could feel in your own diaphragm. 'Remember man, cops like the sound of openin' a fresh can of beer when the case is closed. The sound of openin' a fresh can of worms don't fill their heart with joy, know what I'm sayin'? Now I ain't sayin' there's dirty cops in my precinct, but cops gotta talk to snitches and there's gotta be some give and take. And no news travels faster than a secret.

'You gotta be careful what yo askin' and who yo askin', Scotland. Somebody starts playin' join-the-dots with a bunch of random stiffs and a whole lotta people get trigger-happy. Maybe you ain't even connectin' anythin' to them or to stiffs they got anythin' to do with, but they don't know that and they ain't gonna stop to ask if they get you in their sights.'

'You're saying I should back off? Forget it all?'

'That's up to you, man. Maybe it's too late to back off. But you better be watchin' your back. I was you, I'd get me a gun.'

Parlabane shook his head.

'You know how I feel about guns. I couldn't carry one of those things around with me, forget about it.'

'Yeah, but I'd have one all the same. Keep it where I could get to it in a hurry. I got a spare one in the john. In a plastic bag taped under the cistern lid. Someone catches me off-guard at home, I got a chance if he lets me take a leak or I can just make it to the bathroom. Mitch Cacy keeps one in his ice box.'

'What, so he's got a chance if the bad guy asks for a beer? You're all fucking crazy.'

'You ain't from L.A., Jack.'

Text C: From *Century Road*, BBC 1999.
Two women (A and B) recall a time when they were potato pickers, when they were much younger and lived in the railway town of Retford. They are being interviewed by a man (I).

Key: (.)   Micropause
                  (1.0)   Pause in seconds
                  ]   Overlap

A: Well this was the field with potatoes in

B: This one here

A: Yeah (1.0) we used to have stints didn't we

B: Yeah we had stint (.) you know that how that goes up there (.) erm it (.) that's how it was (0.5) an' yer had a stint as long as that (.) and yer had to pick all yer potatoes

A: An' we used to be together didn't we

B: Yeah

I: You used to work together did you

A: Yeah
                ]
B: Yeah (.) one at one end (.) with yer apron like this (*simulates her apron gathered up and picking off the ground and putting into the apron*)

A: Yeah you used to pick 'ard at it as well

I: That what you used to do (0.5) pick 'em into your apron

B: We used to have (.) a khaki apron

A: Wrapped round
                ]
B: Sack tied right round yer

A: then yer had to pick it (.) an' pull (.) an' pick yer potatoes into it (.) an' empty it into hampers when you'd got a load on

B: I fell asleep one time   ➡

A: You used to carry 'em round yer waist

B: I'm sat here now an' my arm's going like this (*mimes her arm swinging as if in the act of picking potatoes*) while I'm asleep (.) so (.) our John says (.) what you doin' Mam (.) an' I say (.) an I says (.) oh I'd be tatie pickin'

Practice Synoptic Paper 2

A sample student response follows these questions.

Question 1 (1 hour 45 minutes)
Analytical comparison

Read the three texts printed on the following pages. These texts are linked through their common theme of football. **Text A** is a poem written by Ted Hughes. **Text B** is part of a live commentary of a football match on a local BBC radio station. **Text C** is a report from the Sports section of the *Sunday Times*.

Compare all **three** texts, commenting in detail on the ways language is used to suit purpose, audience and context. Your analysis should include consideration of:

❏ the writer's/speaker's choice of vocabulary and grammar
❏ the use of phonological features
❏ the ways in which the writers/speakers convey their attitudes and values to their intended audience
❏ any other areas which you consider are important in your reading, analysis and comparison of these texts.

Question 2 (45 minutes)
Evaluation of analytical methods

Using the three texts you have analysed in Question 1, highlight the ways in which you have interpreted these three texts and evaluate the approaches you have used, saying which you have found the most useful in shaping your responses to the three texts.

Text A

Football at Slack

Between plunging valleys, on a bareback of hill
Men in bunting colours
Bounced, and their blown ball bounced.

The blown ball jumped, and the merry-coloured men
Spouted like water to head it.
The ball blew away downwind -

The rubbery men bounced after it.
The ball jumped up and out and hung on the wind
Over a gulf of treetops.
Then they all shouted together, and the ball blew back.

➡

Winds from fiery holes in heaven
Piled the hills darkening around them
To awe them. The glare light
Mixed its mad oils and threw glooms.
Then the rain lowered a steel press.

Hair plastered, they all just trod water
To puddle glitter. And their shouts bobbed up
Coming fine and thin, washed and happy

While the humped world sank foundering
And the valleys blued unthinkable
Under depth of Atlantic depression -

But the wingers leapt, they bicycled in air
And the goalie flew horizontal

And once again a golden holocaust
Lifted the cloud's edge, to watch them.

Ted Hughes

A football match between local teams inspired Ted Hughes's poem

Text B

Transcription

Key:	(.)	Micropause
	(1.0)	Pause in seconds
	::	elongation of sound
	.h	intake of breath
	[	overlap

Notes: There are two commentators; one is called Ray Simpson (R), the other is called Kevin Smith (K). They are commentating on a Third Round FA Cup match between two soccer clubs, Darlington and Wolverhampton Wanderers.

The numbers on the left are line numbers for easy reference.

1	**R:**	good save by Preece .h he's dropped a a backheader (.) backpass from Andy
2		Crosbie (0.5) .h and Platalainen po:unces on the gift (2.0) and (0.5) my:: wo:rd
3		(2.0) its Third Division against First Division and Kevin tonight (0.5) we've
4		seen Third Division defendin' (1.5)
5	**K:**	we::ll I think there you've seen a bit of park play (1.0) absolutely stunned the
6		crowd here (1.0) even the Wolves er supporters couldn't believe what they
7		were er witnessin' there (1.0) absolutely gobsmacked (1.0) again (.) we've seen
8		an individual mistake (1.0) again (.) we've seen Darlington makin' it (0.5) and
9		again (.) we've seen them score from it (3.0)
10	**R:**	so Mixu Platalainen makes it two nil (1.0) to (0.5) Wolverhampton Wanderers a
11		gift (0.5) from (.) David Preece (.) fumbled the backpass from Andy Crosbie (.)
12		an' all Platalainen had to do (.) was just pick it up (.) an' knock it (.) into an
13		empty net .h an' should Darlington lose this one (1.0) they will look back on it (.)
14		on the night (.) that they made two mistakes an' went out (.) of the FA Cup
15		(.) the fans in front of us Kevin they're shakin' their heads an'

                                                                                            [
16	**K:**	well ah I er er yeh
17		I mean yer er (.) sometimes I feel sorry for keepers with it bein' the last line of
18		defence (.) if they make a mistake they get punished but (1.0) god yer you just
19		do not expect to see that fer from from er (.) a professional footballer (.)
20		between the sticks (2.0)
21	**R:**	you

                [
| 22 | **K:** | well how Darlington pick theirselves up from this is is is er now (.) a test of |
| 23 | | character (0.5) give what they've got (.) an' go down fightin' |

Text C

No Reward for Gallant Gazza

Michael Hodges

Middlesbrough	**0**
Leicester City	**0**

This was a blurred impression of a football game. The attendance may have matched the number of people to queue for Monet this week, but this game did not deserve public display.

Luckily this was in primary colours. Such was the early to and fro that a clear demarcation between red and blue was needed to maintain perspective.

There were neat strokes; both Paul Gascoigne and Hamilton Ricard showed that Middlesbrough do possess some finesse, even though Brian Deane went out of his way to show how limited it is.

Leicester, playing again with the little and large combination of Tony Cottee and Matt Elliott up front, had little to do with the game until Gerry Taggart was offered an open header at Middlesbrough's goal. Content with missing that, they settled back into the uneasy compromise between the panic and flail their defence produces whenever Elliott plays forward.

Perhaps they were thrown by the blur of Gascoigne's arms; contriving as ever to make the simple look Herculean.

The artist formerly known as Gazza daubed his full palette of passes on ➡

the game, but also pumped his limbs madly, grabbed his breath painfully and, in short, generally made the game watchable.

In so doing he was helped by Robbie Mustoe, as good in midfield as he is unsung and a possessor of the rare ability of knowing when to pass.

But the more Middlesbrough got the ball to Deane and Ricard, the less likely they seemed to be able to score – if anything they were more cackhanded than their markers. Colin Cooper did loop a header through the throng, but it was cleared off the line. Then, after Mark Schwarzer had saved an Elliott free-kick with his chin, Ricard slipped Leicester's zig-zagging back line.

Though Kasey Keller's save was good, Ricard should have scored – but on the accumulative evidence of the game, it was perhaps appropriate that he did not.

The shapes, at least were interesting. Martin O'Neill, sensing the bigger picture was a canvas with 0-0 written all over it, brought Elliott back to his usual stamping ground and let captain Steve Walsh wander forward.

Perversely he had more shots in five minutes than Elliott had contrived in 45. Cottee appeared to like the new set-up and was frisky enough to increasingly open up the home defence but it was Gascoigne who continued to be the best user of the ball.

Fit enough now to only need a half-time rest for recovery, he repeatedly cut inside his man and produced excellent passes. Sadly they were usually given away immediately, for if Gascoigne was playing like an artist, his colleagues were the artisans.

Middlesbrough pressed until the end, but to little more than occasional effect. Truly this was stuff to annoy the academy; plenty of content, but little form.

Student response: Analytical comparison

When first confronted with these texts, my initial reaction was that they shared very little in common other than that they all focus on the topic of football. The texts relate to each other in that they are all pieces *about* football, but the content of the pieces and the approach that they take on football is very much determined by the form they are written in, their context and purpose, and their respective audiences.

Hughes' piece is written in the form of a poem and uses the language of a poem. I believe the content mirrors the form in the way that Hughes writes a *poem* about the *poetic* side of football. Hughes is, for all intents and purposes, writing about a football match, but does this in a manner that clearly distinguishes his piece as a poem and sets it apart from Text C, where Michael Hodges writes a post-match report. Hughes, however, highlights a side of football that can be seen as 'poetic' and 'romantic'.

This approach is established through the use of images such as men 'spouting' to head the ball, the 'merry-coloured', 'rubbery' men and the wingers 'leaping'. This vocabulary attempts to exaggerate the game, so that the reader sees it not as simply a game of football, but as something fantastic and superhuman. There is evidently a bond between the players and the situation. Images like players 'treading water to puddle glitter' and the location being 'blued unthinkable under depth of Atlantic depression' add mystery and wonder to a poem that is essentially about a common, everyday game. This is not what Hughes would have us believe, though. He portrays it in such a way that someone reading this who had not played football would think that the game was an Earth-moving, perhaps even spiritual, experience. It is this approach which sets it apart from the other pieces. He writes about the romantic, spiritual side of football. Further use of the elements fire and water add to the spiritual angle of the poem. The weather is described as originating from 'fiery holes in heaven', and when it rains it has the quality of cleansing the players in a religious manner: 'their shouts bobbed up . . . washed and happy'.

But it is the feeling of the superhuman, perhaps even preternatural, feats of the players that permeate this poem, where the players 'bicycled the air' and the goalkeeper 'flew horizontal'. Hughes leaves us with the notion that he is observing men who are sent from the gods and that they have the ability to transcend the weather.

If we then compare the type of language used in Hughes' poem to that used in the BBC radio commentary, we can see clear contrasts. Far from focusing on the romantic side of football, this piece is very much a reflection of its form. It is informative, to the point, and describes only the action that the audience needs to know. Indeed, the audiences of the two are very different. Whereas Hughes' readers are likely to be those who want to broaden their horizons by reading about other experiences, the radio commentary is of parochial interest, probably to the fans of the two clubs.

On the radio, the commentators do not stray from the action to describe how the sun in the sky resembles a 'golden holocaust lifting the cloud's edge', they simply describe what is happening. This is reflected in the use of dynamic verbs: 'dropped' and 'fumbled'. These simple past tense verbs help to convey the action in the commentary. In Hughes' poem we see the romance of the situation and game, a quasi-religious event between players and spectators; in the commentary, the immediate action of the game is conveyed through elliptical utterances, spoken at speed: 'good save by Preece' and 'absolutely stunned the crowd'.

The commentators use football jargon: 'net', 'backpass' and 'two nil'. However, the lexis is even more narrow when the commentators use colloquial terms which reflect their own knowledge of soccer's accepted terminology: 'between the sticks' for 'in goal' and 'park play' for 'lack of professionalism'. These commentators assume the audience understand this terminology simply because they are a specialist audience. In some ways, this linguistic usage is the equivalent of Hughes' metaphors.

The use of non-standard terms underscores the parochial nature of the spoken mode. Such features as the end-clipping of third-person plural verb forms 'shakin',' 'defendin',' and 'fightin',' the non-standard use of the third-person plural reflexive pronoun form 'theirselves' instead of the standard 'themselves', and the use of slang terms such as 'gobsmacked' all serve to emphasize that this is the spoken mode where the speakers slip into their dialect grammar. The non-fluency features show the speed of the language production, especially in lines 15 and 16 where the adjacency pair is not as clearly delineated as it might be, with Kevin Smith struggling to express his feelings after Simpson has handed over to him: 'well ah I er er yeh I mean yer er'. This contrasts very obviously with the careful alliterative construction in Hughes' poem, used to reflect the basic movement and appearance of the game:

'bareback . . . bunting . . .
Bounced, and their blown ball bounced'

If we then compare the vocabulary we have just analysed in the first two texts to that used in the post-match report, we can see that this text lies somewhere between the poles established by the first two. It differs from the first two pieces in that this text is written with hindsight, with a chance to reflect and ascertain clear views on what has happened. In the case of the poem and the commentary, though in very different styles, the action is described as it happens. The writer and speakers therefore create a certain rhythm and tempo by which we read the pieces, a feature not evident in this final text.

The author in this case has had time to reflect and to insert little anecdotes and analogies that aid the readability and entertainment of the piece, whilst clearly marking it apart from the poem and commentary. We are again presented with another approach to football. Whilst Hughes, Simpson and Smith have all managed to portray the magnificence, action and relentlessness of the game of football, Hodges, through his words and images, strikes these down and reminds us that it is 'just a game'. Perhaps the best example of this point is in the description by Hodges of Paul Gascoigne when in possession of the ball. He describes 'the blur of Gascoigne's arms; contriving as ever to make the simple look Herculean.'

We can see here the difference in approaches of all the texts. Hodges has had time to gather his thoughts, to put all the action into the perspective of the game and the bigger picture, and so what results is a comment that diminishes the magnificence implied by Hughes and causes Simpson and Smith's relentless action to falter slightly. Where Hughes' approach is poetic, and Simpson and Smith's all action, Hodges, whilst admiring and praising certain aspects of the game, creates in the reader a feeling of 'back to reality'. Ironically, he does this by using an extended metaphor of the game being an impressionist painting. Hodges speaks of 'the primary colours' of the two teams in 'red and blue', he speaks of the individual's 'neat strokes', of Gazza 'daub(ing) his full palette of passes on the game' and the 'interesting . . . shapes' created by the teams. This gives the whole text a cohesive quality which the commentary does not have; its cohesiveness arises from its sequential nature, with phrases being linked by simple co-ordinating conjunctions 'and' and 'an' all'. The final concluding and perhaps climactic sentence reiterates the idea that this is just a game by working out the extended metaphor that the game had 'plenty of content but little form' and that it purports to be more artistic than it actually is, and ends up 'annoy(ing) the academy'.

In all the texts there is the common focus of football. However, they then deviate and differ through their varying approaches to the game. They conspire to both support and condemn each other through their attitudes – Hughes through his exaggeration: 'the humped world sank foundering' and overtly poetic language: 'The glare light / Mixed its mad oils'; the commentary through its use of prosodic features: 'po:unces' and 'my:: wo::rd' to indicate the speaker's disbelief; and the cohesive quality of the post-match report, through its extended artistic metaphor which is both reductive and belittling of the game of football.

The pieces are, as I mentioned at the beginning of this analysis, reflections of their forms and expected audiences. The poem looks at the poetic side of football. The running commentary looks at the running-action of football. The match report analyses both these features and presents us with an overall picture. Though linked through common focus, the audience, purpose and context of the pieces contrive intriguing and distinguishing contrasts, marking seemingly similar texts clearly apart from one another.

Evaluation of analytical methods

Examining the answer I have just written, and focusing on the way in which I compared the three texts, serves to highlight the fact that there are other routes through this particular type of comparison.

The main idea I took was to look at the texts in terms of their purpose and what the writers and speakers do with their subject matter. Hughes writes about football as if it were some kind of superhuman activity. I concentrated on the imagery of the poem, picking out those images that best served this reading: 'the wingers leapt' and the players 'trod water to puddle glitter'. Coupled with the references to the elemental forces of fire, water, air and earth, my interpretation of the poem becomes religious, hinting at the prodigious actions of the men. However, there are other ways in which the poem could be interpreted and this could form an interesting route through the other two texts. The poem could be seen as an observation on a sport that is exclusive for men, and prohibits women's participation. Whilst this is patently not true in reality, in these texts the focus is on men playing the game; in Hughes' poem he exaggeratedly glorifies their abilities by focusing on their actions: 'plastered hair, they trod water' and the men 'spouted like water'. Their abilities are such that the weather, no matter what it throws at them, does not diminish their actions and it finally 'watch(es) them', presumably in awe of their exertions. This reading would concentrate on Hughes' adjectival use: 'golden' and 'fiery' to reflect the qualities indirectly associated with the men, and the world 'foundering' at their feats (or perhaps feet!).

When I looked at the spoken commentary, I decided to examine it as a direct contrast to the poem: it is lexically sparse, with many function or grammatical words used. I emphasized the local angle also, whilst concentrating on the action of the piece and the way the commentators describe what is happening: 'Platalainen makes it two nil' and 'Preece (has) dropped a backheader'. These simple sentences are in direct contrast to the carefully crafted poetic form of Hughes, and show the spontaneity of the spoken form. An obvious point is that the commentary uses field-specific lexis such as 'backpass', 'park play' and 'between the sticks', all contributing to the narrowness of the purpose and audience, where the commentators make assumptions about the listeners' knowledge of soccer. It is possible to take a similar approach with this text and view it as being exclusive, especially in terms of the knowledge the audience must have. The two commentators are both males (as in the other texts also), emphasizing this sport as a male-dominated domain. Dynamic verbs such as 'pounces', 'punished' and 'fightin'' are all violent and have aggressive connotations; their use by the men in this piece perhaps signals the basic animalistic side of the sport, which will always make it a male preserve, simply because men are the stronger sex!

I also wanted to emphasize in my essay the lack of construction in the commentary, although there is obviously some organization through turn taking and sequencing of events by simple clause co-ordination. The care that both Hughes and Hodges take with their pieces was something I wanted to bring to the fore. I do not think the Michael Hodges' piece is as carefully structured as Ted Hughes' poem, but it is patently more controlled than the commentary, an obvious difference between the two modes.

In my analysis, I wanted to underline the use of the extended image and metaphor of the impressionist painting as the major cohesive device used by the writer. This device seeks to demystify football and, by making an implicit comparison to a superior art form, Hodges promotes this match as being essentially 'artless' whilst ostensibly having all the necessary artistic attributes. He ranges a little further in his references also, drawing on classical references ('Herculean'), contemporary musical references ('the artist formerly known as Gazza', an allusion to the singer Prince), and a contemporary public event, the queues for the Monet exhibition in London. As with the other two texts, this serves to narrow the potential audience, since these references are purely arbitrary and once again point towards a male world, using masculine points of reference to supplement a piece of writing already dominated by masculine names: Tony, Matt, Paul, Gerry, Martin and Steve. These names have no connotations of femininity about them; they are also names which are stereotypical of the soccer world as well as showing the footballers' fondness for shortening names to add to their masculinity.

I believe the line of showing how each text gives a particular angle on the game of soccer is an interesting and rewarding one; there are other interpretations, such as the feminist view I have hinted at here, but I think my original perspective allowed me to compare the texts in a worthwhile manner.

Examiner's comments

This answer shows the variety of approaches that can be adopted when engaging in comparative analysis. The student concentrates on matters of lexis, grammar, purpose, audience and values in his answer. He perhaps plays down quite an important and rich field for comment, that of phonological usage, although he does allude to it in the comments on prosody in the commentary and alliteration in the poem. His evaluation is quite unusual, and certainly very mature, as he cites possible feminist interpretations of the texts as an alternative approach. He could easily have referred to mode theories or different approaches to the purpose of each text in this section, as other possible routes through his comparison. This does not detract from the fact that this is a first-class answer, one which would undoubtedly gain an A grade.

SECTION III: PREPARING FOR ASSESSMENT

---

9 Revising Set Texts

If you are studying English for AS-level you will study two set texts for the exams. If you are studying for the full A-level you will study two or three further texts – four or five in all. Work on these texts will obviously play an important role in your final assessment, so it is essential that you revise them very carefully in preparation for the exams. The grade you achieve will depend on the quality and effectiveness of your preparation, so it is well worth spending time planning how you are going to set about it.

The first thing to bear in mind is that you need to allow plenty of time for revision. Probably one of the first mistakes that students make in terms of exam preparation is to leave it too late to start revision. It is certain that if you leave your revision until the last minute you will seriously damage your chances of doing as well as you are able. Students who do well show a mature, informed understanding of the texts they have studied and a high quality of insight and analysis of the issues that they raise and explore. Well-planned and structured revision has a key role to play in allowing you to develop these elements.

Now we will look at some of the things you can do to help revise your set texts and prepare for the exam.

Reading the texts

By the time you come to your revision period it is likely that you will have read your texts a number of times. This reading and re-reading of the texts is essential to the development of your understanding of them and to gaining the level of insight you need into the issues they explore.

It is surprising, however, just how many students think that reading their texts a couple of times – or even worse, once – will be sufficient. Very occasionally, from students' responses in the exam, it appears that they have not read the text at all! Fortunately these instances are rare, and it is clear that successful students know their texts extremely well, not only in terms of what the text 'is about' but also in terms of its various features. They also 'know their way around' the text and where to find the sections and details that they need in order to answer the question.

When we talk of 'reading the text' you should be aware that there are various kinds of reading, depending on your objective. It may be that when you read the text for the very first time you read it through fairly quickly, achieving an overview of what it is about. When you begin to study it in detail, you may read it more slowly so as to follow the plot carefully, examine the ways in which the characters emerge and begin to form views on the style and the ways in which language is used. Subsequent readings may be different again. You may skim through the text quickly to refresh your memory of the whole thing, or scan it looking for particular references or ideas. These various kinds of readings are very important for several reasons.

- ❏ They help you to become familiar with the text, not just in terms of the plot but also in picking up on the details.
- ❏ Most texts on the AS- or A-level specifications are complex works, and often you find that every time you read them you notice something new.
- ❏ You tend to come to an understanding of a text over a period of time. The kinds of texts you will have encountered on your course need to be thought about carefully and this takes time.
- ❏ This kind of reading is part of a developmental process which enhances your knowledge and understanding of your set texts. You need to build in time to reflect on what you have read, to absorb the material and then return to it again.

Time management

Time is a vital factor in your revision programme and it is essential that you allow yourself sufficient time to thoroughly revise all your texts, and for plenty of practice in the kinds of tasks you will encounter in the exam. It can be very useful to draw up a revision programme to cover all the texts you have studied. Initially this programme can be quite general, but as you get close to the exam it is a good idea to make it much more specific. Begin by compiling a detailed list of the areas of each text that you will need to revise. Remember, too, to build in time to write timed essays on your texts. For example, here is the revision programme on *Measure for Measure* drawn up by a student who has studied that text as part of her A-level course:

Measure for Measure — Areas for Revision

1   Overall synopsis of play.
2   Themes and issues:
    - ❏ justice/mercy
    - ❏ 'seeming' — appearance and reality
    - ❏ morality
    - ❏ hypocrisy

> ❑ *social setting*
> ❑ *attitude to women*
>
> 3   *Characters:*
>> ❑ *Isabella*
>> ❑ *Angelo*
>> ❑ *The Duke*
>> ❑ *Escalus*
>> ❑ *Claudio*
>> ❑ *Mariana*
>> ❑ *Lucio*
>> ❑ *Pompey*
>> ❑ *Mistress Overdone*
>> ❑ *Froth and Elbow*
>
> 4   *Technical features:*
> *Language*
>> ❑ *verse/prose*
>> ❑ *imagery*
>> ❑ *puns*
>> ❑ *different ways different characters use language*
>> ❑ *different ways the same characters use language*
>> ❑ *different effects achieved through the language of the play*
>> ❑ *thematic links developed through language*
>
> *Stagecraft*
>> ❑ *structure of play*
>> ❑ *staging devices*
>> ❑ *time sequences*
>> ❑ *pace*
>> ❑ *suspense*
>> ❑ *visual experience created through the language*
>
> 5   *Specimen passages for detailed analysis:*
>> ❑ *Act I scene i lines 24 - 83*
>> ❑ *Act I scene iii lines 1 - 54*
>> ❑ *Act II scene i lines 209 - 282*
>> ❑ *Act II scene ii lines 134 - 187*
>> ❑ *Act II scene iv lines 55 - 124*
>> ❑ *Act III scene i lines 73 - 146*
>> ❑ *Act III scene ii lines 83 - 179*
>> ❑ *Act V scene i lines 485 - 536*

This gives a basic overview of the areas for revision, but you can make your plan as detailed as you wish. It is advisable to do this with each text you study, so you have a complete record of all the work you have to do as well as a plan.

Next, it is a good idea to draw up a full programme with dates and times scheduling when you are to cover each part. You will find a diary useful when doing this. Begin by calculating how many weeks you have before your exams start. This is where you will probably get your first shock – there will be fewer weeks left than you thought. June always seems a long way off in February or March, but in terms of the number of weeks, it isn't! Here are some points to think about when drawing up your revision timetable.

❑ Be realistic – don't overestimate how much you can get through in a given time. It is far better to start your revision earlier than to try to squash everything in at the last minute.

❑ Make sure you cover every text – even the ones that you think you know well. When you start to revise you sometimes find that you don't know all the details of a text as well as you thought you did.

❑ Create a balance between revision activities that are reading-based and those that involve writing tasks.

❑ Build some time off into your revision programme to give yourself breaks. Revision is best done in relatively short 'chunks', otherwise your mind can go into 'information overload'! One to one-and-a-half hours at a stretch is a reasonable length of time to aim for. Over two hours' work without a break can be too long.

Design your individual revision programme to suit yourself and your texts. The following is part of the revision programme for a student who is revising for Poetic Study (Unit 2) and Section A of The Language of Prose and Speech (Unit 3) for the AS. He is revising *The Selected Poems and Letters: Keats* for Unit 2 and *Frankenstein* for Unit 3.

DAY	TIME	TASK
Monday	9.00 – 10.30	Watch short video on Keats's life. Re-read 'Ode to Psyche' and 'Ode to a Nightingale.'
	11.00 – 12.30	Re-read notes on these poems. Note down key points as bullets.
	1.30 – 3.00	Read sections in book on Keats's Odes from library.
	6.00 – 7.15	Do timed essay on the 'Odes' (title provided by teacher.)
Tuesday	9.00 – 11.00	Watch Kenneth Brannagh's film version of Frankenstein.
	1.00 – 3.00	Skim-read Frankenstein.
	3.30 – 5.00	Review notes on whole novel.
Wednesday	10.00 – 11.30	Look at past paper questions on Keats. Make notes on topic areas asked about.
	1.00 – 2.30	Read notes on characters and themes in Frankenstein.
	3.00 – 4.00	Look at past paper questions on the novel and roughly plan answers to two of them.

Thursday	*9.00 - 10.30*	*Do timed essay on Frankenstein.*
	1.00 - 2.00	*Listen to tape of reading of Keats's poetry.*
	2.30 - 4.00	*Look over notes on 'Ode on a Grecian Urn' and 'To Autumn'.*
	4.15 - 5.00	*Make a list of key points on these poems.*
Friday	*Day off*	
Saturday	*1.00 - 2.00*	*Look over remainder of notes on Keats.*
	2.30 - 4.00	*Write an analysis of the ways in which Keats uses language in 'Ode on a Grecian Urn'.*

This student has arranged his time in manageable blocks and has allowed for time off in the schedule, which is important too. The revision activities are organized to give continuity, but they are also varied so that the revision does not consist only of reading. There is also a good balance between the texts.

Having designed your revision schedule, you need to be flexible and, if need be, adapt it to cater for the unexpected.

ACTIVITY Plan out a short revision programme for yourself based on one of the texts you are studying either for AS- or A-level. If you are approaching your 'mock' or end-of-year exams, you could extend your programme and use it for your current revision.

Open Book exams

Some of the examinations you will sit will be Closed Book exams, but others will allow you to take the texts into the examination room with you and use them for reference. It is worth considering how this affects the nature of the questions you will face.

One feature of Open Book exams is that they allow the Chief Examiner to set a wider range of question types. As you will have access to the text, questions can direct you to a specific passage and ask you to analyse closely the ways in which language is used in it. Sometimes the question will ask you to place the passage you have examined within the broader context of the text as a whole or a certain part of it.

For example, you may come across questions phrased something like this one on *The Miller's Tale*:

Beginning with a consideration of the lines 579–638 ('Whan that the firste cok hath crowe, anon . . . And to himselfe he seide, 'I shal the quite''), explore the ways in which Chaucer uses language to create humour in this extract. How far do you agree with the comment made about *The Miller's Tale* that it consists of no more than 'funny scenes and comic circumstances'? In your answer you will need to make detailed references to the structure, vocabulary and semantic and phonological features of *The Tale.*

Annotating texts

Another aspect of the Open Book exam that needs to be addressed is what kind of things can be written in the text, and how much. The best advice is to refer to information you are given in the Exam Board's Specification. Here is what is laid down in AQA Specification A:

> Texts may contain only a brief marginal annotation, within the body of the text itself (i.e. excluding any other areas of the book). Such annotation should amount to no more than cross-references and/or the glossing of individual words or phrases. Highlighting or underlining is permitted. Annotations going beyond individual words or phrases, or amounting to aides-memoire or notes towards the planning of essays are not permitted. Insertion of pages, loose sheets, 'post-its' or any other form of notes or additional material is not permitted.

Annotations are often more useful while you are studying a text and coming to an understanding of it. For example, you might make quite a few notes in a Chaucer text explaining words and phrases when you first start to study the text, but by the time you come to sit the examination many of these notes will be redundant. It is a good idea to make all your notes in the text in pencil and then, before you sit the exam, go through and remove all the notes that are no longer required – and all that may infringe the rules of the exam.

One useful technique for annotating and yet keeping your text uncluttered is to use a system of colour-coded underlining. These will help you to find the parts of the text that you want easily and quickly.

Past paper questions

As part of your revision programme you should try to look at as many past or specimen exam papers as you can. Your teacher might be able to show you some of these or they can be purchased from the Examination Board. The value of looking at them is that they will give you a flavour of the question types you can expect, and also give you a range of topics that have been focused on in the past. However, do not learn 'model' answers and hope to be able to use these in the exam. If you come across specimen or model answers, regard them critically and as *one* possible way of answering a particular question, but do not take them to be the definitive answer.

Remember, in the exam you will be expected to respond using your own ideas and thoughts, and examiners can spot immediately if you are offering a 'model' answer you have learned.

As well as giving you ideas, looking at past papers can also give you a good idea of the kind of language the questions use. Studying this wording can be very useful as it will help you to be absolutely clear what a question is asking you to do and therefore how to respond. The more you know in this respect, the less likely you are to be intimidated by the phrasing of a question or the terminology it uses.

Timed essays

Another aspect that often worries students is the lack of time in an examination, and how they are to get all their ideas down without running out of time. This problem can be avoided with proper preparation and practice beforehand. It is very important, therefore, that you build into your revision programme plenty of opportunity to practise writing under timed conditions. The more you practise doing this, the quicker you become. You will probably do some timed work in class under the direction of your teacher, but you can also practise on your own. Your teacher will help if you ask for further titles to work on at home.

Essay planning

Practice in essay planning should form another key part in your revision process. The best essays are those where the students have thought about what they want to say before they start to write. By planning your essays you can ensure that your argument is coherent and that you are using your knowledge and analytical skills to the best effect. Essays that are not planned can easily become rambling, drifting away from the main point of the question.

In the exam you will have little time to spend on planning – you will feel the pressure to start writing as soon as you can. However, what you do in the first two or three minutes can be vital to the ultimate success of your answer. Practice in the build-up to the exam will help you develop the skills to plan quickly and effectively. There are a number of things you can do to help.

- ❑ Read the question very carefully and make sure you understand all parts of it.
- ❑ Analyse the question and note down the key areas it covers.
- ❑ Identify the aspect or aspects of the text that are relevant.
- ❑ Briefly plan how you intend to deal with the question – making a checklist of the key points to be covered.

❏ Remember that the question is likely to ask you to analyse language use in some way. Make sure that your response contains *analysis* and not narrative or description.

Preparing yourself

There is much you can do during the revision period to prepare yourself for the examinations. Focus on what you will be expected to know and to do. Although you will need 'factual' knowledge of the texts, none of the questions you will face at AS- or A-level will require merely 'factual' responses, and so if you find yourself simply *describing* what happens in the text you can be sure you are on the wrong track. Your answers will require close analysis of language, an informed response to the text and mature, perceptive and sensitive understanding. Well-planned revision can ensure that this is exactly what your responses show.

10 Handling Unseen Texts

Unseen texts are vital elements of many examination papers and you need to prepare for them just as comprehensively as for those papers that deal with set texts.

The Units of AQA Specification A where there are unseen elements are as follows:

❏ Unit 1: Language Production
❏ Unit 3: Section B: The Study of the Language of Speech
❏ Unit 5: Section B: Adaptation of Texts for an Audience
❏ Unit 6: Language in Context (synoptic paper)

If necessary, remind yourself of the details of each of these by re-reading the relevant sections from this book. A good deal of specialist knowledge is linked to each of the Units, and you must be thoroughly familiar with that before anything else. However, there are certain points that you can take into consideration with any unseen examination paper; in this chapter we will look briefly at some strategies that can help you through these unseen questions and allow you to write your answers effectively.

The unseen elements in this course fall broadly into two types: those tasks that require you to write imaginatively and creatively (Units 1 and 5) and those that require you to respond analytically (Units 3 and 6).

Language production questions

Remind yourself of the outline frameworks associated with each Unit and the areas of production that are common to both papers. These frameworks allow you to manage the construction of your texts, but there are some other points you need to be aware of, when you are about to start planning out and then writing your responses.

❏ Always double check that you have identified the key words of the question and that you know what its focus is.
❏ Think about your knowledge of the kinds of text you have seen in your own reading which have similarities to what you have been asked to produce; it is likely you will be able to draw on this to help you.
❏ Plan out your framework for production (as you have already learned to do).

❏ Ensure that your text is interesting and takes due note of purpose, audience, form and context; if you do not find it appealing, it is likely that the examiner will feel the same way.

❏ Do not go over the top in your production or try to write something that is outside your capabilities; you would probably write a wholly unconvincing text. It is much better to play safe and write a text that works and is intrinsically interesting, rather than something that might totally flop!

❏ Use the next chapter to help you prepare for production tasks; you need to read widely so that you have a clear sense of genre, purpose, audience and context.

Remember that the two language production papers also have analytical tasks as part of their commentaries. In this case the analytical commentary can largely be your own construction in terms of its focus, since you are the person who has written the text to be analysed, and you will (it is hoped) know why you have written it in the way you have!

Unseen textual analysis

Students often find unseen textual analysis very demanding and often adopt an 'ad hoc' approach to it; if you do this, it is likely that your marks will be lower than those you could have achieved.

The first aspect of critical analysis that needs to be put into place is your literary and linguistic toolkit; as we have mentioned before, you need the correct tools for the job and to know how to use them. Re-read the sections that underpin your understanding of each Unit; this will give you the background you need to approach the questions.

The next chapter gives some suggestions about the range of background reading you need to engage in; this will form the foundation of your critical responses, as you will be familiar with the kinds of text you are likely to find in unseen analysis questions. If you do not read widely, your analysis is likely to be somewhat stilted and mechanical, since you will not be able to take account of such important matters as context, authorial values and form.

When you analyse an unseen piece, you need to consider the whole of the text; it will have been chosen not because parts of it are interesting, but because the whole of the text has intrinsic appeal, allowing a variety of approaches and possible comments to be made. It is vital that you read for meaning and that you consider *how* the writer (or speaker) conveys his or her thoughts, ideas and concerns as well as *what* those issues are. The relationship between the two is vital, since each one informs the other, and they cannot be considered as separate entities.

Reading for meaning should lead you into the main analytical areas:

considering style, language use and overall form. These should open up rich critical seams for you to mine, comparing usage to other texts if necessary. Once you have opened up these seams, you need to organize your analysis logically; always use a framework and remember to pattern your analysis by using the critical sentence outlined in the opening chapter:

❑ identify the point you want to discuss
❑ give a working example from the text or texts
❑ comment on how it works within the text, referring to your critical framework where necessary.

The major points you need to cover in any unseen critical analysis are as follows.

❑ Construct a logical framework for analysis.
❑ Read for meaning.
❑ Always consider your *how* and *what* questions together in any textual analysis.
❑ Always think about what the writer (or speaker) wants to convey to his or her audience, and how language use achieves this.
❑ Evaluate the success of the text for you and, if necessary, how it compares with other texts.

The key to effective performance in unseen analysis is to be confident in what you are doing, consistent in how you apply your analytical frameworks, and cogent in your written response.

11 The Chief Examiner's Perspective: Helping You to Succeed

Reflecting carefully on the aims of English Language and Literature study at AS- and A-level will serve to highlight what you should be achieving in your integrated studies. All the specifications aim to encourage you to study language and literature as interconnecting disciplines in particular ways that will help deepen your understanding and enjoyment. More specific aims are detailed below.

At AS-level the specification aims to:

❏ encourage you to develop your ability to use linguistic and literary critical concepts and analytical frameworks when responding to written and spoken texts
❏ encourage you to develop as an independent, confident and reflective reader
❏ enable you to relate literary and non-literary texts to the contexts in which they were produced
❏ enable you to develop your skills in speaking and writing for different purposes and audiences.

These skills are built upon at A2, where they become more penetrating in their nature. The specification aims to:

❏ broaden and deepen your knowledge and understanding, through evaluation of different analytical approaches and textual interpretation
❏ enable you to make comparisons and connections between a range of texts, taking into account the social, cultural and historical factors which influenced the texts
❏ enable you to choose appropriate approaches for your analyses.

Having studied all the Units, you are now in a position to reflect upon these aims and contextualize them, observing how the course has enabled you to fulfil each one. The objective of this chapter is to give you some practical advice on how you can build these aims into your everyday studies and how you can use them as hints to ensure your success in exam situations.

Let us remind ourselves of some of the key concepts that you need to assimilate at each stage of the course.

At AS-level you need to:

❏ understand
❏ show knowledge of   } texts and
❏ interpret   } stimulus materials
❏ analyse

At A2-level you also need to:

❏ compare   } texts and
❏ evaluate   } source materials

Recommended reading

The simple maxim that can enable you to do this is: *read widely and discriminatingly*! Students often limit their reading to the texts on which they will answer questions in the examination and those that their teachers introduce them to in the classroom. But other students are in a better position. It is becoming increasingly obvious to examiners that the most successful students are those who take responsibility for their reading and can show a breadth of reading when analysing texts. If you want to succeed you have to do the same – otherwise you put yourself at an immediate disadvantage. The following list shows a range of the types of text with which it is useful to become familiar. Keep a reading journal and make notes on the key textual discriminators: genre, purpose, audience, form, and context.

❏ A range of contemporary and classical literature covering all the genres, using your set texts as a good starting point, especially in contemporary writing.
❏ A range of non-literary materials including:
 – journalistic writing, to include broadsheet and tabloid daily newspapers
 – magazines (e.g. female issues, male issues, vocational, scientific, sporting, musical, consumer, media-related, specialist hobbies or interests, household, new technology)
 – periodicals (e.g. historical, economic, scientific, political, literary, linguistic, medical)
 – comics (adult and children's)
 – advertisements
 – reports
 – manuals and instruction sheets
 – catalogues
 – forms and applications
 – legal and governmental literature
 – essays
 – diary forms

- travel writing
- encyclopaedias, reference and text books
- children's books and literature.
❏ A range of speech events, to include:
  - spontaneous speech
  - scripted speech and rhetoric
  - dramatized speech
  - representations of speech in literature
  - screenplays
  - teletext subtitles
  - interviews.
❏ Use of new technologies, to include:
  - the Internet
  - e-mails
  - hypertexts
  - corpora.

It would be admirable to familiarize yourself with examples of all of these, but there is a limit to your time and resources, so dip into the list. You will begin to recognize common forms and styles, which can then be replicated or analysed in your responses. If you read widely, you are more likely to develop confidence and accuracy of written expression in all your answers, and your language will become more cohesive and organized.

In the examination

When you are in the examination room and under pressure, there are various pointers that you can always count on to help you.

❏ Always use the prompts in the questions to guide you, especially if you are in any doubt as to what is required in terms of frameworks.
❏ Highlight key words when planning out your answer.
❏ Plan your response, and *never* use pre-prepared answers: they rarely hit the pass mark and they stand out like sore thumbs!
❏ Use the terminology you have learned accurately and naturally, as an aid to enhance your critical responses.
❏ When answering questions on set texts, familiarize yourself with the assessment objectives at the beginning of the paper to ensure you know what the focus of your answer needs to be; you will probably need to have an understanding of the interplay between plot, character and textual issues and their representation in terms of language use, form and structure. You must then communicate this in your analysis.
❏ Write about authorial (or speaker's) intention, methods, values and attitudes, and how they are communicated.
❏ Ensure that your responses are informed (by background reading), logical (through the use of frameworks), critical (by the use of the literary and

linguistic toolkit), realistic (within the bounds of the question), and represent your personal voice.

Reflect on your present level of performance by looking at the mark schemes for past papers, especially those you have used as trial papers or practice in class. These can often help inform you about those areas you have missed or misunderstood.

Pitfalls to avoid

There are certain things that you should avoid at all costs; examiners complain regularly about these and they usually show that a student suffers from lack of awareness about the subject and insecurity about writing examination responses.

Never:

- ❏ simply retell the story in the hope that it will do you some good: it won't!
- ❏ start writing immediately; always take five minutes to formulate and plan out your response
- ❏ panic: take a minute, brainstorm your ideas if necessary, then crystallize them and finally plan your answer
- ❏ quote at length; be economical with textual reference and quotation, and always show why you have used a quotation by interpreting it
- ❏ ignore the question and write an answer to a question that was set last year, or by your teacher: you will fail!

It is perhaps appropriate to finish off this section with a mnemonic which spells out those aspects of integrated literary and linguistic study you need to concentrate on to ensure you are as well prepared as anyone else:

D evelop your ability to produce interesting, informative and fluent examples of your writing

E xpand your critical vocabulary so that your answers are informed, logical and represent your own personal voice

P ractise timed essays including planning, drafting and evaluating

E xplore different approaches to answering questions until you have mastered the technique and found your preferred model(s)

N ever go into an examination situation unprepared: it is essential you are familiar with all aspects of each Unit, including texts and frameworks

D o read widely! Read for meaning and always consider the text as a whole.

Literary and Linguistic Toolkit

Accent:	A distinctive manner of pronunciation that marks a regional or social identity.
Adjacency pairs:	A term relating to the structure of spoken language, indicating a sequence of utterances that form a recognizable structure. Adjacency pairs follow each other, are produced by different speakers, have a logical connection, and conform to a pattern. Questions and answers, commands and responses, greetings and responses form adjacency pairs, e.g. **A:** Hurry up. **B:** I'll be out in a minute. **A:** Are you well? **B:** Very well, thank you.
Adjective:	A word that describes a noun – e.g. the *wooden* table; the *red* balloon. They can also indicate degree, e.g. the *tallest* girl was the *slowest*. Adjectives are also sometimes known as **modifiers**.
Adverb:	A word that describes the action of a verb – e.g. the cat jumped *swiftly*; the boy ate *hungrily*. Adverbs are also sometimes known as **modifiers**. Adverbs can also act as **intensifiers** – e.g. the man became *very* angry.
Allegory:	A story or a narrative, often told at some length, which has a deeper meaning below the surface. *The Pilgrim's Progress* by John Bunyan is a well-known allegory. A more modern example is George Orwell's *Animal Farm*, which on a surface level is about a group of animals who take over their farm, but on a deeper level is an allegory of the Russian Revolution and the shortcomings of Communism.
Alliteration:	The repetition of the same consonant sound, especially at the beginning of words. For example, 'Five miles meandering with a mazy motion' (*Kubla Khan* by S.T. Coleridge).
Allusion:	A reference to another event, person, place or work of literature. The allusion is usually implied rather than explicit, and often provides another layer of meaning to what is being said.
Ambiguity:	Use of language where the meaning is unclear or has two or more possible interpretations. It could be created through a weakness in the writer's expression, but often it is deliberately used by writers to create layers of meaning in the mind of the reader.
Ambivalence:	The situation where more than one possible attitude is being displayed by the writer towards a character, theme, or idea, etc.

Anachronism: Something that is historically inaccurate – for example, the reference to a clock chiming in Shakespeare's *Julius Caesar*. The Romans did not have chiming clocks, of course.

Anapest: A unit of poetic metre made up of two unstressed syllables followed by a stressed syllable – e.g. there are four anapests in:

ᵕ ᵕ / ᵕ ᵕ / ᵕ ᵕ / ᵕ ᵕ /
The Assyrian came down like the wolf on the fold
(*The Destruction of Sennacherib* by Lord Byron)

Anaphoric: A form of **referencing** in which a pronoun or noun phrase points back to something mentioned earlier – e.g. the party was a great success and *it* was enjoyed by everyone.

Antithesis: Contrasting ideas or words that are balanced against each other, e.g. 'To be, or not to be' (*Hamlet* by William Shakespeare).

Antonyms: Words that are opposite in meaning (*dark/light, fast/slow*).

Archaism: Use of language that is old-fashioned – words or phrases that are not completely obsolete, but no longer in current usage.

Assonance: The repetition of similar vowel sounds. For example, 'There must be Gods thrown down and trumpets blown' (*Hyperion* by John Keats). This shows the paired assonance of *must, trum* and *thrown, blown*.

Attitude: A particular stance or viewpoint adopted by a writer or speaker.

Audience: The people addressed by a piece of writing, speech, etc. This is closely associated with the idea of **purpose**. Language (either written or spoken) is used in various kinds of ways depending on the audience that it is aimed at and the purpose that it is designed to achieve.

Ballad: A narrative poem that tells a story (traditional ballads were songs) usually in a straightforward way. The theme is often tragic or contains a whimsical, supernatural or fantastical element.

Bias: Language used in such a way as to express a prejudice against someone or something, or which favours a particular point of view.

Blank verse: Unrhymed poetry that adheres to a strict pattern in that each line is an iambic pentameter (a ten-syllable line with five stresses). It is close to the natural rhythm of English speech or prose and is used a great deal by many writers, including Shakespeare and Milton.

Caesura: A conscious break in a line of poetry, e.g. 'Fix' d were their habits; they arose betimes,/ Then pray'd their hour, and sang their party rhymes' (Thomas Crabbe).

Caricature: A character described through the exaggeration of the features that he or she possesses.

Cataphoric: See **referencing**.

Catharsis: A purging of emotions such as takes place at the end of a tragedy.

Chaining: The linking together of adjacency pairs to form a conversation.

Clause: A group of words, usually with a finite verb, which is structurally larger than a **phrase**. Clauses are made up of elements, each of which expresses a particular kind of meaning. There are five types of clause element:

❏ the *subject* – identifies the theme or topic of the clause
❏ the *verb* – expresses a range of meanings, such as actions, sensations or states of being
❏ the *object* – identifies who or what has been directly affected by the action of the verb
❏ the *complement – gives further information about another clause element*
❏ the *adverbial* – adds information about the situation, such as the time of an action or its frequency.

All five elements appear in the above order in the sentence: *The teacher/ had told/ me/ to listen/ three times.*

Cliché: A phrase, idea, or image that has been over-used so that it has lost much of its original meaning, impact and freshness.

Cohesion: Links and connections that unite the elements of discourse or text.

Coinage: The creation and addition of new words to the existing word stock.

Collective noun: See **noun.**

Collocation: Two or more words that frequently appear together as part of a set phrase. They are often well known and predictable, so many could also be described as **idioms** or **clichés**, e.g. *safe and sound, loud and clear, here and there.*

Colloquial: An everyday or non-formal quality in speech or writing, often characterized by the use of slang or non-standard features.

Comedy: Originally, simply a play or other work that ended happily. Now we use the term to describe something that is funny and makes us laugh. In literature, comedy is not necessarily a lightweight form. Shakespeare's *Measure for Measure*, for example, is for the most part a serious and dark play, but as it ends happily it is described as a comedy.

Command: The type of sentence in which someone is told to do something – e.g. *Stand up immediately!*

Common noun: See **noun**.

Complement: A clause element that adds extra information about the subject or object of the clause after the copular verb – e.g. The student was *tired.*

Complex sentence: See **sentence.**

Compound: A word made up of at least two free morphemes – e.g. *babysitter, skateboard, mother-in-law.*

Compound sentence:	See **sentence**.
Conceit:	An elaborate, extended, and sometimes surprising comparison between things that, at first sight, do not have much in common – e.g. in John Donne's poem *A Valediction: Forbidding Mourning* he compares the souls of himself and his lover with the legs of a draughtsman's compasses.
Conjunction:	A word that connects words or other constructions. There are two kinds of conjunctions – *co-ordinating* and *subordinating*.

❏ *Co-ordinating* conjunctions – *and, but* and *or* – are the most common. These can join single words as in fish *and* chips or they can join phrases: Loved by the poor *but* hated by the rich. They can also join sentences by replacing full stops: He agreed to come. He did not speak. He agreed to come *but* he did not speak.

❏ *Subordinating* conjunctions also join but they use a different process. Co-ordinating conjunctions join two equal parts and they remain equals. Subordinating conjunctions join statements by making one less important than the other. One statement becomes the main statement and the other a subordinate supporting one, as in this example, where *although* becomes the subordinating conjunction: *Although* John was clever, he did not do enough work to pass his exams. Other subordinating conjunctions include *because, unless, whenever, if, that, while, where, as.*

Connotation:	The associations attached to a word in addition to its dictionary definition.
Context:	The social circumstances in which speech or writing takes place.
Contextual framework:	The application of a particular socio/historical standpoint used to analyse a text.
Contraction:	A shortened word, e.g. *isn't, don't*
Convergence:	A process of linguistic change in which accents or dialects become more alike.
Conversation analysis:	A study of the key features of informal spoken interaction.
Couplet:	Two consecutive lines of verse that rhyme, e.g. 'Had we but World enough and time,/This coyness, lady, were no crime.' (Andrew Marvell)
Dactyl:	A unit of poetic metre consisting of a stressed syllable followed by two unstressed ones – e.g. there are three dactyls in:

Half a league, half a league,

Half a league, onward.
(*The Charge of the Light Brigade* by Alfred, Lord Tennyson)

Declarative:	A grammatical mood that expresses a statement – e.g. *I am a hardworking student.*

Degree: Comparison of adjectives or adverbs. Most adjectives or adverbs can be compared in one of three ways. The thing they express can be related to a higher degree, to the same degree or to a lower degree. For example, John is *tall* (*absolute* form). Kate is *taller* (*comparative* form). David is *tallest* (*superlative* form). Some examples adopt an irregular form such as *good/better/best, bad/worse/worst.*

Deixis: Words that can be interpreted only with reference to the speaker's position in space or time. These are known as *deictic forms* and fall into three main types. *Personal deixis* includes the use of such pronouns as *you* or *I* that identify who is taking part in the discourse. *Spatial deixis* shows the speaker's position in relation to other people or objects, e.g. *this, that, here, there. Temporal deixis* relates the speaker to time using words such as *tomorrow, now, yesterday.*

Demonstrative: A term used to describe determiners or pronouns that distinguish one item from other similar ones – e.g. *this, that, these, those.*

Denotation: The dictionary definition of a word (see **connotation**).

Denouement: The ending of a play, novel or short story where 'all is revealed' and the plot is unravelled.

Determiner: Words that 'determine' the number and definiteness of the noun. There are three kinds of determiners: *central determiners, predeterminers* and *postdeterminers.*

❏ *Central determiners* consist of the definite article (*the*) and several other words that can take its place – *this, that, each, every, some* and *any*. Words like this are called determiners only when used before the noun. If they are used alone instead of the noun they are being used as a pronoun – e.g. I need *some* paper (determiner). I need *some* (pronoun).

❏ *Predeterminers* can be used before the central determiners. They can include words such as *all, both, half, double* – e.g. *all* this money.

❏ *Postdeterminers* follow the central determiners but come before any adjectives. Cardinal numbers (*one, two, three*), ordinals (*first, second, third*), and quantifiers (*much, many, several*) can be used in this way.

Diachronic: A term used to describe language change that occurs over a period of time.

Diacritics: Marks added to text, or phonetic symbols, to specify various sound qualities such as syllabus stress, length, tone, etc. Often used in literature to indicate poetic metre.

Dialect: A language variety marked by a distinctive grammar and vocabulary, used by people with a common regional or social background.

Dialogue: Language interaction between two or more people.

Diction: The choice of words that a writer makes – another term for **vocabulary** or **lexis,** although less used these days.

Didactic:	A term describing a work that is intended to preach or teach, often containing a particular moral or political point.
Direct speech:	The actual words spoken by a person, recorded in written form using speech marks or quotation marks.
Discourse:	Any spoken or written language that is longer than a sentence.
Divergence:	A process in which accents or dialects move further apart and the differences between them increase.
Double negative:	A part of speech or writing in which more than one negative is used in one verb phrase, frequently used in certain dialects – e.g. *I haven't done nothing.* It has the effect of creating an opposite meaning to that intended.
Dynamic:	A verb that expresses an action rather than a state, and can be used in the progressive form – e.g. *jump/jumping; clap/clapping.*
Elegy:	A meditative poem, usually sad and reflective in nature. Sometimes, but not always, it is concerned with the theme of death.
Elision:	The omission of an unstressed syllable so that the line conforms to a particular metrical pattern – e.g. *o'er* (over) and *e'en* (even).
Ellipsis:	The omission of a part of a sentence, which can be understood from the context – e.g. I'd like to go to the concert but I can't (*go to the concert* omitted because the repetition is not necessary).
End-stopped:	A verse line with a pause or stop at the end of it.
Enjambment:	A line of verse that flows on into the next line without pause.
Etymology:	The study of the history and origins of words.
Euphemism:	A word that replaces a word or term that is unpleasant, could offend or is a taboo word – e.g. *to pass away* meaning to die.
Exophoric:	See **referencing**.
Fabilau:	A short comic tale with a bawdy element, akin to the 'dirty story'. Chaucer's *The Miller's Tale* contains strong elements of the fabilau.
Farce:	A play that aims to entertain the audience through absurd and ridiculous characters and actions.
Feedback:	The reaction speakers receive from their listeners or the information speakers gain from monitoring their own speech.
Field:	An area of meaning (for example, education) which is characterized by common lexical items (*teacher, classroom, headteacher, caretaker, examination,* etc.)
Figurative language:	Language that is symbolic or metaphorical and not meant to be taken literally.
Foot:	A group of syllables forming a unit of verse – the basic unit of metre (see Chapter 2, Poetic Study).

Formality: A scale of language use relating to the formality of the social context within which it is used. Language can be used formally or informally depending on the context.

Formulaic: A term to denote language that is patterned and always appears in the same form – e.g. *Yours faithfully, Bye for now.*

Framework: A critical skeleton that could be applied to analyse texts in various ways to suit the purpose of the analysis. A literary framework could be applied, or a linguistic framework, a contextual framework, etc.

Free verse: Verse written without any fixed structure (either in metre, rhythm or form).

Genre: A particular type of writing, e.g. prose, poetry, drama.

Heptameter: A verse line containing seven feet.

Hexameter: A verse line containing six feet.

Homograph: A word with the same spelling but different meanings – e.g. *fair:* The girl had *fair* hair. The children went to the *fair.* The result was not *fair.*

Homonym: A word with the same sound or the same spelling as another but with a different meaning – e.g. *maid* and *made; May* (the month) and *may* (is allowed to). Note: *Homograph* can be used for words with the same spelling, *homophone* for words with the same sound, but *homonym* covers both.

Homophone: A word that sounds the same as another but has a different meaning – e.g. *rode, road* and *rowed.*

Hyperbole: A deliberate and extravagant exaggeration.

Hyponymy: The relationship between specific and general words where the meaning of one form is included in the meaning of another. For example, *dog* is an hyponym of *animal. Yew, oak, sycamore* are hyponyms of *tree.*

Iamb: The most common metrical foot in English poetry, consisting of an unstressed syllable followed by a stressed syllable.

Idiom: A sequence of words that is a unit of meaning – e.g. *kick the bucket, put your foot in it.*

Imagery: The use of words to create a picture or 'image' in the mind of the reader. Images can relate to any of the senses – not just sight, but also hearing, taste, touch and smell. The term is often used to refer to the use of descriptive language, particularly to the use of **metaphors** and **similes**.

Imperative: A grammatical mood expressing a directive (command, warning, request, etc.).

Incompatibility: A linguistic feature that defines one item and thereby excludes others. For example, it would not be possible to say *I am writing in one colour of ink and it is red and blue.* As it has to be either red or blue, one term excludes the other.

Indirect speech:	The words of a speaker that are reported rather than being quoted directly – e.g. *David said that he was going out.* **Direct speech** would be *'I am going out,' said David.* (See Chapter 3, The Language of Prose.)
Infinitive:	A non-finite verb in the base form – e.g. they might *see*. Often the verb is preceded by the preposition *to* – e.g. *to see*. A split infinitive, which is grammatically incorrect, is where another word is placed between the preposition and the base form of the verb. Perhaps the most famous example is Star Trek's *To boldly go . . .*
Insertion sequence:	A feature occurring in spoken discourse where the original conversation is suspended because of an interruption caused by a speech sequence from another source. When the interruption has been dealt with, the original speech sequence resumes.
Intensifier:	A word or phrase that adds emphasis – e.g. *very, unbelievably, awfully, terribly.*
Internal rhyme:	Rhyming words within a line rather than at the ends of lines.
Interrogative:	A grammatical mood expressing a question.
Inter-textual:	Having clear links with other texts through the themes, ideas or issues explored.
Intonation:	The tone of voice in speech.
Inversion:	Reversing the order of clause elements, so that subject and verb appear in the reverse of their normal order – e.g. *Here is the milkman*, instead of *The milkman is here.*
Irony:	At its simplest level, irony means saying one thing while meaning another. It occurs where a word or phrase has one surface meaning but another, contradictory and possibly opposite meaning is implied. Irony is frequently confused with sarcasm. Sarcasm is spoken, often relying on tone of voice, and is much more blunt than irony.
Lament:	A poem expressing intense grief.
Language acquisition:	The process of learning a first language as a child.
Language change:	The process of change in a language over a period of time.
Language of speech:	Spoken language of any kind.
Lexis:	The vocabulary of a language or particular use of language.
Loan word:	A word borrowed from another language.
Lyric:	Originally a lyric was a song performed to the accompaniment of a lyre (a stringed harp-like instrument) but now it can mean a song-like poem or a short poem expressing personal feeling.
Main clause:	A clause that is not dependent and makes sense on its own. See **clause**.

Malapropism: A mixing up of words that sound similar. Made famous by Mrs Malaprop, a character in Sheridan's *The Rivals*, who said 'He is the very *pineapple* of politeness' (for *pinnacle*) and 'She is as headstrong as an *allegory* on the banks of the Nile' (for *alligator*).

Manner: An adverbial answering the question 'How?', e.g. *slowly*.

Metalanguage: The language used to talk about language.

Metaphor: A comparison of one thing to another in order to make description more vivid. Unlike a **simile**, a metaphor states that one thing *is* the other. For example, a simile could be *The wind cut through me like a knife*, whereas the metaphor might state *The wind cut through me*. (See **simile** and **personification**).

Metonymy: A feature where an attribute of the thing being described stands for the whole thing. For example, the term *crown* could be used to mean the king or the queen; *the turf* could stand for horse racing; and *Fleet Street* could mean the Press.

Metre: The regular use of stressed and unstressed syllables in poetry (see Chapter 2, Poetic Study).

Modal: An auxiliary verb which cannot be used as a main verb – e.g. *can, may, will, shall, must, could, might, would, should*.

Mode: A particular medium of communication – e.g. speech, writing, etc.

Modification: The use of one linguistic item to specify the nature of another. Adjectives act as modifiers – e.g. the *blue* sky – as do adverbs: He ducked *quickly* to avoid being seen.

Modifier: A word that specifies the nature of another word or tells us more about it. **Adverbs** and **adjectives** act as modifiers.

Monologue: Speech or writing produced, and often performed, by one person.

Monometer: A line of verse containing only one foot.

Monosyllabic: Having only one syllable.

Mood: Main clauses can have one of three moods: the *declarative* mood is used to make statements; the *imperative* mood is used to issue orders, commands or make requests; and the *interrogative* mood is used to ask questions.

Narrative: A piece of writing or speech that tells a story.

Neologism: Sometimes called a nonce-word or **coinage** – a new or invented word or expression. Usually they are made up of adaptations of existing words, although the term nonce-word was originally applied to words that had a 'one-off' use such as the combination of *fair* and *joyous* to give *frabjous*, used by Lewis Carroll. Examples of more modern neologisms are *zeroized, shopaholic, computerate*. Of course, when a word has been in use a while it ceases to be new and is no longer considered a neologism.

Non-standard English:	Any variety of language use that does not conform to the standard, prestige form of English accepted as the norm by society. See **standard English** and **received pronunciation**.
Noun:	A word class with a naming function, which can be used as a subject or an object in a clause. They can be grouped in several ways. Here are the main kinds.

- ❏ *Proper nouns*: the names of specific people, places, times, occasions, events, publications and so on – e.g. *London, Lulu, The English Magazine, July, Christmas Day.* They are usually written with an initial capital letter.
- ❏ *Common nouns*: general objects or ideas – e.g. *table, window, book, pen.*
- ❏ *Abstract nouns*: qualities or states that exist only in our minds – e.g. *cleverness, courage, justice, loyalty, mercy.*
- ❏ *Collective nouns*: groups of people, or collections of things as a whole – e.g. *crowd, flock, regiment, convoy, forest, crew.*

Octave:	The first eight lines of a sonnet.
Octometer:	A verse line consisting of eight feet.
Ode:	A verse form similar to a lyric but often more lengthy and containing more serious and elevated thoughts.
Onomatopoeia:	The use of words whose sounds copy the sounds of the thing or process they describe. On a simple level, words like *bang, hiss* and *splash* are onomatopoeic, but it also has more subtle uses.
Oxymoron:	A figure of speech that joins together words of opposite meanings – e.g. *the living dead, bitter sweet.*
Paradox:	A statement that appears contradictory, but when considered more closely is seen to contain a good deal of truth.
Parallelism:	The patterning of pairs of sounds, words or structures to create a sense of balance in spoken or written discourse – e.g. 'I am the way, the life and the truth.'
Parody:	A work that is written in imitation of another work, very often with the intention of making fun of the original.
Participle:	The non-finite form of verbs that can occur after an auxiliary verb – e.g. was *running* (present participle); had *run* (past participle). Can also occur before a head noun – e.g. the *running* man, or the *completed* task.
Particle:	A grammatical function word that never changes its form – e.g. *up, down, in, after.*
Pastoral:	Generally, literature concerning rural life with idealized settings and rustic characters. Often pastorals are concerned with the lives of shepherds and shepherdesses, presented in idyllic and unrealistic ways.
Pathos:	The effect in literature that makes the reader feel sadness or pity.

Patterning: Language used in such a way as to create discernible patterns, perhaps through **imagery**, or a repeated symbol or motif, or use of **parallelism**, etc.

Pentameter: A line of verse containing five feet.

Periphrasis: A round-about or long-winded way of saying something.

Personification: The attribution of human feelings, emotions, sensations or physical attributes to an inanimate object. Personification is a kind of **metaphor**, where human qualities are given to things or abstract ideas.

Phatic: A term describing language used to make social contact, which is intended more to convey general sociability than to communicate meaning – e.g. *Nice morning, isn't it?*

Phonetic alphabet: Symbols and **diacritics** designed to represent exactly the sound of spoken language.

Phonetic transcription: A detailed transcription, using phonetic symbols, concentrating on the details of pronunciation.

Phonetics: The study of spoken sounds and the way in which they are produced.

Phrase: A group of words smaller than a **clause** which forms a grammatical unit, but does not contain a finite verb and therefore does not make complete sense on its own.

Pitch: The auditory level of sound.

Pleonasm: The unnecessary use of words – e.g. *here and now, this present day and age*. Also called **tautology**.

Plot: The sequence of events in a poem, play, novel or short story that makes up the main story line.

Polysyllabic: Having more than one syllable.

Preposition: A word expressing a relationship of meaning between two parts of a sentence, most often showing how the two parts are related in space or time – e.g. We had a meal *in* a restaurant. I'll take you *to* the cinema.

Pronoun: A word that stands for a noun – e.g. Kate went to the cinema and *she* bought an ice cream. My car is red but my friend has a maroon *one*. Pronouns include *he, she, they, we, her, him, all, both, each*.

Prose: Any kind of writing that is not verse – usually divided into fiction and non-fiction.

Protagonist: The main character or speaker in a poem, monologue, play or story.

Pun: A play on words that have similar sounds but quite different meanings. For example, in Shakespeare's *Romeo and Juliet*, after he has been mortally wounded by Tybalt and is dying, Mercutio says 'Ask for me tomorrow, and you will find me a grave man.'

Purpose:	The reason why a piece of writing has been written or a speech made – e.g. to entertain, to explain, to persuade, to argue.
Quatrain:	A stanza of four lines, which can have various rhyme schemes.
Received pronunciation:	Sometimes know as RP, the prestige British accent that has a high social status and is not related to a specific region or influenced by regional variation.
Recursive:	Said of a grammatical rule that is capable of repeated application.

Referencing: References point to something else in the discourse. Pronouns are often used to make these references, although comparative structures that express certain similarities or differences can also be used. In this sentence a pronoun is used: The student worked hard, so *she* had little spare time. In this sentence a comparative structure is used: The second team was good but *the first one* was better.

There are three main kinds of reference:

- ❏ *Anaphoric* references point *backwards* in a text. The reader or listener must refer to a previous reference to make sense of the pronoun or comparative structure. Both examples given above are of this kind of reference.
- ❏ *Cataphoric* references point *forwards* in a text. In other words the reader or listener must refer to a future reference in order to understand the structure used, e.g. *Those* were *the days* my friend.
- ❏ *Exophoric* references point *beyond* the text. The reader or the listener has to make a connection with something outside the text, e.g. The fish was *this* big. Some kind of context or sign is needed here so that the statement makes sense.

Refrain:	Repetition throughout a poem of a phrase, line or series of lines as in the 'chorus' of a song.
Repetition:	A device that emphasizes an idea through repetition.
Representational features:	Language use where one thing is used to represent another, as in **symbolic language** or the use of **imagery**.
Rhetoric:	Originally, the art of speaking and writing in such a way as to persuade an audience to a particular point of view. Now it is often used to imply grand words that have no substance in them. There are a variety of rhetorical devices such as the rhetorical question – a question that does not require an answer, as the answer is obvious or implied in the question itself.
Rhyme:	Corresponding sounds in words, usually at the end of each line of verse, but not always.
Rhyme scheme:	The pattern of the rhymes in a poem.
Rhythm:	The 'movement' of a poem as created through the metre and the way that language is stressed within the poem.

Satire: The highlighting or exposing of human failings or foolishness within a society, by ridiculing them. Satire can range from gentle and light to extremely biting and bitter in tone, e.g. Swift's *Gulliver's Travels* or *A Modest Proposal*, or George Orwell's *Animal Farm*.

Scansion: The analysis of metrical patterns in poetry.

Semantic features: Features that provide speech or writing with a linguistic meaning.

Semantic field: Areas of meaning identified by a set of mutually defining words. For example, *red*, *blue*, *green*, *yellow* are all words identified with colour. *Regiment*, *soldier*, *battalion*, *barracks*, *parade* are identified as describing military things.

Semantics: The study of the meaning of language.

Sentence: A grammatical structure made up of one or more clauses. Usually in written language it begins with a capital letter and ends with a full stop or a feature that performs the function of a full stop, such as a question mark. In analysing spoken language, **utterances** are often referred to rather than sentences.

In terms of purpose, there are four kinds of sentences.

❏ Command – *Get up, now!*
❏ Question – *How are you?*
❏ Statement – *I am going out tonight.*
❏ Exclamation – *Stop that immediately!*

There are also three kinds of sentences in terms of their structure.

❏ *Simple sentence* – all the above examples are of simple sentences. A simple sentence has just one finite verb (a finite verb is a verb that has a subject.)
❏ *Compound sentence* – consists of two or more simple sentences joined together by a co-ordinating conjunction – e.g. *I hope to pass my exams and then go on to university.*
❏ *Complex sentence* – has one main clause and any number of subordinate clauses joined to it by subordinating conjunctions – e.g. *The strikers will continue to hold their demonstrations and will not give up their struggle easily.*

Septet: A seven-line stanza.

Sequencing: The rules governing the succession of utterances in discourse.

Sestet: The last six lines of a sonnet.

Side-sequences: In spoken discourse, an explanation of something that has already been uttered.

Simile: A comparison of one thing with another in order to make description more vivid. Similes use the words *like* or *as* to make the comparison.

Slang: Distinctive words and phrases associated with informal speech. Very often it is used within certain social groups or age groups.

Soliloquy: A speech in which a dramatic character, alone on stage, expresses his or her thoughts and feelings aloud for the benefit of the audience, often in a revealing way.

Sonnet: A fourteen-line poem, usually with ten syllables in each line. There are several ways in which the lines can be organized, but they often consist of an **octave** and a **sestet**.

Spondee: A unit of poetic metre containing two stressed syllables.

Standard English: The form of English considered to be and accepted as the norm in society, and used as the medium of government, education, law, etc. Language that differs from this standard is known as **non-standard**.

Stanza: The blocks of lines into which a poem is divided. Sometimes these are referred to less precisely as verses, which can lead to confusion as poetry is sometimes called 'verse' too.

Stream of consciousness: A technique in which the writer puts down thoughts and emotions in a 'stream' as they come to mind, without imposing order or structure.

Structure: The way that a poem, play or other piece of writing has been put together. This can include the metre pattern, stanza arrangement, the ways the ideas are developed, etc.

Style: The individual way in which a writer has used language to express his or her ideas.

Stylistics: The study of lexical and structural variations in language according to use, audience and purpose.

Sub-plot: A secondary story line in a novel or play. Often, as in some plays by Shakespeare, the sub-plot can provide some comic relief from the main action, but sub-plots can also relate to the main plot in quite complex ways.

Sub-text: Ideas, themes, or issues that are not dealt with overtly by a text but exist below the surface meaning.

Syllable: A word or part of a word that can be uttered in a single effort of the voice. Patterns of stressed and unstressed syllables make up the rhythm pattern of the language.

Symbolic language: The use of words or phrases to represent something else.

Synecdoche: A device in which a part is used to represent the whole – e.g. There were several new *faces* at the meeting.

Synonyms: Different words with the same or nearly the same meanings – e.g. *shut* and *close* or *ship* and *vessel*.

Syntax: The study of the structure of sentences.

Tag question: An interrogative structure added to the end of a sentence which requires a reply – e.g. Terrible weather, *isn't it?*

Tautology: Saying the same thing twice over in different words – e.g. *The visitors arrived one after the other in succession.*

Tetrameter: A verse line of four feet.

Text: A piece of spoken or written language with a definable communicative function.

Theme: The central idea or ideas that a writer explores through his or her text.

Tone: The tone of a text is created through the combined effects of a number of features, such as **diction**, **syntax**, **rhythm**, etc. The tone can be a major factor in establishing the overall impression of a piece of writing.

Topicality: The topic of a spoken encounter is directly related to its **manner** and its participants. The topic can determine the level of **formality**, and topic shifts can occur when speakers move from one topic to another. These mark key points in the discourse.

Transcription: A written record of spoken language, which may use symbols to represent the distinctive features of speech.

Trimeter: A unit of poetic metre containing three feet.

Trochee: A unit of poetic metre containing a stressed followed by an unstressed syllable.

Turn-taking: Organization of speakers' contributions in a conversation. Turns may be fairly equal, or one of the participants may dominate.

Utterances: A piece of spoken language. Also used to describe a spoken 'sentence', since it can be difficult to apply the normal rules of a written sentence to speech.

Verb: A word that expresses actions, states of being or processes. There are three types of verb that can occur within a verb phrase.

- ❑ *Full* (or *lexical*) verbs have a clearly stateable meaning. These act as main verbs, such as *run, jump, go, look.*
- ❑ *Modal auxiliary* verbs express a range of judgements about the likelihood of events. These function only as auxiliary verbs – *will, shall, may, might, can.*
- ❑ *Primary* verbs can function either as main verbs or auxiliary verbs. There are three of them: *be, have* and *do.*

Vernacular: The native language a community uses for speech.

Vocabulary: The words of a language –the same as **lexis**.

Zeugma: A device that joins together two apparently incongruous things by applying a verb or adjective to both of them which really applies to only one of them – e.g. 'Kill the boys and the luggage' (Shakespeare's *Henry V*).

Index